D0856536

COLLECTED ESSAYS

OF

EDMUND GOSSE

SEVENTEENTH CENTURY STUDIES

AMS PRESS
NEW YORK

SEVENTEENTH CENTURY STUDIES

BY

EDMUND GOSSE, C.B.

LONDON
WILLIAM HEINEMANN
1914

Library of Congress Cataloging in Publication Data

Gosse, Sir Edmund William, 1849-1928.
    Seventeenth century studies.

    (Collected essays of Edmund Gosse, v. 1)
    CONTENTS: Thomas Lodge.--John Webster.--Samuel
Rowlands. [etc.]
    1. English poetry--Early modern (to 1700)--Addresses,
essays, lectures. I. Title. II. Series: Gosse, Sir
Edmund William, 1849-1928. Collected essays, v. 1.
PR543.G6 1972   821'.4'09   70-136381
ISBN 0-404-02885-3

Reprinted from the edition of 1914, London
First AMS edition published in 1972
Manufactured in the United States of America

International Standard Book Number: 0-404-02885-3

AMS PRESS INC.
NEW YORK, N. Y.   10003

PREFACE

TO THE FIRST EDITION
(1883)

IN writing this book my object has been to do for some of the rank and file of seventeenth century literature what modern criticism has done, on a much larger scale, for Shakespeare, Milton, and Dryden. Those great figures have been taken out of their surroundings, and have been discussed upon their own merits, biographically, æsthetically, historically. But in scarcely any instances, and in these on no consistent plan, has this been done for the smaller writers. Yet it is in these less monumental figures that the progress of literary history is most clearly to be marked, and it has seemed to me not undesirable that the truth which we try to tell definitely and exhaustively in a set of volumes about Milton or Dryden, should be told as definitely in a single chapter about Cowley or Otway. I have therefore tried to make each of the ensuing studies an exhaustive critical biography in miniature, yet each in some

way connected with that which precedes it, and all
treated on the same relative scale.   It was necessary,
in order to do this, to take more pains than is at first
sight apparent in the choice of names, some which
presented themselves seeming to be too full of individuality, and very many more to be not full
enough.

The volume was begun in 1872, and, with necessary intervals, has occupied me ever since.   The first
list of contents upon which I decided, ran thus:—
Lodge, Webster, Dekker, Donne, Randolph, Herrick,
Cowley, Orinda, Etheredge, Otway.   In the second
half of this list it has not seemed necessary to make
any modification; in the first half three names occur
which will not be found represented in this book.
Perhaps I may be allowed to mention the reason of
this alteration, as it helps me to explain the scope of
my inquiry.   Whether Dekker or a somewhat earlier
name would best fit my purpose was still undecided
when the Council of the Hunterian Club asked me to
introduce to their subscribers their magnificent reprint
of Samuel Rowlands.   I was obliged, for this purpose,
again to read through the entire works of that author,
and I then saw that he was even a more typical figure
than Dekker, his immediate successor.

It was with reluctance that I resigned Donne and
Randolph, and from opposite reasons.   It seemed that

the one was too small and the other too large for the species of portraiture which I had chosen. Upon reflection I decided that, in spite of his promise and his virile grace, the author of *The Jealous Lovers* was too vague a figure to be painted at full length in a gallery of portraits. In the study on the Cotswold Games he is introduced, not too inadequately, I hope, in the centre of the manly school of Ben Jonson. Again, as I read more and more deeply in the literature of the seventeenth century, I became convinced that I could not adequately deal with Donne within such narrow limits. That extraordinary writer casts his shadow over the vault of the century from its beginning to its close, like one of those ancient Carthaginian statues, the hands and feet of which supported opposite extremities of the arch they occupied. Donne is himself the paradox of which he sings; he is a seeming absurdity in literature. To be so great and yet so mean, to have phrases like Shakespeare and tricks like Gongora, to combine within one brain all the virtues and all the vices of the imaginative intellect, this has been given to only one man, and that the inscrutable Dean of St. Paul's. To write fully of his work would be to write the history of the decline of English poetry, to account for the Augustan renascence, to trace the history of the national mind for a period of at least a century.

I felt Donne to be as far beyond the scope of my work as Ben Jonson would have been.

All critical work, nowadays, must be done on the principle of the coral insect. No one can hope to do more than place his atom on the mass that those who preceded him have constructed. It will not be supposed that I am so presumptuous or so ignorant as to forget what has been written for seventy years past on the poetry of the seventeenth century, or how much genius, industry, and judgment have been expended on its elucidation. It must, however, be remembered that this minute care has usually been reserved for greater men than those with whom I have to deal. When I began this volume only three of the poets discussed in it had been edited, only one in the exact modern method. When the ensuing study on Herrick first appeared in 1874, Mr. Palgrave had not produced his *Chrysomela*, Dr. Grosart had not collected and edited the works, Mr. Edwin Abbey had not reprinted and adorned the *Hesperides* with illustrations that form a brilliant and sympathetic commentary. Since my successive studies have been written, Lodge, Rowlands, Dover, and Cowley have for the first time been edited, in each case, however, for private subscribers alone. Crashaw now exists in two stately quartos, edited by Dr. Grosart ; but Orinda, Etheredge, and Otway are still attainable only in the original editions. As long as the books themselves are so difficult of access, so long will hasty criticism continue to repeat the acute, but often entirely false and unfounded generalisations of writers like Hallam, who enlightened our darkness before literary analysis had become a science.

As far as actual historical discovery goes, it is hard for any one nowadays to glean after Dr. Grosart. However, I may claim in some of the studies, in those on Lodge, Rowlands, and Etheredge in particular, to have added some essential facts to our previous knowledge. This, however, has not been my principal aim. I have rather desired to enrich the biography of each poet by a careful analysis of the evidence concealed in his work, and in the writings of his coevals, a field which, particularly as we descend the century, has been singularly little worked. I hope, moreover, that in the critical part of the work it may be found that I have not unsuccessfully introduced certain elements, the influence of contemporary politics, the relation to foreign literatures, the relative aspect of divergent schools, which have been hitherto neglected.

By first printing each study in a provisional form, I may have laid myself open to the charge of seeming to disguise the unity of my work. I cannot, however, regret a practice which gave me the great advantage of getting my work revised by the most competent hands. It is impossible to ask friends to weary themselves with the examination of manuscript, but the busiest scholar will revise a friend's work in print. I have submitted these essays, in their earlier form, to several persons who have made a special study of English poetry, and their strictures and corrections have been of inestimable service to me in my final revision. To all these friends my best thanks are due, but, particularly to Mr. Leslie Stephen, who was in most cases the first reader of these studies, and but for whose indulgence—that of the kindest of editors—they could scarcely have seen the light ; to Mr. Swinburne, for whose censure and encouragement, particularly in the early part of the design, I cannot be too grateful ; to Dr. Grosart, for gifts of books and correction of various matters of detail ; and lastly, to Mr. J. Henry Shorthouse, for sympathetic notes on Crashaw and on Orinda.

CONTENTS

THOMAS LODGE

IF a full and continuous biography of Thomas Lodge could be recovered, it would possess as much interest to a student of Elizabethan manners and letters as any Memoir that can be imagined. It would combine, in a series of pictures, scenes from all the principal conditions of life in that stirring and vigorous age. It would introduce us to the stately civic life of London city, to Oxford in the early glow of humanism and liberal thought, to the dawn of professional literature in London, to the life of a soldier against Spain, to the adventures of a freebooting sailor on the high seas, to the poetry of the age, and then to its science, to the stage in London and to the anatomical lecture-room in Avignon, to the humdrum existence of a country practitioner, and to the perilous intrigues of a sympathiser with Catholicism trembling on the verge of treason.

Lodge is therefore in many respects a typical figure. His genius, from the purely literary point of view, is sufficiently considerable to make him interesting in himself, and to give him a noticeable presence in the shifting pageant of the times. But what mainly distinguishes him from four or five other composers of

A

delicate lyrics and amorous romances is the length and
picturesque variety of his career.   Of this career,
unhappily, we possess but the outline.   A few dates in
wills or at the close of prefaces, a few nimble conjectures, a page of biography in the *Athenæ* of Anthony
à Wood, these we have to piece together as best
we may, and to endeavour to recover from them the
lost presence of a man; nor are we without this consolation, that, for an Elizabethan poet, Lodge stands
out before us at last with some measure of distinctness.

The year of the birth of Thomas Lodge is a matter
of pure conjecture.   At the death of his mother in
1579 he was not yet twenty-five, and at the death of
his father in 1583 he had almost certainly passed that
age.   The various circumstances of his early career
combine to make it probable that he was born in 1557.
He was the second son of people in affluent circumstances, his father, Sir Thomas Lodge, a grocer, having
been Lord Mayor of London in the plague-year, 1563.
The poet in after years took care to sign himself
"Gentleman," and to hold himself a little above the
crowd of playwrights.   His family pedigree was, or
professed to be, an ancient one, and he claimed descent
from Odoard di Logis, Baron of Wigton in Cumber-
land, a nobleman of the twelfth century.   The poet's
mother, Anne, Lady Lodge, was the daughter of a
previous Lord Mayor of London, Sir William Laxton,
who died before the poet's birth, in 1556; his grand-
mother, Lady Laxton, who lived to see him grown
up, seems to have shown him a particular partiality,

and to have selected him for preference among her daughter's children, who were six in number. In 1571 he entered Merchant Taylors' School, as has lately been discovered.[1] According to Wood, Thomas Lodge made his first appearance in Oxford about 1573, "and was afterwards servitour or scholar under the learned and virtuous Mr. Edward Hobye of Trinity College, where, making early advances, his ingenuity began at first to be observed by several of his compositions in poetry." This Edward Hobye was perhaps the son of that accomplished Sir Thomas Hobye, who, a quarter of a century earlier, had Englished the *Courtier* of Count Baldassar Castiglione.

About 1575 there were three distinct schools or haunts of polite letters in England, each of them silent to the world, but each preparing to make itself widely felt, and each fitting out soldiers for the great conflict of the wits. At the court of Elizabeth, Sidney, Greville, and Dyer were turning over the masterpieces of Greek and Italian literature, and dreaming, at least, of some form of stately English emulation. At Cambridge, amid a breathless circle of private admirers, Spenser

[1] To the courtesy of the Rev. Charles J. Robinson I owe the communication of this entry, from the Minutes of the Court of the Merchant Taylors' Company, held 23rd March $157\frac{0}{1}$:—

"Item the foresaide M^r and Wardens have admitted Thomas Lodge, fil', Thome L. militis, Edmond Greenock, fil...... G... .., Thomas Morgan, fil...... M......, William Widnell, fil, William W., mercator scissor, Robert Smythe, fil, Robert S. Jarrett Keyne, fil, John K., fishmonger, Samuel Lane, fil, John L., vintner, are admitted of the number of those l. schollars that are limited to be taughte within o^r schole."

The reference is to fifty scholars who were to pay 2s. 6d. a quarter.

was testing his powers of versification, as yet with little notion of the direction they would ultimately take. At Oxford, when Lodge went up to Trinity, John Lyly had already been four years at Magdalen, and though still only twenty years of age, had attracted considerable notice by his neglect of purely academical studies, and by his proclivities to poetry and romance. Among the youths who were clustered around him were George Peele, afterwards a famous playwright, and Abraham Fraunce, a writer of more reputation than merit. Probably in the same year which saw Lodge's advent at the University, Thomas Watson came to Oxford, and joined the coterie.

It would be very interesting to follow the intellectual development of this set of Oxford students, who seem, in some obscure way, to have found at Cambridge an ardent friend and adherent in Robert Greene. Their early exercises in verse and prose have all been lost, unless, indeed, as seems not unlikely, some portion of Lyly's epoch-making *Euphues* was composed before its author took his degree in 1575. Lodge was beyond question deeply influenced by Lyly. To the close of his career his style continued to be coloured with Euphuism, and on two separate occasions he blazoned the name of Lyly's masterpiece on a title-page of his own. To his intimacy with Peele he owed, in all probability, his interest in the stage, and his zeal for the revival of dramatic art; and Watson, whom he was destined to surpass in every branch of poetry, may have led him first in a lyrical direction with his amorous and precocious *Hekatompathia*. His own writings show that he was deeply read in the classics, that he had mastered French, Spanish, and Italian, and that he was familiar with all the learned subtilties which at that time engaged the leisure of the Universities.

All that we positively know of Lodge's Oxford career is that he was at college with Edmund and Robert Carew, sons of Lord Hunsdon, and that he remained at Trinity until he took his degree of Bachelor of Arts, on the 8th of July 1577, being then probably twenty years of age. He did not remain at Oxford to take the higher degree of Master of Arts; but returning to London, was admitted, on the 26th of April 1578, into the Society of Lincoln's Inn. His elder brother, William Lodge, had belonged to the Society, in which his father also had held office since 1572. In the winter of 1579 he had the misfortune to lose his mother, Lady Lodge; in the course of that year she had drawn out her will, in which she makes particular mention of her son Thomas, bequeathing part of her property towards "his finding at his book at Lincoln's Inn," and the rest to him at the age of twenty-five, with this provision, that should he "discontinue his studies," and cease to be what "a good student ought to be," this property should, on his father's decision, be divided among his brothers. It is unsafe to argue from this caution that Lodge was already a youth of unsteady character; on the contrary, he must have shown particular powers of intelligence to be thus selected among six children as his mother's sole legatee. There was probably some understanding on this point entered into between the father and mother, for in Sir Thomas Lodge's will the five other children are provided for, but the poet is not mentioned. It was perhaps recognised that Thomas had already received his share of the family estate direct from his mother.

The death of his mother seems to have been the occasion of his first essay in publication. *An Epitaph of the Lady Anne Lodge* was licensed on the 23rd of December 1579, and the name of its author was entered as "T. Lodge." This poem, which was probably an unbound pamphlet, has totally disappeared. Lodge's next venture has shown more vitality, but caused him at the time great disappointment and vexation. In 1579 the Rev. Stephen Gosson, a young divine of more effrontery than talent, published a furious counterblast against poetry, music, and the drama. This volume, which was named *The School of Abuse*, was in fact a puritanical attempt to nip in the bud the whole new blossom of English literature. It was not inspired, as were the attacks of Jeremy Collier a century later, by the righteous anger of a not very imaginative man who saw the wickedness of the stage without noticing its poetry; it was merely the snarl of a dull cleric who hated all that was urbane and graceful for its own sake. What was perhaps the strangest thing about it was that it abused poetry, and music, and stage-plays before these things had really begun to exist in England, so that its author was forced, in the absence of actual foes, to fight with such phantoms of literature as Webbe and Puttenham. *The School of Abuse* had hardly been published when

the *Shepherd's Calendar* appeared, and demonstrated
its absurdity. Young Thomas Lodge had the want
of wisdom to fly in defence of the fine art against this
lumbering opponent, and to pit his Oxford rhetoric
against the apparatus of a professed pedant. A much
greater honour, and a much more complete disaster,
awaited Gosson in the fact that Sir Philip Sidney was
about to deign to answer his attack on the arts in his
final *Apology for Poetry*. This latter work, not printed
till 1595, was written in the autumn of 1581. It was
probably about a year earlier that Lodge wrote and
hurried through the press his reply to Gosson. Of
this reply only two copies have come down to us,
each in a mutilated condition, without title-page or
introduction. There seems to have been a refusal of
publication, for Lodge himself says, in his preface to
the *Alarum against Usurers*, in 1584 :—

"About three years ago, one Stephen Gosson published a
book, intitled *The School of Abuse*, in which, having escaped
in many and sundry conclusions, I, as the occasion then fitted
me, shaped him such an answer as beseemed his discourse,
which by reason of the slenderness of the subject, because it
was in defence of plays and playmakers, the godly and reverend,
that had to deal in the cause, misliking it, forbade the publishing,
notwithstanding he, coming by a private imperfect copy, about
two years since, made a reply."

Lodge's *Defence of Poetry* need not detain us long.
It is a production of the old inflated type, without a
touch of modern freshness, full of pompous and only
too probably spurious allusions to the classics, vague,
wordy, and, in its temper, offensive. The author's

opponent is "shameless Gosson," a "hypocrite," a "monstrous chicken without head," and is addressed throughout with unmeasured and voluble contempt. The whole tract consists, as we possess it, of only twenty-four leaves, and within this small compass all the arts are defended from their clerical assailant. It is illustrative of the poverty of native literature in 1579, that not a single poem or play in the English language is quoted or referred to. That the little tract should have been suppressed is unaccountable, yet not more so than such an act of purposeless tyranny as the extinction of Drayton's *Harmony of the Church* ten years later. We know too little of the circumstances attending the censorship of the press under Elizabeth to hazard a conjecture regarding its mode of operation.

During the next few years we have great difficulty in following Lodge's fortunes. According to our supposition that he was born in 1557, he must have inherited his mother's fortune in 1582, since it was to pass to him when he reached the age of twenty-five. It is possible that before this he had become alienated from his family, and had even suffered poverty. In 1581 Lodge revised for the press, and issued with a commendatory poem of his own, Barnaby Rich's romance of *Don Simonides*. In this poem he speaks of his muse as dulled by his "long distress," and remarks that "a doleful dump pulls back my pleasant vein." I confess that these phrases seem to me to suggest illness rather than material ill-fortune, and I think that this view is justified by the famous phrase

of Stephen Gosson, who, returning to the attack in
1582, spoke of Lodge as "hunted by the heavy hand
of God, and become little better than a vagrant, looser
than liberty, lighter than vanity itself." Here, I think,
we may perceive a mixture of fact and supposition.
Gosson had doubtless heard of that "distress" under
which Lodge was labouring, and at once proceeded, in
the cowardly manner of disputants in that age, to
exaggerate it to Lodge's confusion. Gosson knew so
little about his opponent that he calls him William,
some copies of *Plays Confuted* containing a slip, on
which is the word "Thomas," pasted over the
"William." Gosson's testimony is of little value, and
if we listen to his vague accusation, we are no less
bound to remember that, when Lodge found next
occasion to take up his pen, he refuted the charges of
Gosson in a manly and straightforward epistle to those
who knew him best, the Gentlemen of the Inns of
Court :—

"You that know me, Gentlemen, can testify that neither my
life hath been so lewd, as that my company was odious, nor my
behaviour so light, as that it should pass the limits of modesty :
this notwithstanding, a licentious Hipponax, neither regarding the asperity of the laws touching slanderous libellers, nor
the offspring from whence I came, which is not contemptible,
attempted, not only in public and reproachful terms to condemn
me in his writings, but also to slander me."

Lodge was not so vagrant a person but that he had
married by this time, and in 1583 possessed property,
which he devised in his will to his wife Joan, and to his
daughter Mary. In December of the same year, his

father, Sir Thomas Lodge, died and was buried at St. Mary, Aldermary, with civic honours.

With this event the early career of the poet closes, and it is at this point that we must refer once more to the *Alarum against Usurers*, in which a number of passages occur which have been supposed, and not without a show of probability, to be autobiographical. In that work, published in 1584, Lodge comes before us as a writer possessing much more command over language than he had displayed in his attack on Gosson. The *Alarum* is a prose treatise against "coney-catching," the first of a class in which Greene, and afterwards Dekker, were to attain a great popularity, in which the temptations and miseries of London life were painted in gloomy colours, and the results of dissolute living were traded on to produce a literary effect. In Lodge's case it has been taken for granted that the palinode was sincere and personal, and that in this pamphlet he wore the white sheet publicly for notorious offences of his own. Nothing is more rash than a supposition of this sort, and nothing more dangerous in biographical criticism than to identify the literature with the man. Lodge describes a young gentleman from the University, whose mother tenderly cherished him, and whose wit was praised and his preferment secured, until his father brought him to the Inns of Court, where he fell among evil companions, and sank into giddy and debauched habits. His mother is now dead, his father's allowance to him is insufficient to meet his expenses, and he is deeply involved with usurers.

There is no doubt a great temptation to the biographer to distribute the incidents of this picturesque study along the scanty lines of Lodge's own memoir, but a more careful perusal of the *Alarum* shows the extreme danger of this course. The tract is inspired, probably, by some experience of the evils of which it treats; but it is not possible that, if the poet had been notoriously an evil-liver of this boisterous kind, he would have chosen to analyse his experience in so full and open a manner, in a book which bore his name, and which was elaborately dedicated to his colleagues of Lincoln's Inn. It is much more likely that his experience as a lawyer opened up to him the abuses which he describes, and that the real object of his tract was a purely philanthropic one, a desire to bring the scandalous tyranny of the money-lenders before the notice of Parliament.

Bound up with the *Alarum against Usurers*, in 1584, were two other works of a widely different nature. The *Delectable History of Forbonius and Prisceria* is a romance in prose and verse, which shows that Lodge responded with instant promptitude to Greene's start-word in *Mamillia* the year before. In these florid and cumbrous stories the English novel put forth its first bud; it is in these imitations of Italian romance that our long series of fiction commences. One or two writers, and particularly Whetstone in his *Promos and Cassandra* in 1578, had given a kind of timid suggestion of a story; but it is Greene to whom the merit is due of first writing a book wholly devoted to fictitious adventure in prose. Lodge, on

his side, made an improvement on Greene by introducing into *Forbonius and Prisceria* poetical interludes
and a system of correspondence in sonnets, which
were immediately adopted by Greene, and bequeathed
by him to his imitators.

Hitherto Lodge's achievements in verse had. been
slight and far from promising, but in this book he
begins to express himself with that mellifluous smoothness which afterwards characterised his poems.   The
prose style of the romance is founded on that of
Lyly's *Euphues*, of which Lodge was then, and remained, by far the most successful adapter.   His
memory was no less well stocked, and his fancy no
less graceful than those of Lyly himself, and he added
to Lyly's rather cold ethical abstraction of style a
southern glow of feeling.   In *Forbonius and Prisceria*,
however, we see rather a suggestion of this latter
quality than the presence of it, and the merits of the
romance are negative rather than positive.   The third
division of the volume is the best; it is a vigorous
satirical poem in rhyme royal entitled *Truth's Complaint
over England*.   In accordance with prudence, no less
than with the fashion of the age, the exact meaning of
the satire is concealed under an allegorical narrative.
Britain is expostulated with for her unjust madness,
for her prejudice against truth, and for being " hard-
hearted, flinty-minded, and bent to abuse."   In the
face of Lodge's later relations to the Catholic party,
it is difficult to understand these reproaches otherwise
than by supposing the satire to be a prudently concealed protest against the Anti-Romanist action of

Parliament, and the new stringent laws against the Jesuits. To have openly attempted to stem the rapidly-increasing flood of prejudice against the Papacy would merely have been to endanger the poet's own head, and we must suppose *Truth's Complaint* to have been one more of those cryptic contributions to politics which the Elizabethan poets loved to devise, and the only satisfaction of which must have been the pleasure of making an oral commentary to private friends.

As far as I am aware, there is no reason to suppose that any earlier edition of Lodge's next work, *Scilla's Metamorphosis*, than that which we now possess of 1589, was ever published. Yet I confess I should be little surprised if it was found to belong rather to 1585 or 1586. It seems to me to be a product of the poet's early London life, before the date of his wanderings, and the tone of the preface, no less than the style of the contents, bears out this supposition. It is dedicated, like the *Alarum against Usurers*, to the Gentlemen of the Inns of Court, and the author styles himself "of Lincoln's Inn, Gent." The preface, which is written in a cumbrous and affected style unworthy of Lodge in 1589, complains of the spread of poetic composition, which enforces him to publish his verses and assert his individuality. This petulance may either have been provoked by the success of such miscellanies as Clement Robinson's *Handful of Pleasant Delights*, or may be the expression of a passing irritation at the success of Lodge's personal friends, Lyly, Greene, Watson, and Peele, all of whom had come before the public with some prominence during the last few years.

The rapidity with which Greene, in particular, had poured forth his romances, might well have suggested to Lodge that " our wits nowadays are waxed very fruitful, and our pamphleteers more than prodigal ; " and the ease and skill with which the same writer had adopted and enriched that manner in poetry which Lodge had invented, may have provoked the latter to irritation.

Glaucus and Scilla, as the poem of *Scilla's Metamorphosis* is more properly named, was, however, a work in which its author owed little to his predecessors, and had nothing to fear from his contemporaries. It is no small merit in Lodge that in this work he was the inventor, or the introducer, into English literature, of a class of poem which has thriven amongst us, and which counts Shakespeare, Keats, and even Wordsworth (in *Laodamia*) among its direct cultivators. This was the minor epic in which a classical subject is treated in a romantic manner. Lodge sustains his theme through nearly one hundred and fifty stanzas, and if his narrative manner leaves much to be desired, his style is fluent and coloured, and his fancy is well supported. But the great interest of this poem, and one which has never fully received the attention it deserves, is the influence which it had upon the mind of Shakespeare. It is not too much to say that *Venus and Adonis* is a direct imitation of *Glaucus and Scilla*—an imitation, indeed, which vastly outshines its original, but none the less was distinctly composed in emulation of the older poem. The stanza in which the two poems are written is the same, and the relation between the volumes of 1589 and 1593

becomes quite startling when we realise that these
verses occur in the earlier poem :—

> " He that hath seen the sweet Arcadian boy
> Wiping the purple from his forced wound,
> His pretty tears betokening his annoy,
> His sighs, his cries, his falling on the ground,
>> The echoes ringing from the rocks his fall,
>> The trees with tears reporting of his thrall

> "And Venus starting at her love-mate's cry,
> Forcing her birds to haste her chariot on,
> And full of grief at last with piteous eye,
> Seen where all pale with death he lay alone,
>> Whose beauty quailed, as wont the lilies droop,
>> When wasteful winter winds do make them stoop.

> " Her dainty hand addressed to daw her dear,
> Her roseal lip allied to his pale cheek,
> Her sighs, and then her looks and heavy cheer,
> Her bitter threats, and then her passions meek ;
>> How on his senseless corpse she lay a-crying,
>> As if the boy were then but new a-dying."

This is very close to the earliest manner of Shakespeare ; and, if we return from *Glaucus and Scilla*
to *Venus and Adonis*, we shall be struck by the
resemblance in many points. There can be no doubt
that the young Shakespeare borrowed from Lodge his
tone, the mincing sweetness of his versification, and
the fantastical use of such words as "lily," "purple,"
crystal," and "primrose." None of the predecessors
of the greatest of our poets had so direct an influence
upon his early style as Lodge, and this must certainly
be accounted not the least of the claims of the latter
to our attention.

The remaining poems in the volume of 1589 are worthy of careful examination. A poem "In commendation of a Solitary Life" is a very delicate and refined composition, and one which might be taken as a typical example of the poetry of reflection in the age of Elizabeth. "A Beauty's Lullaby," on the other hand, is confessedly a work of the author's youth, and returns to the unwieldy versification and confused volubility of a preceding generation, in which rhetoric had taken the place of fancy. "Sundry sweet Sonnets," with which the collection closes, contain a variety of interesting lyrical experiments; the little madrigal, beginning "A very Phœnix, in her radiant eyes," and the song of which this is a verse—

> " The birds upon the trees
>   Do sing with pleasant voices,
>   And chant in their degrees
>   Their loves and lucky choices,
>   When I, whilst they are singing,
>   With sighs mine arms am wringing,"

should be omitted from no anthology of Elizabethan verse; the sonnets are most of them written in that spurious form of sixteen lines invented by Watson in his *Hekatompathia*, but in a single instance Lodge gives us here a sonnet of fourteen lines. He founds it, evidently, upon French usage, for it is in alexandrines. The proper Elizabethan sonnet had not yet been presented to the public, though Sidney's had doubtless been widely circulated in manuscript.

The progress of poetical taste was so rapid in the ninth decade of the sixteenth century that we may trace it almost year by year. It seems to me impossible that so very intelligent and sensitive a poet as Lodge could have written these "Sundry sweet Sonnets" after Sidney's death in 1586. He might very well publish them later, indeed; and yet I feel much inclined to think that *Scilla's Metamorphosis* was but reprinted in 1589. Of its author's adventures and manner of life between 1584 and 1590 we know only this, that he was engaged in at least one freebooting expedition to Spanish waters. In the very interesting preface to *Rosalynde* he tells us that he accompanied Captain Clarke in an attack upon the Azores and the Canaries. His expressions are so eloquent, and breathe so exactly the grandiose spirit of the age of Elizabeth, that we may quote them with advantage. "Having," he says to his friend Lord Hunsdon, "with Capt. Clarke made a voyage to the Islands of Terceras and the Canaries, to beguile the time with labour, I writ this book, rough, as hatched in the storms of the ocean, and feathered in the surges of many perilous seas." No account of this particular expedition has been preserved, and we may believe that it did not materially differ from many others of which a record has been kept by Purchas or Hakluyt.

The romance of *Rosalynde: Euphues' Golden Legacy*, which appeared in 1590, is the next, and by far the most important of Lodge's longer productions. "Room," says the author, "for a soldier and a sailor, that gives you the fruits of his labours that he wrought in the ocean, when every line was wet with a surge, and every humorous passion counterchecked with a storm." It is very pleasant to imagine the young poet, in the same picturesque dress in which his fellow-soldiers fought the Spanish Armada, stretched on the deck of his ship while she sailed under a tropical sky, and setting the amorous passions of the Forest of Arden to the monotonous music of the ocean. But for us the great interest of this, the best of Lodge's works, consists in the fact that Shakespeare borrowed from it the plot of one of the most exquisite of his comedies, *As You Like It*. With the exceptions of Rosalynde herself, of Phœbe, and of Adam, the trusty servant, Shakespeare has altered all the names which Lodge gives to his persons. Sir John of Bordeaux (Sir Rowland de Bois) has two sons, Saladyne (Oliver) and Rosader (Orlando); the younger of these departs from his brother's house in dudgeon, and arrives at the court at Torrismond, king of France (Frederick), who has banished his brother Gerismond (the Duke), the rightful monarch, to be an outlaw in the forest of Arden. At the usurper's court Rosader meets the wrestler Norman (Charles), and challenges him to try a fall in the presence of Rosalynde and her friend Aliena (Celia), the false king's daughter. It will be remembered that Celia adopts the name Aliena in the forest. All then follows as in *As You Like It*, except that there were in Lodge's story no equivalents to Jacques, Touchstone, and Audrey.

We put Lodge at a great disadvantage when we compare his crude invention with Shakespeare's magical insight and perfect vision; it is more fair to compare the *Rosalynde* as a story with the tales of Lodge's

immediate contemporaries. In it, and in the *Menaphon*
of Greene, which was probably written about the same
time, though published in 1589, we find the two coty-
ledons between which sprang up the shoot which has
spread into the mighty tree of English fiction. In
these languid and cumbrous stories it may be difficult
to trace any promise of the subtlety of *Far from the
Madding Crowd*, or of the vivid realism of *A Modern
Instance*, but the process of evolution which has led
from Greene and Lodge to Mr. Hardy and Mr. Howells
has been consistent and direct. Already in these
Euphuistic romances we trace in embryo certain
qualities which have always been characteristic of
Anglo-Saxon fiction, a vigorous ideal of conduct, a
love of strength and adventure, an almost Quixotic
reverence for womanhood. Before their time anything
like a coherent tale in prose had been unknown in
English ; chronicle-history had been attempted with
occasional success, but purely imaginative invention
had not. If we compare the *Rosalynde* of Lodge with
the *Menaphon*, which is Greene's masterpiece, we are
first struck with the strong similarity between the
methods of the two friends. They had acted and
reacted on each other, until it would be difficult,
without much reflection, to be sure whether one rich
dreamy page were the work of Greene or of Lodge.
The verses would always help us to discriminate, and
by-and-bye we should perceive that in the conduct of
his story Lodge is more skilful and more business-
like than Greene, who becomes entangled in his own
garlands and arabesques.

The *Rosalynde* is really very pleasant reading for its own sake, and as the author appears to have invented the plot, we may give him credit for having conceived a series of romantic situations which Shakespeare himself was content to accept. The life in the forest of Arden is charmingly described. Shakespeare gives us a sheepcot fenced about with olive-trees, but in Lodge the banished king is found feasting with the outlaws under a grove of lemons, and Rosader, while he rests from hunting lions with a boar-spear, inscribes his sonnets on the soft bark of a fig-tree.

These anachronisms cannot disturb those who enter into the spirit of either romance. The light which is blown down the deep glades of Arden, and falls lovingly on the groups in their pastoral masquerade, is that which never shone on sea or land, but which has coloured the romantic vision of dreamers since the world began. And it is very curious that the generation which saw the whole of Europe plunged into civil and international wars, when the roar of cannon became a common sound in the ears of Christendom, and when the whole religious and social polity of man was undergoing noisy revolution, should be the one to turn with special fondness to the contemplation of Arcadias and Eldorados, out of space, out of time; and that, on the very eve of the Armada, Lodge should have sailed under the battlements of Terceira with his brain full of Rosader's melancholy amoret in praise of beauteous Rosalynde's perfection.

The verse in the *Rosalynde* demands particular notice. It is as far superior to the prose in excellence

as Lodge himself was to Gosson or Gabriel Harvey.
Such a stanza as

> With orient pearl, with ruby red,
> With marble white, with sapphire blue,
> Her body every way is fed,
> Yet soft in touch and sweet in view ;
> Nature herself her shape admires,
> The Gods are wounded in her sight,
> And Love forsakes his heavenly fires
> And at her eyes his brand doth light,"

and the pieces beginning "First shall the heavens
want starry light," "Love in my bosom like a bee,"
and "Turn I my looks unto the skies," are of the
first order of excellence. Nothing so fluent, so opu-
lent, so melodious had up to that time been known
in English lyrical verse, for we must never forget that
when these exquisite poems were given to the public,
the *Faery Queen* itself was not yet circulated. In
these love-songs a note of passion, a soaring and
shouting music of the lark at heaven's gate, was heard
for the first time above the scholastic voices of such
artificial poets as Watson, and for a moment, to an
observant eye, Lodge might have seemed, next after
Spenser, the foremost living poet of the English race.
Only, however, for a moment, since the vaster luminary
of Shakespeare was on the horizon, attended and
preceded by Hesper and Phosphor, Marlowe with the
pride of his youth, and Sidney with his posthumous
glory. And then the full morning broke, and Lodge
in his sweet colours of the sunrise was set aside, and
forgotten in a blaze of daylight.

Something of this must have been dimly felt by Greene and Lodge. They did not confess that they were superseded, and from Lodge at least we have no word of petulance at the success of younger men. But from this date there is less effort made to breast the accomplishment of the age, and we find in both poets a recurrence to the established forms of their art. Greene, indeed, during the brief remainder of his life, abandoned the pastoral romance in favour of those treatises of "coney-catching" of which Lodge had set him the example in his *Alarum against Usurers*. That the friendship between these eminent men had become close we have many evidences. Lodge, who must have been reading Ronsard or Baïf, addressed an octett in French to Greene in 1589, as an introduction to the *Spanish Masquerado* of the latter poet, in which he addresses him as "mon Greene" and "mon doux ami." The success of *Rosalynde* in 1590 was instantaneous, and this romance continued to be printed for nearly a century. Lodge was encouraged to take up literature as a profession, and his publications during the next five years were very numerous. On the 2nd of May 1591 he issued from "my chamber," presumably in London, a piece of hackwork, the *Life of Robin the Devil*, a pseudo-historical account of the vices, adventures, and penitent end of Robert le Diable, second Duke of Normandy, whose brief career closed on the 2nd of July 1035, and whose eccentric vigour of character had collected a whole train of myths about his memory. This pamphlet was evidently a professional piece of work, but it is very far from being one of Lodge's less successful pieces. The poems which he scattered through its pages display, it is true, much less originality and brilliance than those in *Rosalynde*, but the story, such as it is, is well told, and there are prose passages, such as the voluptuous description of the "Bower of Editha," which are equal to the best which Lodge has left us. It is perhaps not unworthy of remark that it is in this book that we first detect that sympathy with the Catholic creed, and with Roman forms of penitence and ritual, which became more and more marked in Lodge's writings, and which have led to the shrewd conjecture that he was already secretly a member of the Roman communion.

At the close of *Rosalynde* Lodge promised that if the public encouraged his labours, he would next prepare his *Sailor's Calendar*. This work, which, if it ever appeared, has been hopelessly lost, was probably an account of the author's expedition to the Azores with Captain Clarke, and would doubtless have been rich in such autobiographical touches as we can ill be content to miss. In October 1764 there was sold from the library of Mr. John Hutton, of St. Paul's Churchyard, a black-letter volume by Lodge, entitled, *A Spider's Web*, which has not turned up since. Several of his existing works remain in unique exemplars, and there are, therefore, it is possible, other lacunæ in our list of his productions. The next book which comes under our notice is one of the rarest of all, and its entire disappearance would denude its author of little of his glory. Before, however, we consider the *Catharos*, which apparently was published late in 1591, and during its author's absence from England, we must deal with the circumstances which led him abroad.

Thomas Cavendish was a young squire of Suffolk, who, upon attaining his majority, had fitted out a ship, and had gone with Sir Richard Grenville on a privateering expedition to the West Indies. His courage was extraordinary, his judgment above that of a boy of twenty-one, and his power over men almost magical. In July of the following year he set out, at his own cost, on an enterprise which greatly impressed the imagination of the age, the circumnavigation of the globe, and this he accomplished in September 1588. He ravaged the coasts of many peaceful and savage nations, and returned to England with silken sails and every ostentation of wealth. So brilliant had been his success that he was encouraged, although his constitution had suffered in his adventures, to undertake a still more important piratical enterprise. On the 26th of August 1591, "three tall ships and two barks," with Thomas Cavendish at their head, set sail from Plymouth, bound for the coast of China and the Philippine Islands. Cavendish sailed on board the *Leycester*, and among the company of gentlemen who manned the second ship, the *Desire*, a galleon of 140 tons, in which Cavendish had made his previous voyage, was Thomas Lodge, the poet, who was now about thirty-four years of age. There may have been in him a hereditary love of this species of adventure, for his father, the sober Mayor of London city, had in the poet's infancy taken part in a peculiarly infamous expedition of the kind, the voyage of Robert Baker to Guinea in 1562, with the *Minion* and the *Primrose*. It was in the course of this expedition, and of that which followed it in 1563, that the traffic in negro slaves was set in motion.

It was necessary for Cavendish to avoid those particular portions of the globe which he had ravaged in his voyage of circumnavigation, and we hear of his landing first on the coast of Brazil, which he had formerly avoided. He ordered an attack on the town of Santos, while the people were at mass; the surprise was accomplished, but no use was made of the success, and the failure of Cavendish's judgment was soon made apparent. From the 15th of December to the 22nd of January 1592, the little fleet remained at Santos doing nothing; the captain of the *Roebuck*, the third galleon, was told off in command of those who preferred to spend this time on shore, and Lodge was among the latter. The Englishmen took up their abode in the College of the Jesuits, and Lodge occupied himself, as he tells us, among the books in the library of the Fathers. He had by this time, perhaps on one of his previous expeditions, made himself master of the Spanish language. Something which he met with in a book at Santos suggested to him the idea which he proceeded to weave into a new romance.

Meanwhile the English fleet were driven from their position by want of food, and proceeded down the coast of Brazil to the Straits of Magellan. "Here," says Lodge, "I had rather will to get my dinner, than to win fame;" and, indeed, a spirit of dissension and mutiny began to render life on board the English ships almost unbearable. Cavendish, who could bear his men through unruffled success, but who was too young and too inexperienced for calmness in misfortune, seems to have lost his head altogether. The cold was extreme, the ships were separated by violent storms, and at last Cavendish left the *Leycester* and came on board the *Desire*, where Lodge was, bitterly denouncing his own men, and refusing to sail with them any longer. The officers of the *Desire* held parley accordingly with those of the *Leycester*, and Cavendish was persuaded to go back to the latter. Lodge seems to have shared the common dislike of Cavendish, for in 1596 he speaks of him as one "whose memory, if I repent not, I lament not."

In the midst, however, of these sufferings and disturbances, while they lay storm-bound among the icy cliffs of Patagonia, Lodge occupied himself by writing his Arcadian romance of the *Margarite of America*, which he printed four years later. In the preface to that book he says: "Touching the place where I wrote this, it was in those Straits christened by Magellan; in which place to the southward many wondrous Isles, many strange fishes, many monstrous Patagoñes, withdrew my senses: briefly, many bitter and extreme frosts at midsummer continually clothe and clad the discomfortable mountains; so that there was great wonder in the place wherein I writ this, so likewise might it be marvelled that in such scanty fare, such causes of fear, so mighty discouragements, and so many crosses, I should deserve to eternise anything." The weary months spent to no purpose within the Antarctic seas must have fretted the spirits of all the companions of Cavendish. At last it seems to have become plain to them that autumn was coming on, and that they would not get through to the Pacific at all. The *Desire* set off alone on her return voyage, and Lodge, if he was still on board of her, landed, after disappointment, suffering, and almost starvation, on the coast of Ireland, on the 11th of June 1593. The crew of the ship had been reduced to sixteen, and of these only five were in tolerable health. Cavendish himself died of a broken heart, at the age of twenty-nine, before he completed what Purchas calls "that dismal and fated voyage, in which he consummated his earthly peregrinations."

This voyage appears to have cured Lodge of all his youthful vivacity, although his wandering spirit soon broke out again. During his absence of twenty-two months great changes had occurred. Three of those poets with whose names his had been most closely united had died during that interval; these were Watson, Greene, and Marlowe. But he found that his memory had been supported during his absence, in one case, certainly, by a friend whom he should never see again. In 1591, immediately after his departure, had been published his *Catharos*, or, as the sub-title names it, *A Nettle for Nice Noses*. This has become one of the rarest, and must always have been one of the most insignificant of his productions.

Three friends, Diogenes, Philoplutos, and Cosmosophos, whose names betray their didactic purpose, carry on a dreary dialogue on the subject of the seven deadly sins as they are practised in Athens, or rather London. Diogenes is a cynic moralist, who claims that his own life is καθαρός, *pure*, and who bitterly reflects on the conduct of his fellow-citizens. The *Nettle for Nice Noses* has no literary merit; it is an early example of the rabid and pedantic prose satire of the Elizabethan age, a style of cheap literature which pandered to the respectable lower middle class, and fostered its prejudices. Here and there we find a touch of Lodge's eloquent Euphuism, but as a whole this is among the tamest of his books.

Infinitely better and more characteristic is the romance of *Euphues' Shadow*, which appeared the following year, and the editing of which was one of the last performances on earth of Robert Greene. Lodge, as appears from the preface, wrote from America to Greene, begging him to see this book through the press and to select a patron. The title of the romance directly recalls the famous work of Lyly, and it is in *Euphues' Shadow* that Lodge comes nearest to his great precursor. Those far-fetched references to the classics, those applications to man's estate of a fabulous zoology and botany, those involved and sonorous sentences, each a very microcosm in itself, all the features of Lyly's extraordinary style are reproduced by Lodge with the most startling precision. We have the beast Varius, with his rich skin but rank flesh, the bird Struchio, the populous and pompous

city of Pasan, the horn of the serpent Cerastes, the
virtues of the herb Abrotamum, almost before we
have fairly started in the story ; and the manner of
Lyly is caught with singular art and precision. Probably this was done on purpose, for it is certain that
after a few pages the author becomes weary of this
antithetical apparatus and panoply of examples, and
sinks to the rich, easy style that was native to him.
The lyrics, which are more sparsely than usual
scattered over the pages of this romance, are not in
Lodge's brightest vein, and no one of them would be
selected as among his most characteristic pieces.

It is probable that both of Lodge's surviving plays
were first acted during his absence from England. We
know that this was the case with *A Looking Glass for
London and England*, in which Greene had been his
collaborator. This drama was performed by Lord
Strange's servants on the 8th and 27th of March 1592,
and again on the 19th of April and the 7th of June of
the same year. A passage of Greene's posthumous
Groat's Worth of Wit has been rashly considered
to refer unquestionably to Lodge. After exhorting
Marlowe, Greene proceeds : "With thee I join young
Juvenal, that biting satirist, that lastly with me
together writ a comedy." It is perhaps not much to
the point that the *Looking Glass* is not a comedy at
all, but a tragedy; but it is almost certain that when
Juvenal is mentioned Nash is always meant. Nash
had made himself many enemies by his pasquils, and
was widely known, which Lodge was not, as a "biting
satirist." It is possible that Nash may have assisted

Greene in writing his *George à Greene*, or in composing some other comedy which no longer exists. At all events, our desire to clutch at every shred of biographical allusion must not blind us to the fact that by Juvenal Greene can hardly have intended Lodge, or any one but Nash.

In a tract printed in 1867, Dr. C. M. Ingleby carefully sifted and collated all the evidence for the popular assumption that Lodge was himself a player, and he showed it to rest upon absolutely no basis at all. That somebody called Lodge failed to pay his tailor's bill, and left Henslowe responsible for the debt, is one of those tantalising little facts which may mean everything or nothing, and upon which it is exceedingly dangerous to dogmatise. Lodge had certainly very little dramatic faculty, and there is no evidence to show that at any period of his life he tried to eke out this talent by actual stage experience. Of his two plays, the *Looking Glass for London and England* is by far the more interesting. It is very primitive in form; the serious part of the plot deals with the arrogance and license of Rasni, king of Assyria. Neither in manner nor in metrical peculiarity are these descriptions of the pride of Nineveh like anything else to be found in the works of Greene or Lodge. Whichever of them wrote the opening scenes of the *Looking Glass* was fresh from witnessing the performance of Marlowe's *Tamburlaine the Great*, and was anxious to outdo the young master himself in the "swelling bombast of bragging blank verse." It is probably Lodge to whom we owe the rant of these "drumming decasyllabons,"

which occasionally soften to a richness that reminds
us of the lyrics in *Rosalynde*. This is the language
in which the King of Cicilia thinks fit to describe King
Rasni :—

> " If lovely shape, feature by nature's skill
> Passing in beauty fair Endymion's,
> That Luna wrapped within her snowy breasts,
> Or that sweet boy that wrought bright Venus' bane,
> Transformed into a purple hyacinth,
> If beauty nonpareil in excellence
> May make a king match with the God in gree,
> Rasni is God on earth, and none but he."

Unfortunately, although the authors of the *Looking
Glass* borrowed from Marlowe something of his boisterous music and his high key of passion, they possessed
none of his sounder dramatic qualities. The piece is
a strange old-fashioned farrago of bombast and satire ;
when Rasni and the Ninevites are not mouthing, low
comic personages in the streets of London are talking
Elizabethan slang. A certain Osias serves as chorus,
and shifts the clumsy scenes. Jonas is thrown straight
out of the mouth of the whale on to the stage, and the
vengeance of Heaven falls on Nineveh with a grotesque
attempt at realism. Yet poor as is the *Looking Glass*,
it is a better play than Lodge's sole unassisted effort
at dramatic composition, *The Wounds of Civil War*,
first printed in 1594. The dull and tame scenes of
this historical drama, in which there is hardly an
attempt at action, and where there is even a melancholy
absence of rant, hardly allow themselves to be read.
At one point Lodge remembers who he is, and Marius,

in exile on the Numidian mountains, recites with great satisfaction a sonnet and a long madrigal, like those carved on the trees of Arden by Rosader and Montanus. It may be said that there is no female character in *The Wounds of Civil War*, for though Cornelia and Fulvia cross the stage, and then at the close recross it, they have no further business to perform. The play contains its sole historical interest in the fact that it was the precursor of those tragedies of Roman history which form so splendid a part of the works of Shakespeare and Ben Jonson.

During 1593, the year of his return from South America, Lodge's pen was particularly active. It is probable that he resumed his legal connection, for, on the title-page of his *Life and Death of William Longbeard*, he once more styles himself "of Lincoln's Inn." This tract is a pseudo-historical romance of the same kind as Lodge's previous *Robin the Devil*, but more hastily put together, and eked out with a variety of short stories about famous pirates, and the melancholy fates of learned men. The tale which gives its name to the volume is adorned by a variety of odes and sonnets, which are pretty in themselves, but preposterously out of place in such a prosaic narrative of crime and its reward. Lodge was better occupied during the same year by contributing lyrics to the miscellany called *The Phœnix Nest*, which was printed by John Jackson, and nominally edited by a certain R. S. In the induction to his next publication, *Phillis*, Lodge seems to claim for himself the responsibility of the *Phœnix Nest*, in which we find no fewer than thirteen of his pieces which occur nowhere else. *Phillis* itself, however, is a far more important publication than either of these. It is, in fact, from a critical point of view, the best of all Lodge's works, *Rosalynde* excepted. Among the cycles of Elizabethan sonnets it takes an early place, being preceded by Sidney's *Stella*, Daniel's *Delia*, and Constable's *Diana*, and accompanied by Barnaby Barnes' *Parthenope*, and Watson's posthumous *Tears of Fancy*. Lodge's sonnets are particularly rich in single lines, such as :—

"The falling fountains from the mountains falling,"

and in short passages of extraordinary felicity, such as :—

"The rumour runs that here in Isis swim
    Such stately swans, so confident in dying,
That when they feel themselves near Lethe's brim
    They sing their fatal dirge when death is nighing ;
And I, like these, that feel my wounds are mortal,
    Contented die for her whom I adore,
And in my joyful hymns do still exhort all
    To die for such a saint, or love no more."

But it is rare to find a sonnet which preserves this level of excellence throughout. That beginning

"How languisheth the primrose of Love's garden,"

has found its way into the anthologies, and

"I wrote in Myrrha's bark, and as I wrote,"

with its beautiful pine-wood scenery, is almost as worthy of popularity. The use of the double rhyme gives a unique sweetness to many of Lodge's sonnets, and in almost all of them, even where the construction is most lax and the sense most obscure, the diction is particularly rich. The volume contains, besides sonnets, some of Lodge's best songs and lyrics, in particular "Love guides the roses of thy lips," "My Phillis hath the morning sun," and "My matchless mistress, whose delicious eyes," each of which might be quoted as a type of the erotic poetry of the age. The whole book was dedicated to Lady Shrewsbury. It closes with a long, dreary, and excessively obscure elegiac poem called *The Complaint of Elstred*, which may have given Shakespeare a faint suggestion of the form of his *Lover's Complaint*, and which tells those histories of Locrine and Sabrina, which were dramatised two years after with the assumption of Shakespeare's name, and in a subsequent generation occupied the attention of Milton.

When Joseph Hall brought out his *Virgidemiarum* in 1597, and boasted with youthful braggadocio—

> "follow me who list
> And be the second English satirist,"

he forgot or neglected to remind his readers that Lodge had, in 1595, published in his *Fig for Momus* four or five satires which led the way for future essays in this vein so distinctly that to overlook them was an act of bad faith or of bad history. This was another case in which Lodge set a fashion which has been followed by every English writer of the same kind. The satire in heroic couplets has passed from Lodge through Hall, Donne, Dryden, Pope, Churchill, Crabbe, and Byron, to such rare later efforts as have been essayed, without any change of outward form, and Lodge deserves the credit of his discovery. His satires seem to have attracted no notice in his own age, for he was never encouraged to print that "whole centon of them," which, he says, were in his possession.

The *Fig for Momus*, which was sent out to the world on the 6th of May 1595, was in several ways a tentative volume. Lodge proved himself an innovator again by publishing in it, for the first time in English, epistles in verse to private persons, founded in form upon those of Horace. Of these epistles several address eminent men in terms of friendship. One to Michael Drayton, to whom an eclogue in the same volume is inscribed under the pseudonym of Rowland, shows the existence of an intimate affection between Lodge and the young author of *Idea*, and is an early testimony to the dignified esteem with which Drayton was regarded by his contemporaries. An eclogue in the *Fig for Momus* is dedicated to Samuel Daniel, an Oxford man who had gone up to Magdalen after Lodge's time, and who had lately made himself noticeable for a very pure and intelligent vein of reflective poetry. Daniel and Drayton were men of the best class, gentlemen who held themselves aloof from the vulgar struggle of the wits, and it is significant that they, and no longer the rough sort of professional pamphleteers, should appear as Lodge's friends and associates.

He was now approaching the age of forty; the new canons of literary taste which he had been among the first to institute, were now being adopted by authors of far greater power and freshness than he. Shakespeare was in motion ; the riotous crew of the dramatists were lifting up their voices, and Lodge breathed along his oaten flute with less confidence, and betrayed a certain growing agitation year by year. The *Fig for Momus* marks his latest appearance as a poet, since the sonnets of the *Margarite of America* certainly, and those published in *England's Helicon* probably, were the work of several years prior to their publication. Lodge's satires, eclogues, and epistles are very monotonous in style, and do not command attention by their vigour and concision. The thought is rarely bright enough or the expression nervous enough to demand definite praise. The best that can be said of them is that they are lucid and Horatian, escaping the faults of those succeeding satirists who thought themselves tame unless they took Persius, or even, perhaps, the *Alexandra* of Lycophron, as the model of their obscurity.

In 1596 Lodge's activity as an original writer culminated, and practically closed. We possess no fewer than four distinct volumes published by him in that year. On the 15th of April he gave to the world his prose disquisition of *The Devil Conjured*. It is a tedious soliloquy on virtue, put into the mouth of a "virtuous and solitary Hermit called Anthony," and bears a sort of whimsical resemblance in its conception, though certainly none in its execution, to the *Tentation de St. Antoine* of Flaubert. The author himself thought highly of this performance, and even went so far as contemptuously to describe his former poems and romances as mere corncockles, while this was the real wheat of his brain. The preface, indeed, is a palinode; there can be little doubt that he had now "got religion," and that his early amorous writings, though always innocent, seemed to him to call for penitence. It appears from the dedication to Sir John Fortescue, that Lodge was now suffering from reports, and it is probable that he was already suspected of being a Catholic.

This element in his nature is still more apparent, though yet not openly avowed, in *Wit's Misery and the World's Madness*, another prose disquisition, of a pseudo-philosophical kind, which he issued from his house at Low Leyton, on the 5th of November of the same year, 1596. The Lodge family had always been associated, more or less vaguely, with this village, which lies in the Hundred of Becontree, in Essex, about six miles to the north-east of London. The messuage or farm of Malmaynes, in the same hundred, was originally given by Lady Lodge in her will to her son Thomas, but the gift is set aside in a codicil, and certain lands on the borders of Suffolk and Essex, at or near Nayland, are bequeathed to the poet instead. Sir Thomas Lodge's house, however, had been at or near Low Leyton, and it may be conjectured that by some means or other his second son had come into possession of it. By this time, it would seem, Lodge's first wife was dead, and he had married Mrs. Jane Albridge (or Aldred), a widow lady, a Catholic, whose first husband had been a dependent of Lodge's early patron, Sir Francis Walsingham, and who had herself been useful to the Catholics at Rome and other places in the days of their darkest persecution. This Mrs. Lodge has retained a minute niche in history as a cat's-paw in the hands of the detractors of the Earl of Arundel during his imprisonment in the Tower in 1586.

Bearing these circumstances in mind, it is by no means extraordinary that a leaning towards Catholic psychology of the more obvious kind, such as we find it expressed in the *Devil Conjured* and in *Wit's Misery and the World's Madness*, should have taken the form of direct Romanism in the "*Prosopopeia,* or Tears of the Holy, Blessed, and Sanctified Mary, the Mother of God." It has been doubted, I cannot conceive upon what grounds, whether this little treatise, although signed with the familiar letters T. L., is actually by our Thomas Lodge. It is true that in two copies these initials have been reversed by the printer, but, in my opinion the style of the text is sufficient to demonstrate that this is one of Lodge's genuine tracts, and the open profession of Catholic doctrine is no more than what we have been gradually prepared for by the whole tenor of the poet's career. If there is any cause for astonishment, it is that Lodge should have ventured to come forward under so thin a disguise, at a time when it was still dangerous to avow dissent from the Church of England.

In the midst of this busy year, 1596, and in spite of all his denunciation of his early amatory writings, Lodge bethought him of the romance which he had

composed in the Straits of Magellan in the winter of
1592, and he published it on the 4th of May under the
title of *A Margarite of America*. This is one of the
prettiest of his stories. It has absolutely nothing to
do with America, save the accident of its composition
there; it is a tragical narrative of the loves of Arsa-
dachas, son and heir to the Emperor of Cusco, and
Margarita, whose father was king of Muscovy, and
who dwelt in a fortress "situate by a gracious and
silver-floating river, environed with curious planted
trees to minister shade, and sweet-smelling flowers."
Lodge has expended his richest fancy on this work;
the heroine's father cannot be murdered in his bed,
but that this article of furniture is described as of
black ebony, set about with rubies and carbuncles;
the lady herself, summoned to her fate, pauses that
she may decently array herself in a grass-green robe,
embroidered with daisies; and if a political meeting
is to be held by the nobles of Cusco, it has to be
arranged in "a fair arbour, covered with roses and
honeysuckles, paved with camomile, pinks, and violets,
and guarded with two pretty crystal fountains on
every side." The passages of verse, sonnets, and
canzonets are of the same sweet and mellifluous order,
and recall the interludes of the *Rosalynde*. It does
not seem to have been observed that the elaborate
piece beginning—

> "With Ganymede now joins the shining sun,"

is an example, the earliest in English literature, of a
sestina formed on the exact plan of that form of verse,

as invented by Arnaut Daniel and employed by Dante. An examination of the length of the lines and of the arrangement of the tornada shows that Lodge was following an Italian, and not a Provençal model. The latter, indeed, he could scarcely be expected to meet with. When we except the *Rosalynde* and the *Phillis*, *A Margarite of America* is perhaps the work of Lodge's which will best reward the ordinary reader.

Lodge now retired from the profession of poetry, and adopted that of medicine. According to Anthony à Wood, he took his degree of Doctor of Physic at Avignon. This must have been at least as early as 1600, for in that year certain passages from his known poems were quoted in *England's Parnassus* with the attribution "Doctor Lodge." He also contributed original poems to *England's Helicon*, a miscellany of the same year. As a physician, he rapidly attained a great reputation, and was ranked among the leading Englishmen in the profession. On the 25th of October 1602, "Thomas Lodge, Doctor of Physic, of the University of Avenion," was incorporated in the University of Oxford. In the same year he produced a version of the works of Josephus, which was so popular that between 1602 and 1670 it passed through no fewer than seven editions. In 1603 Lodge appeared for the last time before the public as an original author, with a *Treatise of the Plague*, dedicated to the Lord Mayor and Corporation of London, and applicable to the epidemic at that moment raging in the city. Contemporary allusions to him are not rare in the occasional literature of the early part of the seventeenth century.

In the first act of that curious play *The Return from Parnassus*, which, though not printed until 1606, was acted in 1602, Lodge is thus referred to as a physician and as a Euphuist:—

> " For Lodge and Watson, men of some desert,
>   Yet subject to a critic's marginal ;
>   Lodge for his oar in ev'ry paper boat,
>   He that turns over Galen ev'ry day,
>   To sit and simper ' Euphues' Legacy.' "

In a manuscript " Poetical Common Place Book of a Cambridge Student," which was perhaps begun in 1611, there is a coarse satirical piece against " London Physicians," in which Lodge is thus mentioned :—

> " And old Doctor Lodge,
>   That leaues of to doge,
>   Will you neuer leaue ? "

This not very intelligible apostrophe possibly points to the fact that, in spite of his reputation—and in his *Troia Britanica*, in 1609, Heywood had given him a place among the six most famous English doctors— Lodge was occasionally put to great straits for a livelihood. In the meantime I may be allowed to print for the first time a letter which exists among the Domestic State Papers, and which reveals something of the intrigues in which Lodge and his Catholic wife were unquestionably engaged :—

" S^r, havinge mett wth so convenient a messenger I canno but congratulate yor departure hence to liue in such contentment as their I heare you doe. wch as I wish more and more to increase so doubt I not but that you will alwayes be mindefull of ye well wisshinge frendes you have left behinde yo^u. In my

last lettre to you, I requested that Mrs Lodge might haue continued heare at leaste for some six or seaven monethes, but
sithence that tyme havinge bin at the Moscovia house and not
findinge that her stay heare might doe me the good I expected,
and that I hould it no reasonable request so longe to disjoyne
man and wief, I leave the orderinge of y^t busines to yor owne
further consideracōn.   Wisshinge that Mr. Griffin for that my
selfe shall be often absent from hence wer fully authorized by a
lettre of Attorney from you, to haue the managinge of that
busines from tyme to tyme.   And that further you will write
yor lettres as occasōn shall be offered to the M^r of the company
and yor lettres of particular direction to Mr Griffin or others to
such effect as I shall from tyme to tyme require it.   The
shippinge wch went forth two yeare sithence is not yet all returned and theirfore no accoumpt past as yet of that viage, yet
it is proffered that the fiftye pounde may goe in adventure this
yeare againe wch argueth that the principall remayneth whole,
but yet cannot be gotten out, and theirfore I hould it best againe
to adventure it, and so Mrs Lodge in yor absence hath undertaken to doe.   And some bodye must from tyme to tyme be
heare to let the company what they will adventure or els the
stocke for y^t yeare lieth deade.   Notw^{th}standinge all the diffi-
cultyes this age seemeth for this p^rsent to inviron us wth all,
y^t we shall still be hable to drawe breath in England, and I
hope ere it be longe to see you willinge and desirous to looke
homewarde, for though much hath bin attempted against us in
parliament yet, hitherto nothinge is done harder then of oulde,
nor as I hope will be.   I pray you S^r advertize me howe I
might place Robin their, and what the charge would be to kepe
him at his booke or what you thinke of it, if I could gett him
placed wth Sr Willm Standley, and lett me heare sometymes from
you I pray yo^w we lye still at o^r oulde lodginge.   And thus
wth my hartye commendacōns & my wiues to you wth yor servants
dutye I ende London this ix^{th} of March 1605.

> " Yo^r lovinge frende

> " W. JENISON.

" To the worshipfull his louinge frende
" Mr Thomas Lodge, Doctor in Phisicke."

Our next glimpse of the poet-physician shows him to us once more setting out upon his travels. A memorandum on the Privy Council Registers, dated January 10th, 1616, mentions "A passe for Tho. Lodge, Doctor of Physic, and Henry Sewell, gent., to travel into the Arch-Duke's Country, to recover such debts as are due unto them there, taking with them two servants, and to return agayne in five moneths." It has been suggested that the real object of this journey was to avoid process on the part of Alleyn, who arrested Lodge immediately upon his return. Lodge seems to have left England again as soon as this trouble was over, and to have remained abroad, probably practising in the Low Countries, until 1619. In his treatise called *The Poor Man's Talent*, first printed in 1881, he describes a remedy "which," he says, "I have often tried in the Royal Hospital at Mecklin upon soldiers that grew lame by cold." But inquiries made at Malines have unfortunately resulted in the discovery of no record of his name or functions.

Of Lodge's remaining years few memorials are in existence. That he was in easy circumstances may be gathered from the fact that in 1612 he raised a monument in the Church of Rolleston, Notts, to the memory of his younger brother, Nicholas Lodge, lord of that manor, in whose will a legacy of two gold bracelets is made to the wife of the poet. In 1614 Lodge published a translation of the works of Seneca, and a copy of this book is in existence, given by Lodge to Thomas Dekker in the year of publication. About

1623 he compiled *The Poor Man's Talent*, a medical text-book for the use of his wife's old patroness, Anne, Countess of Arundel. In this work Lodge uses expressions which could only proceed from the mouth of a Catholic, and such a phrase as " I will set down a remedy which St. Dominic revealed to a poor devout woman," leave us no room to doubt that by this time, at all events, he had definitely joined that communion to which he had all his life been leaning.

Lodge became a very prominent practitioner during the last years of his life. His private house was still at Low Leyton, but he saw his London patients originally in Warwick Lane, afterwards in Lambert Hill, and finally, shortly before his death, in Old Fish Street. He died, it is said, of the plague, in 1625, being then in his sixty-seventh or sixty-eighth year, and on the 12th of October of that year administration of his effects was granted to his widow, Jane Lodge, who must herself have been an elderly woman at the time, her name having come forward in connection with the Arundel family just forty years before.

Thomas Lodge was a strange compound of strength and weakness, of imitation and originality. His intelligence and activity gave him a prominence in the literature of the time which his mind was hardly vigorous enough to sustain. He would have, as his satirist says, "his oar in every paper boat," and could not conceive the possibility of failing in any department of literature. As a fact, however, he is a signal failure in drama, in satire, and in philosophy, and his unsuccessful efforts in these directions occupy a large section of his entire works. His almost servile attitude towards the bold affectations of Lyly would make us at one moment deny Lodge all true originality, if we were not immediately confronted by the fact that he was himself a pioneer in half-a-dozen fields of poetical invention. The introducer into English of the romantic epic, of the heroic satire, and of the heroic epistle, cannot be overlooked in any historical summary of our literature. But Lodge's real excellence is as a lyrical poet, and in the richness of his fancy as a prose romancer.

His prose style, judged by severe modern canons, or even compared with the poetical style of his own age, is not less intolerable than that of most of his contemporaries. English prose, as an instrument for the clear expression of unaffected thought, had hardly begun to exist. Lodge's best romances are as lucidly and gracefully written as was at that time possible. They never can, however, take again a living place in literature; but this honour must not be denied to the best of their author's songs and sonnets. In that glowing age no one could express the jubilant exuberance of love with a fuller note, with a more luxurious music, with more affluent and redundant imagery. His intellectual languor prevents the complete, or rather the continuous expression of this golden ecstasy, and we are often left to wonder that a lyrist who was so thrilling a moment ago can now be so insipid. But in a few of his best songs he sustains his flight till the music is perfect, and in these he reaches the topmost level of success. The author of "Like to the clear in highest sphere," was as genuine a poet as ever breathed, and whether in these moments of great inspiration, or in his hours of lassitude and extravagance, Lodge is always the very type and exemplar of a man of letters in the irregular and romantic age of Elizabeth.

1882.

JOHN WEBSTER

AMONG those shrouded figures of the Elizabethan poets, to whom present popularity was a doubtful thing, and future fame scarcely dreamed of, who had no Vasari to perpetuate the humours and adventures of their lives, those who defied the world most have left the most definite personal impression behind them. Robert Greene, the dissolute bully, the remorseful rake, whose red beard flares in his own graceless stories, would hardly have been suspected as the outward man of that lyric spirit that wrote "Ah! were she pitiful as she is fair," and that dreamed the strange pure Utopia of the *Menaphon*. If Greene, and Dekker, and Marlowe, the three scapegraces of the period, present such violent and unexpected features in their private lives, what eccentricities may not have characterised those other men, whose deeds cried out less loudly against them, and whose works have now no setting of biographical fact? Among these latter figures, perhaps the most shadowy and indefinable is the one that bears the good English name of John Webster. When was he born? No one has recorded. When did he die? It is not known. His presence seems to hover about London, and is doubtfully connected in some gloomy fashion with the Church of St.

47

Andrew's, Holborn. One miserable satirist has per-
petuated his own obscure name by vilifying our poet
with coarse and ridiculous abuse; and this summary,
with the dates of his productions, comprises the entire
biography of a man who ranks as one of the most
illustrious dramatists of modern Europe.   Meagre
enough, truly, is this life-history, so meagre, indeed,
that editors have distended it with babbling discus-
sions as to the authorship of certain tracts, violently
Puritanic, and published when the poet must have
been extremely aged; of which controversy we need
say nothing here, merely remembering that it is not
very long since Mr. Sheridan Knowles, a dramatist of
no mean talent, surprised us in his old age by a like
change of opinion.   All we can profitably do in the
absence of characteristic anecdotes is to examine the
priceless legacy of verse that this phantom-bard has
left us, and seek there for the lineaments we cannot
find elsewhere.

A most unfortunate practice among many of the
dramatic authors of the Elizabethan age, and one
ensuing on their carelessness of posterity, was to unite
together in the composition of single plays, a course
still pursued by some playwrights in France.   In most
instances this destroys all possibility of studying the
individual style of each poet; in the case of Dekker,
who carried the system of poetic partnership to excess,
it has seriously impaired the reputation of a writer
who, if we could only be sure that we had him in our
grasp, was probably inferior to few of his time in certain
great qualities.   Happily Shakespeare, Ben Jonson,

and Webster, the three brightest stars in the galaxy, usually avoided the practice, and hence the study of their style is easy. Webster, for instance, besides all combined work, has left four perfect dramas in which there is not a suspicion of any hand but his own. These four, all diverse in their detail, but uniform in the salient characteristics of style, are a tragedy of intrigue, a tragedy of the fatalist or Æschylean type, a tragi-comedy and an historical play. So strongly marked is the style in all these productions, that coming fresh from the study of them, I felt able unhesitatingly to identify and separate from the rubbish of a minor author a complete idyll of pure comedy. It is embedded in a play by Rowley, called *A Cure for a Cuckold*, which has always been printed as a joint work of the two dramatists. So clumsily are the two plays united, that they can be separated scene by scene, without there being any doubt of the authorship of either. Webster's little drama, a thoroughly characteristic and very lovely work, has nothing whatever to do with the vulgar under-plot which suggested, properly enough, the existing title, and I cannot bear that a piece so pure and refined should be stigmatised by so repulsive and unmeaning a name. If some editor would but adopt my discovery, and reprint this little comedy without any dross of Rowley, a new name might be thought of to distinguish it by. But I hope presently to return to this point.

After Shakespeare, Jonson comes, and after Jonson, Webster. We acknowledge no claimants to a share of their peculiar honour. In spite of the sweetness

D

and wit of Beaumont and Fletcher, their want of originality, individuality, and sustained power places them in the second rank of dramatists, though they are honourably pre-eminent there. No one else, save Marlowe, who belongs to an earlier epoch, and stands alone, dares pretend to the foremost rank. Webster is far beneath Ben Jonson in scope and freshness of invention, in learning, and in the more obvious forms of comedy; in versatility and in natural ease of dialogue we must confess him also inferior to that great master. But, like Shakespeare, he is transcendental; his strong muse wings itself out of the common world, and sees things with the eye of a visionary. His scenes force us to a great solemnity; the very jesting is bitter and of a sad echo; without rousing any of the meaner passions, unalloyed by fear or any weak insistance on the forms of death, he yet leads through his sterner works such a mournful masque of cumulative anguish, that nothing but the great destiny on which all is seen to hang can reconcile us to the unutterable sorrow. The soft moderns of whom Théophile Gautier said in his scorn, " Ils n'admettaient que deux couleurs dramatiques, le bleu de ciel ou le vert pomme," will do well to fly with averted faces from John Webster, whose canvas is lurid with the colour of a thunder-cloud, and red with blood and flame. Those whose nervous systems still permit them to meditate on great physical and psychical crises will discover in him a tragical writer second only to Shakespeare, and in his *Duchess of Malfy* a masterpiece excelled, we venture to say, only by *King Lear*.

Twice Webster has placed before us the sublime spectacle of a human soul, delicately organised, full of power and splendour, ruthlessly followed by a silent, dogged, remorseless fate to the inevitable close. Of most of his characters, we can say from the first, that they are "fey;" their doom is inscribed on their own faces. In the *White Devil*, Vittoria, like Faust, by renouncing principle for pleasure, gives up her soul to demons, who thenceforth never leave hold of their prey, but suggest and tempt, draw the gilded chains tighter and tighter, and at last drag her downward, with her last cry ringing in our ears—

"I am lost for ever!"

In the *Duchess of Malfy*, on the contrary, we have a soul of exquisite virtue snared in a network of adverse influences, and by them overpowered, and to outward appearance miserably vanquished. But out of these adversities comes health, not indeed to the heroic victim, but to those around, who see, in the words of our poet, that—

"Man, like to cassia, is proved best, being bruised."

Though the most obvious, this insight into the true heart of tragedy is not the only excellence prominent in Webster. Strange indeed would it be if to this grandeur of invention were added no gifts of graceful and witty expression. Over the inevitable rosemary and yew he binds at first the vine-leaf and the laurel, and the conceptions of pleasure and a suave courtly life are fulfilled with a success only forgotten when we are fearfully face to face with the realities of grief and death. In one play he has continued the happier strain to the close, and in another, after leading us to the brink of doom, he has relented and given back the lives half-forfeited. In this, as in so much else, he has shown himself a delicate as well as a sublime artist, one who "can breathe through silver" as well as blow through bronze, and one must seek his parallel rather in such later masters as Goethe and Hugo, than in such contemporaries as Ford and Tourneur, whose force makes us forgive, though it cannot conceal, their crudeness.

Where Webster fails is not in crudeness. He was the most literary among the Elizabethans after Jonson, and he carried into his art some of the affectations of the purely literary spirit. The infinite tact of Shakespeare he vainly endeavoured to equal by study and art, as did Jonson, but Webster's source of failure was diametrically opposite to his rival's. Ben Jonson's plays stand or fall according to the success or the reverse of the principal character in each. At most, one or two *personæ* are modelled with care and completeness; the rest are shadows and stage-puppets. Webster erred in the other extreme; in the eager effort to elaborate all parts of his production, he lost in general effect. In the *Devil's Law Case*, the attention becomes completely exhausted in following the development of a dozen characters, any one of whom would have been decisive enough to serve a minor playwright for hero or heroine. So Lionardo is said to have been held in constant check by the desire to work out an ideal

of perfect beauty, not being willing to acknowledge
that to inferior portions of a great work inferior attention must needs be given. Hence Webster, in his
turn weighted with the desire to give an impossible
perfection to his studies of human nature, paused and
loitered till life went by, and left less work of his to
be garnered than any of his contemporaries. It is
indeed little that we possess, but who shall overvalue
its unique preciousness, or consent to lose one of the
weighty lines? This is the reward of careful writing;
we should all consent without much sorrow to the
loss of many lines of Heywood and Middleton. There
is no possibility of estimating what we have lost of
Webster. *The Guise* may or may not have been a
rifaccimento of Marlowe's *Massacre at Paris*, but there
are other plays of Webster's mentioned in the diary
of Henslowe that could hardly have failed to be characteristic. *The Two Harpies*, for instance, has a fas-
cinatingly weird sound about it, and may have been
something very wild and Æschylean.

The versification of Webster is vigorous and often
musical. It strikes a golden mean between the stiff
march of Marlowe's serried lines and Fletcher's languid
excess of laxity. Before Shakespeare the dramatists
were all buckled up in plate-armour; after him they
lounged about ungirdled and loose-shod. Webster
and Jonson were permitted to walk abreast of their
divine rival. It is noticeable that Webster somewhat persistently eschews soliloquy, the department
of the drama best adapted for the display of musical blank verse. How much wild melody he could

throw into his lines, the celebrated speech of Francisco shows :—

"I left them winding of Marcello's corse," &c.

And sentences full of a peculiar delicate music surprise one in each of Webster's works. His earliest known lines, those prefixed to a work of Anthony Munday's, are very striking for a power of versification at that time rare. We have it on Webster's own declaration that he was a very slow and careful composer, and it is evident that he studied the effect of sound in his dramas.

It cannot possibly be needful in these days, when whoever will may buy Webster's entire works for a few shillings, to tell the stories of his plays. That is quite beside our purpose. It will be better as briefly as possible to show what are the prominent character-istics, the main successes, the most obvious beauties of each of the dramas, and to interpret as far as lies in our power a great artist whose masterpieces remain comparatively unknown and misapprehended. In 1612, when, as far as we can guess, Webster was about thirty-five years of age, the *White Devil*, the earliest of his dramas, was printed. It is to be regretted that either his exceeding slowness of composition, or the evil reception this play met with from the public, did not permit Webster to carry out what we like to think was his original project. The play, as it at present stands, is not divided into acts and scenes, slurs over incidents, and even represents prominent crises by dumb show. It reads like the first draft of a trilogy, and it may be held that the poet's original intention was to treat the subject in a trilogical manner, ending the first two dramas at the murders of Isabella and Marcello respectively. Expanded thus by the masterly hand of its inventor, the tragedy would have possessed an immense power over every careful reader; an influence weakened at present by the thinness of execution. The death of Isabella, now almost comic in the conjuror's description, would have brought a world of grand ideas to the poet's mind, when he had to wind up a solemn drama with it, and the elaboration of minor characters, in which he so delighted, would then have been appropriate and needful. As it is, there is more in this great sketch than we can ever hope to fathom.

The scene is laid, where our old dramatists love to lay it, in Italy, and the characters are all true to their Italian birthright. Vittoria herself, the White Devil, with all her grace and subtlety, her implacable warm passions, her never-failing wit and splendid duplicity, is a woman not to be found out of sight of the Apennines. What passes through those bright rosy lips can never be trusted; sift every word by fact and effect, if you would guess the truth. If we had not heard her charnel-house dream, horribly suggestive of robbery and murder, no storming of Monticelso, no reproaches of Brachiano, would induce us to condemn one so overpoweringly frank and brave. We are reminded of Shelley and his Beatrice Cenci, and the old poet is no whit put out of countenance by the comparison. The trial-scene has been the admiration of every critic. Charles Lamb's quaint praise of it is known to every one, but we hold he exaggerates the effect of Vittoria's "innocence-resembling boldness" upon our minds; surely Monticelso's altogether extravagant abuse has as much to do with the favour we feel for her as her own rather brazen confidence.

The character of Flamineo is one of the cleverest creations of Webster; he is a thorough rascal, yet he interests us exceedingly, and is consistent throughout. Less cruel than Iago, he is almost as base, and equally heartless, but there is a slight flavour of loyalty about him; the regard he bears in his mean way for his sister prevents our absolute disgust. He is the very incarnation of sordid prosiness; nothing awes, nothing checks him, except positive danger to himself. When Cornelia breaks in like a ghost upon the scheming trio, with her prophetic denunciation and bitter reproach:

> " Never dropped mildew on a flower here
>   Till now !"

the effect on Vittoria is sudden though brief repentance, on Brachiano a pang of accusing conscience, but on Flamineo nothing whatever save surprise at his colleague's weakness and annoyance at his mother's interruption. This marvellous serenity is thoroughly characteristic of him: when the murders are completed, and his accomplices agitated and doubtful, Flamineo's activity and frivolity are as amazing as ever: he puts Marcello, his virtuous young brother, out of the way with the most cheerful alacrity. When Brachiano is poisoned, he becomes slightly alarmed, but is soon cracking his bitter jests over the corpse. Brachiano's ghost, following the exhibitions of his mother's frenzied grief, awes him for a little while, and then how grandly does he address the ghost, pointing to heaven, "yon starry gallery," and hell, "that cursed dungeon!" Brachiano having gone back to his own place, whichever that was, Flamineo relapses again into callous frivolity, and resumes his avaricious designs.

The scene with his sister at last is very masterly. She is the only creature on earth whom he hesitates to put out of his way by murder. Vittoria's calmness and presence of mind do not leave her when her brother threatens her with the horrible private slaying. Her repartees are as shrewd as ever, only a little sadder. When she supposes that she has shot her brother, and is undeceived by his suddenly leaping at her, for the first time she quails. She is weak, and her weakness is discovered. But when Ludovico bursts in with his rabble, all her courage returns, and she is a queen again. Pale and stern and beautiful she dies, with the words of wonderful despair on her lips:

> " My soul, like to a ship in a black storm,
> Is driven, I know not whither!"

Very different is Flamineo's death; he, too, has no cowardly shrinking, he is stolid as ever, and how bitter are his words of dying mockery! This final scene is the very acme of depravity; the blossom of sin fully ripened into the fruit of punishment, but with infinite grace and sweet underlying pathos the poet has made a streak of dawning light break out in the east. From the utter darkness of the finale, we can for a moment before the curtain falls glance at the young Giovanni, virtuous and brave, rising like the morning star, to herald peace and good-will to men.

Monticelso, the Cardinal, who afterwards becomes Pope, is strikingly drawn. In the trial, with truly clerical want of tact, he lets his indignation at the sin of the fair culprit overstep all bounds, and create a sympathy for her. However wicked she was, our sympathies arraign themselves at once on the side of a lady attacked with such intolerable coarseness. Francesco, who is not half so honest as Monticelso, is able to seem a more righteous judge. Yet we cannot but admire the impulsive Cardinal; his speech to Ludovico in earnest reprimand of his intended crime, is a masterpiece in Webster's moral manner. When he perceives that his warning produces no impression on this inveterate ruffian, how fine is his sudden impatience :

> " Instruction to thee
> Comes like sweet showers to overhardened ground,
> They wet, but pierce not deep.   And so I leave thee,
> With all the Furies hanging round thy neck ! "

Brachiano is too hardened a reprobate to excite any sympathy, and he lacks the intellectual interest that is excited by Flamineo's vagaries.   His death is frightful and shrieking; he is mocked and tormented to the last, Vittoria alone showing any regard for him.   For her his death is a prophetic warning; from that moment she is doomed.

> " I am lost for ever ! "

is her cry of despair and remorseful agony.

The episode of Marcello's death and funeral is the

most poetical passage in the play, rendered with something of the lyrical sweetness of Dekker in his best moments. We are made to feel it to be necessary for the fulfilment of the tragic idea, that he, the one good fruit among these apples of Sodom, should be removed, so that the family, the salt of virtue thus taken from them, might perfect their moral putrefaction. The dirge sung over him by Cornelia is universally admired, and more widely known perhaps than any part of the works of John Webster.

The play is full of fine lines and scattered images. We shall not find many more striking than this announcement to Francesco of the murder of Isabella:

> " My lord, untie your folded thoughts,
> And let them dangle loose as a bride's hair:
> Your sister's poisoned!"

The best words with which to sum up the scope and destination of the play are those of Brachiano, when for the first time he catches sight of the baleful influence on himself and others which Vittoria has, and addressing her says:

> " Thou hast led me like a heathen sacrifice,
> With music and with fatal yokes of flowers,
> To my eternal ruin!"

The *Duchess of Malfy* has been, without question, the most popular work of Webster, the one most often read and praised, and even laid open to the general public in elegant extracts and the like, a delicate form of semi-literary luxury altogether foreign to the genius of this man, yet not perhaps quite unknown to him in the shape of *Miscellanies* and *England's Parnassus*. Not in any of these lyrical hodge-podges, where Sylvester's sonnets elbow Sidney's, and the most laboured dulness is mingled with the most refined wit, does the name of John Webster flourish. For him was reserved till a later age the honour of genteel mutilation in *Collections for the Young*, and even here little appears but the death-scene of the Duchess. The true lover of his fame regrets even this exhibition. The scene we refer to no more represents the play than a single joint represents a man. It is a fragment, horribly edged and repulsive, in elaborate incompleteness. It is necessary that we be fully aware of the previous character of all parties, and the strokes of fortune or crime that have gradually placed them in so critical a position. Only when such a knowledge is complete, and it can become so only after long and thoughtful study, do we perceive the aim of the drama, and the great lesson running through the whole of it.

This, surely, may be summed up thus: men are placed by God in varied positions, dependent one on another, and usually so hemmed in by the conventions of society, that they act with sameness, and more by fashion than by principle. But now and then one and another are called out to take an individual position, and act in ways altogether novel and startling. Then it is that the real nobility of character or the reverse makes itself apparent. A knob of cassia may lie quiet in a box beside a lump of gum-arabic, and no difference or slight be perceived between them. Let them then be taken out and crushed, "bruised," as Webster has it; the cassia fills the air with aromatic fragrance, the other has lost the little comeliness it possessed. This refinement of a noble mind by suffering is the keynote to the *Duchess of Malfy*, and the wretchedness that comes upon her only illuminates and purifies her lovely character.

Where Webster found the story appears to be uncertain. There exists a dramatic version of it, *El Mayerdomo de la Duquessa de Amalfi*, among the works of Lope de Vega, and it forms the subject of one of the *Novelle* of Bandello. In Webster's version the Duchess is presented before us as a woman of supreme rank and high spirit, whose power of mind and healthiness of purpose have kept her uncontaminated by the frivolous conventionality of a court-life. She dares to act for herself; though a sovereign, she does not forget she is a woman, and sees nothing ignoble in the faithful love of a subject. She loves Antonio, a lord of her court, a man of the utmost integrity and as high-minded as herself. As Mr. Dyce has pointed out, this is a position of great peril for the author, but he triumphs in the difficulty. The scene in which the Duchess declares her passion is one of the most wonderful in the works of any dramatist. Her fine flutterings when she has dismissed her maid, Cariola, and is awaiting her treasurer, the amusing and yet touching way in which they each manœuvre, and hint and probe their mutual desires,

Antonio's modesty and intelligence, his brave little justification of his true-heartedness—

> " Were there nor heaven nor hell
> I should be honest.   I have long served Virtue,
> And never taken wages of her—"

her exquisite delicacy of condescension, his just but not abject expressions of unworthiness, unite to form one of the most beautiful pictures a dramatist ever painted.

It is difficult to admit that Antonio deserves the charge of dulness and poorness which some critics have brought against him; his mind is of a fine calibre, if not very deep, yet very serious and honest; his sententiousness may be somewhat in the vein of Polonius, but is very consistent with his general character, thus forming another instance of the scrupulous care with which Webster worked up even his minor *personæ*.   All through we cannot but feel that the Duchess is at all points his superior; in the intensely pathetic parting (close of Act III.) she is loftier than he, even in her despair :

> " My laurel is all withered ! "

After this Antonio becomes a nonentity; his appearances are unaccountable and useless, and his death a burlesque.   Yet in his dying speech the old Antonio accent is audible again, sententious to the last.

Bosola is, no doubt, the cleverest male invention of Webster.   He is the peculiar of the author; his speeches, humours, turns of thought, are Websterian exclusively. How strange are his pungent bitterness and sombre railing! Did the Clerk of St. Andrew's, Holborn, talk so among his contemporaries, and mystify them, we wonder? Some of Bosola's acrid sayings are unfathomable. We must not think because he is the bane of every one, that he is a thorough rogue. His better nature constantly peeps out. He knows and cares nothing for the Duchess; he thinks no great harm can come of Ferdinand's spy system; he is that prince's liege servant, and to be paid well for these inscrutable services. So he proceeds to watch the Duchess, and informs accordingly. We listen with wonder to his lashing tongue, but soon perceive that his fantastic conceits perplex more than offend the victims of his sarcasm.

In Act IV., when the blow has fallen, melted at last, Bosola lays aside his cynicism, and speaks out boldly to Ferdinand. At the death-scene, he is executioner, but evidently hates his cruel work, and to carry off his part, he is obliged to return more extravagantly than ever to his fantasies. In the brutal butchering in Act V., Bosola is nothing, and his dying remorse and regret vapid and worthless. Never did grand play end so wretchedly, unless *Hamlet* be similarly condemned.

In all that pertains to the unnamed Duchess, Webster stands out among his later tragic rivals as Chopin did among the Romantic poets and painters of his time. It is as though he interpreted the thoughts of the others in an art more subtle and refined than theirs. The character of the heroine is revealed with splendid effect in one scene in Act III. A happy bride, gay and witty, she sits in her chamber braiding her hair; falling into a fit of musing, and left unconsciously alone by her playful companions, her thought is turned from the joyous present to the dim future. Before her pass the images of Eld and Death, and she sees her own bright head whitened with the orris-powder of grey hairs. Such a moment is chosen for the horrible in-rushing of her implacable brother. She is discovered; the die is cast; calmly she accepts her fate, but all dreams of life and love are done with; she can never smile again. From this moment her character grows broader and more spiritual, till at last she seems physically dead. Her natural vivacity is all gone, and her replies have a hollow and passionless accent, as if they came from another world, and as though the sweet lips that utter them were dust laid out of sight. How queenly she dies, in contrast with poor Cariola's screaming and scratching!

Nowhere does the subtle magician, the painstaking analyst of obscure humanity, triumph more than when he depicts the brother of the Duchess. Never could there be more temptation for a dramatist not fully master of his work to present a puppet rather than a man to a not too critical audience. Yet Webster, bent upon the perfection of his work, has expended on these detestable persons the most careful skill. Throughout the plot we are reminded of a later, and yet more pro-foundly moving tragedy, the *Clarissa* of Richardson, and the resemblance is increased by the likeness of the Duke and Cardinal to the insolent brother and aggravating sister of the peerless "Clary." In both cases a willing blindness and a stupid regard for the supposed family honour unite with avarice in urging the persecution of one who blooms in a barren family like a lily among thorns. It is somewhat astonishing that during the two years between Acts II. and III. the Duke, notwithstanding his knowledge of the Duchess's marriage, does not act against her. At last his weak brain dissolves into frenzy, and this is really the only true feature in the fifth act. His death is confounded in the final general butchery.

In considering this strange drama as a whole, its marvellous originality must strike us at once. The treatment adopted for this wild story by Webster is such as would have occurred to no other mind. Three men of that period assimilate more or less closely with our poet, and form a group whose members revelled in the sombre and the violent. But how differently would this story have been treated by each of them; The southern imagination of Marlowe would have expended a wealth of voluptuous colour on so passionate a subject, but we should have missed much tenderness and subdued grace, much conceited wit, and hardly have gained, perhaps, in general impressiveness. Marlowe was strongly imbued with the sense of the glory of colour that served to render deathless the great Venetians of a century before; Webster, on the other hand, had little feeling for it. He views hope and love and beauty from their purely emotional side; he is exquisitely human, and in his sadness, remorseful and unupbraiding. We find no traces in Webster of such personal swayings of passion as surge in the pages of

E

Marlowe; but neither can be found in him the utter weight of woe that characterises the other two members of the "Satanic School." Cyril Tourneur, in his two remarkable and unworthily neglected plays, exhibits an unfathomable grief, suggestive of the despair of a lost soul. His lines linger as if falling from burdened lips. Life seems to him a mere stage for sorrows; he knows not joy even by hearsay; actual physical enjoyments are to him mere gall and ashes, even in desire. What weight of horror must have lain on the mind of this remarkable and obscure person! We picture him to ourselves as a masculine Emily Brontë, afflicted with an incurable malady of the soul. We shudder to think with what blackness of plumes, with what darkness of congealed and mysterious blood, he would have illustrated the story of our Duchess. Last of the gloomy quartette comes Ford, a soul in a different mould still— delicate, passionate, weak, worn out with the yearning of obstinate desire—puling for the moon like a child, and refusing in morbid feebleness of appetite the ordinary diet of men—the Charles Baudelaire of his age. With him, too, our mighty Webster has little in common but the superficial colour; and it is doubtful whether Ford would have even cared to accept the story as it now stands for the illustration of his ideas. In theatrical arrangement, in study and clearness of character, it is not needful to point out by how very much both Ford and Tourneur are the inferiors of the subject of this essay.

The *Duchess of Malfy* is full of faults; and it would need but a shallow wit to point them out. Webster erred, as we have said, in attempting an altogether impossible perfection, and in consequence worked some portions up with the minute accuracy of a miniature, and left some mere gaps of crude colour. But it is not with his faults, but with his excellences, that we are engaged. We can hardly account for the want of taste and art shown in the fifth act, unless on the not unplausible assumption that the poet, having destroyed the lovely Duchess, in whom all his intellectual interest had centred, found his energies droop and his vivacity decline when she no longer formed the heart of the action.

The Devil's Law Case, which seems to contain a reference to the Massacre at Amboyna in 1623, and which nevertheless bears that date on its title-page, follows the *Duchess of Malfy* by about six years. In some respects it is an exceedingly faulty production; there is no great central idea on which the plot wheels as on an axis; there are no characters whose personal charm constrains our admiration; the structure of the piece is as bad as it well could be; the *dénouement* is vague and unsatisfactory; the spirit running through it is a mixture of spurious tragedy, and comedy which arouses no glimmer of a smile. On the other hand, it abounds above all the works of its author in lines and passages of unique and peculiar beauty, and some of its *personæ* are drawn with a consummate art and consistency.

Before we can enter on any disquisition on the *Devil's Law Case*, it is necessary to blot from our memories the irritating presence of the lawyers, who are introduced with such a waste of subtlety. The fatiguing loquacity and intrigues of Crispiano and Ariosto must be forgotten; and before our eyes we must place the five prime movers in the play—namely, the members of Romelio's family: himself, mother and sister, and the two suitors. The plot, which at first merely dazes and confounds, stripped of its accessories, is simply this: Jolenta, secretly plighted to Contarino, is in vain required to marry Ercole by her brother Romelio, a merchant. The mother of Jolenta and Romelio, Leonora, secretly loves Contarino, and therefore urges Ercole upon her daughter. The rivals fight a duel, in which both are seriously wounded; and Romelio, finding that Contarino has left his property to Jolenta, thinks to make sure by stabbing him in his sick-bed. Leonora, to revenge her lover, brings a charge of illegitimacy against her son. The charge is overthrown; and she is about to suffer for libel, when Ercole and Contarino, who have recovered, appear in succession, and all the persons form a tableau.

What is the upshot of it all is not clear. A dull and repulsive plot this must certainly be confessed to be, but yet, in the hands of Webster, it admits of no little talent in character painting. The family of Romelio resemble one another in many points—they are all passionate, perverse, and reserved. They all combine in deceiving one another; from the beginning they bring this coil of trouble on themselves by being so very crafty towards one another. Leonora hints her love to Contarino in so mystical a way that he never suspects her aim. He, on the other hand, thinks himself wondrously clever in asking for her picture—meaning her daughter. Thus they outwit each other. The mother and children are amusingly self-willed. The scene in which Romelio tries to force Ercole on Jolenta is a masterly one. Jolenta is quite calm and decided; she uses the exact phrases that are most suited to irritate Romelio; the latter blusters, threatens, embarrasses modest Ercole, but gains little by it all. Leonora's little selfish by-play is cleverly brought in. At last poor Jolenta is overwhelmed, but she is still inflexible; she merely yields to the physical oppression of the moment, and is peculiarly gracious to Contarino in sheer wilfulness.

So these precious relatives quietly flout one another, and consequently upon their schemings a difference arises between the suitors, and Contarino challenges Ercole to fight a duel. This quarrel has been highly lauded by Charles Lamb, as being " well arranged and gentlemanlike." It has additional interest in the play because the two rivals who thus engage are by far the most pleasing characters introduced. Ercole, especially, is a man

> " Whose word is still led by a noble thought,
> And that thought followed by as fair a deed."

Romelio is a very different being, "a glorious devil, large in heart and brain, that did love" money only. He is almost invariably made to speak in a poetical strain; he is a voluble theorist in virtue. It is therefore quite consistently that the exquisite passage on honourable activity flows from his lips :—

> "Virtue is ever sowing of her seeds
>   In the trenches for the soldier ; in the wakeful study
> For the scholar ; in the furrows of the sea
> For men of our profession ; of all which
> Arise and spring up honour."

With such flowrets of morality does the glib merchant adorn his conversation.   No wonder poor Contarino is lost in admiraion, and even the reader is startled to find what a very different sort of person Romelio is behind the scenes.   His avarice is grasping and pitiless, his lust of gold akin to Barnabas in the *Jew of Malta.* The same man who could with fluent solemnity preach the cause of virtue to Contarino, says to his sister presently, of the same gentleman and Ercole :—

> " I have a plot shall breed
> Out of the death of these two noblemen
> The advancement of our house ! "

He is a magnificent Pecksniff, who has so long persuaded the world to believe in him that at last he believes in himself.   Even murder has no terror for him, and as "an Italianated Jew" he plays the rogue finely.

Poor Leonora in the frenzy of her irrepressible love is very pitiable, and her grief makes her eloquent. When she is lying, worn out, on the floor, and answers the questioning priest by saying,

> " I am whispering to a dead friend ! "

she rises to sublimity of that subdued kind characteristic of the Elizabethan dramatists. Her sudden and unnatural rage against her son is very fantastic, and treated in a most repulsive way. Indeed, the last two acts of the *Devil's Law Case*, describing Leonora's suit, which is devilish enough in all conscience, are unredeemed by any beauty of plot or character. But although the persons lose all hold over our attention, the passages of pure poetry are more numerous than ever; Romelio turns ballad-monger and becomes Skeltonian in his lyric cynicism. This Satanic play is one from which the reader is inclined to draw copious extracts for frequent pleasurable reference, but hardly to toil through its obscure labyrinth again. It is not a long work, fortunately; as Romelio remarks, with his usual acumen,

"Bad plays are the worse for their length !"

As if desirous that posterity might judge of his skill in every branch of the higher drama, Webster's next effort was an historical one. *Appius and Virginia* was the most popular of his works on the stage of that day, and was the only one that seems to have been resuscitated after the Restoration. Still later it was rewritten in the popular style of the day by the illustrious John Dennis, while another critic of the times of Charles II., who had all the lofty disdain of a Gallomaniac for the rough polish of Webster, informs us that "the ingenious Mr. Betterton altered and bettered this piece." We may forgive the pun and eschew the elegant emendations of these later wits. The subject so eloquently told by Livy was a favourite one with the English public. One of those curious interludes which form the connecting link between the old moralities and the regular drama, had treated the story in a jingling way, but Webster did not draw his inspiration from that trickling fountain, nor apply to the ever-bubbling well of his own invention, but kept very close to Livy, and was only saved by his strong impersonifying habit of mind from falling into the mere historic dulness of such plays as *Perkin Warbeck* or *Sejanus*.

It is difficult to imbue the most pathetic history with poetic life; the rigidity of fact leaves too little room for the play of imagination. Even in Shakespeare, Falstaff and Pistol and Bardolph have for us more living reality by far than the once actually breathing Worcester and Hotspur, and the poet is more easy in painting them. One of the sweetest singers of our century, speaking to Love, the sovereign Power, says :—

> "All records, saving thine, come cool and calm,
>   And shadowy, through the mist of passèd years ;
> For others, good or bad, hatred and tears
> Have become indolent."

And all the life and worth left in such a record as this Roman tale consist in the light of immortal passion gleaming around the men and women, whose hopes and fears and tremulous pleasures were identical with those we daily experience.

It is manifest that to produce a really lasting drama, founded on an historical basis, the dramatist must remember this fact, and insist most prominently on

the emotions of his *personæ*. Webster in writing
Appius and Virginia either pandered to the popular
taste of the hour, or failed to attain his own high
standard. This play is classical and cold; to say it
is illuminated by no flashes of pathos and originality
would be to deny its authorship, but the general effect
is frigid. The love of Icilius and Virginia, with which
might have been inwoven much fervid colour and
passionate fancy, has been coolly passed over. The
character of the heroine is sketched with so light a
pencil that we are left in uncertainty as to the features
of her soul. The interest of the play centres around
the good and the bad heroes, Virginius and Appius
Claudius. The former is on all occasions displayed
as a mirror of virtue; the latter, with much novelty
and freshness of treatment, as a worldly-wise rogue.
The crafty decemvir, with his Janus-head of virtue
in word and vice in action, is a creation worthy of
Webster's subtle intellect. A word or hint shows us
the laborious course of plottings which have placed
him at last on the curule chair. He is no novice, but
a perfect adept, in the art of cozening. Yet having
attained the full height of his ambition, his care
slackens and the first and fatal error is made from
this pinnacle. The faithful accomplice of his crimes,
the execrable Marcus, starts at the discovery of his
patron's weakness. He sees the danger which Appius
is too much dazzled by success to see. All this intri-
cate imagining we owe to Webster and not to the
unvarnished tale of Livy. We can only swiftly indicate the power and beauty which are expended on the

character of Virginius, but even he is too declamatory and cold.   There is a vein of languor running through *Appius and Virginia* which is quite foreign to its author's stalwart and active genius; and it is impossible to put away from one the conviction that its composition was a labour forced upon him by personal need or the entreaty of a manager.   "It is far more " correct," in an Augustan and Drydenic sense, than his other dramas, and was accordingly, as we have seen, the only one successfully revived at the Restoration.

The play brought out by Kirkman in 1661, under the title of "*A Cure for a Cuckold,* by John Webster and William Rowley," has never hitherto obtained the attention it deserves.   Mr. Dyce is sceptical, as well he may be, of Kirkman's probity, but thinks there are traces of Webster in it; Mr. W. C. Hazlitt does not hazard any opinion save that "it is not a *White Devil* or a *Duchess of Malfy,*" which is self-evident.   No one has yet pointed out, what we claim as a discovery, that, far from the obscurity of mingled authorship which usually attends a compound play, the respective scenes of this may, with a little care, be labelled "Webster," "Rowley," without a shadow of reasonable doubt.   We take it that the matter stood thus: William Rowley, the passably clever author of *A Shoemaker's a Gentleman,* a dramatist who never rose to any eminence in serious composition, had on his hands a short town-comedy, suited to the vicious taste of the day, to which he had given the appropriate name on Kirkman's title-page.   But this not being long enough for representation, and from its nature not being capable of much expansion, Rowley asked Webster, as a dramatist in high repute, for a comedy whose plot might be interwoven with his own. Webster glanced at his friend's little play, found its subject uncongenial to him, but consented to write a short high comedy, which Rowley might join with his own low comedy as well as he could.

The consequence is that the spirit of the two dramas clashes continually; consistent alone, viewed together they are most inconsistent. Webster's characters are noble, sententious, gentleman-like; Rowley's are ribald, vulgar, ignoble. This is seen to perfection in the cases of Woodroff, Luce, and Franckford, who are supposed to bear the mutual relationship of brother, sister, and husband. Woodroff, whose action is confined to the upper section of the play, is a serene and virtuous figure in Webster's finest style. His sister Luce and her husband, whose station is almost wholly in the lower section, are coarse and vulgar, with a vulgarity wholly foreign to our poet. Not to enter wearisomely into this matter, we will merely beg the reader to judge for himself whether the bridal party in *A Cure for a Cuckold* and the various incidents that follow upon it are not obviously the exclusive property of Webster. They may be judged as a complete work by themselves, and to release us from the offensive existing title, correct enough as far as regards Rowley's section, we would suggest the adoption of a new title for this play. Perhaps, in the absence of authority, we may be allowed to suggest provisionally that of

Love's Graduate, a name justified by a speech of Clare's in the opening scene, and by the general succession of events with regard to her.

The purity and stateliness of the verse impress one from the first. No such musical lines fell from the pen of William Rowley; the blank verse of that author is extremely tame, and has a tendency to fall into rhyme at the most inappropriate moments, as if the shadow of the decadence had already fallen on him, and he prophesied of Dryden. He confines himself to prose in his share of the present work. To return to *Love's Graduate*. The first act is occupied with a bridal party, convened to the marriage of Annabel and Bonville. The guests converse with all the suavity and florid grace appropriate to the occasion; as we always notice in Webster's work, there is a lack of passionate utterance, but there is a quiet joyousness and golden indolence akin to the hazy beauty of a summer afternoon, which atone for the characteristic lack of amorous fervour.

This little idyll, so long and so completely neglected that it seems like some Pompeian jar, faultless and fragile, suddenly revealed uninjured, with its bright frieze of dancers as fresh as when they were painted, has a special claim to respectful consideration. In it, while detecting everywhere those peculiarities of style and feeling which we have learned to look for in Webster's work, we also discover traits nowhere else discernible. This sense of quiet enjoyment, which we have pointed out as characterising the opening act, is hardly to be found, in so full a measure at least, in any of the plays we have already examined. If, as we believe, *Love's Graduate* is the product of his later years, it would give us some ground for supposing that ease and competence mellowed the gloomy spirit of his youth, and developed to more perfection the graceful and reflective instincts of his imagination.

The interest mainly centres round the quartette, Annabel and her newly-married consort, and the un-linked lovers, Lessingham and Clare. The last of these is very cleverly contrasted with Annabel; if two words nowadays misused *ad nauseam* may be brought into legitimate service, Annabel's mind is of an objective type, Clare's subjective. The bride is clear-headed and joyous, untroubled by doubts or anxieties, sociable, merry, and without reserve; her friend is tortuous and melancholy, dealing in symbols and conceits, reserved, inscrutable, introspective. Lessingham is more interesting than agreeable; he is very honest and well-meaning, but weak in will and purpose; we find him too passionate to be really generous, and at last, led away by his tempestuous emotions, he becomes malicious and cruel. To work out all this with success needed a master's hand; Webster delighted in developing such fantastic and wayward characters as these. Bonville, again, stands as much in contrast to Lessingham as Annabel does to Clare. He is very virtuous and noble, but less subtle of intellect than his friend, and capable of the injustice that is the child of imperfect mental sympathy.

The third act contains a scene, in our estimation, finer than any out of the two great tragedies, and

second to few in them. The quarrel on Calais sands
between Lessingham and Bonville is one of the most
complete triumphs of Webster's subtle genius. It bears
just sufficient likeness to the well-known duel in the
Devil's Law Case to prove their common paternity,
but in pathos and stately power it far excels it. The
occasion is peculiar. Lessingham is commanded by the
mysterious Clare to kill his best friend if he would win
her love, so he induces Bonville on the very day of his
marriage to come to Calais, where only English duels
could be fought, to be his second. When they get
there, no one is in sight, and Lessingham has to explain to his astonished and indignant friend that he is
himself the antagonist. The situation is a most thrilling one. The long stretch of ribbed and barren sand ;
the unbroken solitude of sea, shore, and sky ; the two
men fearlessly standing face to face before they bury the
love of years in a feud where the passion of anger has no
place. The only sound in all the wide expanse is the
long wash " of the cruel and inconstant sea, that beats
upon this beach." While they prepare to fight for life
and death, their words, bold and solemn as the dying
speech of a good man, wake the echoes of that un-
peopled place. What they say, with what a sad and
noble compromise they rescue their lives from that
fratricide, it is not my part to tell. Let the reader
search out for himself, and store up this strange duel
in his memory.

The finale is more happily managed than is usual in
Webster's plays. In the beginning of the last act a
general misunderstanding has involved every one in

confusion. The reputation of the excellent Annabel has to be cleared, and her father, Woodroff, defends her in a noble little speech. The final quarrel, after which all the threads are unravelled, is most natural and animated, and on the stage would be extremely effective. This little drama would be well worthy of reproduction on the boards of one of our theatres.[1]

In that high garden of the gods of song where the Muses walk among the statues of the dead poets they have loved, there is one delicious terrace that looks over the western sea. Here, when the grass is still dewy, and the shadow of the eastern mountains still upon the garden, Melpomene comes daily to lay a fresh garland on the bland brows of Shakespeare. All the unfamiliar faces of the Elizabethans gaze out of the shade of the laurels, reposing in marble after their stormy life on earth. But before she reaches the great Master, the Muse steps aside to lay vervain on a head whose outlines, in the extreme shadow, are quite invisible to us; it is to the author of the *Duchess of Malfy* that she pays this gracious homage, and we long to stand where she does, and see what face and form, what lips and hair and eyes clothed the godhead of this poet of poets. This we shall never see; the laurels will for ever hide this singer's throat and forehead. The more let us devoutly examine what he has

---

[1] A reprint of Webster's share in this play, edited by the Hon. S. E. Spring-Rice, was issued in 1884 from the private press of the Rev. C. H. Daniel, of Worcester College, Oxford. Mr. Spring-Rice has paid me the compliment of adopting my title of *Love's Graduate*.

left behind him, and write on the blank slab that hides his dust some such words as these, which some one has used regarding him :—

> " His was a soul whose calm intensity
>   Glared, shadeless, at the passion-sun that blinds,
>   Unblinded, till the storm of song arose ;
>   Even as the patient and Promethean sea
>   Tosses in sleep, until the vulture-winds
>   Swoop down, and tear the breast of its repose !"

1874.

SAMUEL ROWLANDS

IN an age when the newly-awakened taste for letters
had suddenly thrown open to men who could wield
a pen every door that led to the arena of literary pub-
licity, Samuel Rowlands made less effort than most of
his contemporaries to gain the plaudits of the cultivated,
or to secure the garland of lasting fame. His name
appears in no list of honoured poets in his own generation; in the next, his writings found no editor, and his
life no biographer. He comes down to us merely as
a voluble pamphleteer, of whose numerous works some
are altogether lost, and others, become nearly unique,
are purchased by the curious at such prices for a single
copy as the author never made by a whole edition.
Of the minor masters of the Greek stage, of Ion or of
Iophon, we have plentiful record, though their works
are gone; but in the case of the lesser stars of the
Elizabethan galaxy the work of oblivion has been
reversed—we have their works, but not the record of
their lives. In no case has history been more per-
sistent in silence than when summoned to give us
news of Samuel Rowlands. Of almost every other
writer we have succeeded in discovering something;
but of him nothing. We do not know when he was
born, or when he died, whether he was a scholar of

either university, whether he had taken orders, or
whether he had married a wife. It is left to us, therefore, as to those who map the heavens, to draw an
approximate outline of his life by the conjunction of
those works or stars that form his constellation. They
are very numerous, they extend over a period of thirty
years, and they give some, but very slight, internal
evidence of their author's personality.

In all probability Samuel Rowlands was born soon
after 1570. We may roughly conjecture that 1573,
the year that saw the birth of Donne and of Ben
Jonson, saw his also. Should this be correct, he was
from six to eighteen years younger than the five
famous friends in whose steps he was to walk, with a
gentler, tamer tread than theirs. When he was about
ten years old, Lodge, Peele, and Greene began to
write, and it was not long before Nash and Marlowe
joined the company of the penners of love-pamphlets.
These men, united rather by their boisterous friendship than any innate similarity of genius, were among
the first professional men of letters in England. Lodge
and Greene began as Euphuists at the feet of Lyly;
they were drawn by the example of Nash into the
practice of satire, and into the compilation of catchpenny pamphlets on passing events. They very
quickly ran through their brief careers, and had already
died or retired from public life before Rowlands began
to write. But their influence had been immense; they
had inaugurated a new epoch in popular literature;
and though the main current of such writing proceeded to flow in the channel of the drama, they still

counted their followers in the younger generation. Of these followers Rowlands, and fifteen years later Braithwait, were the most important, and to both of these authors, entirely neglected for more than two centuries, public interest has of late returned. That either the one or the other was a writer of much merit, or deserved in any strict sense the name of poet, may easily and safely be denied, but neither lacks that quality of force that renders an author worthy of more than mere antiquarian attention.

Like Drayton, and other secular poets of that age, Rowlands commenced his career with a volume of devotional pieces. *The Betraying of Christ*, which bore the more apt sub-title of *Poems on the Passion*, appeared in 1598, and went through two editions within that year. We have guessed the age of the author at twenty-five, and certainly the style of his verses gives us no sign of precocity or extreme youth. The poems are indeed remarkably smooth, with the even grace and monotonous polish of a writer to whom the art of verse presents no difficulties and contains no surprises. They are composed in an heroic stanza of six lines, rhyme royal with the fifth line omitted, and this form, one of the simplest that can be devised, remained a favourite with Rowlands until he ceased to publish.

But it was not with nerveless paraphrases of the New Testament that he was destined to catch the popular ear. In 1600 he produced two works which greatly extended his reputation, and made him, if not famous, at least widely notorious. The first of these, entitled *A Merry Meeting, or 'Tis Merry when Knaves Meet*, was successfully suppressed by the authorities, and has only come down to us in an expurgated edition of 1609. It was so offensive in its personality, so acrid in its satire, that it was ordered to be burned publicly, and in the Hall Kitchen of the Stationers' Company. A month later the poet hurried through the press another collection, *The Letting of Humour's Blood in the Head Vein*, and this has fortunately survived in at least four copies. It is a very creditable production, full of the animation of the time, with none of its pedantry, and a little of its genius. The greater part of the book is occupied with small satirical pieces, called Epigrams, describing, mainly in the six-line stanza, those fantastic figures of the day which the poets delighted to caricature. These are very well written, clear, pointed, and even, never rising to the incisive melody of a great poet, but never sinking below a fairly admirable level, while for the student of manners they abound in picturesque detail and realistic painting. The following lines from an address to the poet's contemporaries, stripped of their antique spelling, give a fair notion of the modern tone of the book, and its easy elegance :—

> " Will you stand spending your invention's treasure
> To teach stage parrots speak for penny pleasure,
> While you yourselves, like music-sounding lutes,
> Fretted and strange, gain them their silken fruits?
> Leave Cupid's cuts, women's face-flattering praise,
> Love's subject grows too threadbare nowadays,
> Change Venus' swans to write of Vulcan's geese,
> And you shall merit golden pens apiece."

The dislike of the theatre here so strongly expressed
continued to the last, and Rowlands seems never to
have been tempted to try his skill in the lucrative field
of the stage. It is not improbable that his facile pen
and experience in the humours of low life would have
enabled him to develop a comic talent which might
have ranged between that of Dekker and that of Heywood ; but he would have missed the tenderness of
the former, and the flowery fancy of the latter. The
end of the volume called *The Letting of Humour's Blood*
is composed of satires in the Roman style, in heroic
couplets. Here again Rowlands shows rather his
quickness in seizing an idea than his faculty for
originating one, since the trick of writing these pieces
had been invented by Lodge in 1595, and had been
imitated by Hall, Guilpin, and Marston before Rowlands adopted it. He is, however, in some respects
the superior of these preceding writers. In all probability he was not, as they were, men of any classic
learning, and he was seduced by no desire of emulating
Persius into those harsh and involved constructions
which make the satires of Donne and Marston the
wonder of grammarians.

The early works of Rowlands gave promise of
much greater attainment than their author ultimately
achieved. His fourth book, *'Tis Merry when Gossips
Meet*, published in 1602, is an admirable piece of
comedy, bright, fresh, and limpid, and composed in a
style only too dangerously smooth and rapid. It opens
with a fine tribute to Chaucer, "our famous reverend
English Poet," and proceeds to give a valuable piece

of contemporary manners in a conversation between a gentleman and a bookseller, in prose. The gentleman has no taste for new books; he prefers the old ones. He says, "Canst help me to all Greene's books in one volume? But I will have them every one, not any wanting." The modern book-hunter starts at the idea of a volume containing all Greene's works in the original quartos; even the bookseller of 1602 finds that he has some half-a-dozen lacking. Then the gentleman is urged to buy a book of Nash's, but he has it already; at last he is persuaded to buy the very poem to which this conversation is a preface, and we are interested to learn that he pays sixpence for it, less than one-thousandth part of the sum that would be asked to-day for a clean copy.

The poem is in Rowlands' usual six-line stanza, but it is singular among his works as being in a dramatic form. It is, in fact, a dialogue between a Widow, a Wife, a Maid, and a Vintner. The Widow meets the Wife, whom she has not seen for a long time, outside a tavern, and while they stand talking the Maid goes by. The Widow stops her, and vows that they must all three drink a glass together before they part. The Wife and the Maid object, but their objections are overruled by the boisterous joviality of the Widow, who drags them into the tavern. They are shown upstairs into a private room, and the Vintner brings them claret. Over their wine they discuss old times and their present fortunes in a very humorous and natural way. The Widow is a coarse, good-humoured woman, full of animal spirits, and still rebellious with the memory of her red-haired husband, who used her ill; the Wife, on the other hand, praises her husband, an easy soul who lets her have her way; the Maid talks very little at first, but as she warms with the wine, she describes the sort of husband she means to have. Presently they finish the claret, and the Wife and the Maid wish to go, but the Widow will not hear of it, bidding the Vintner rather burn some sack and fry some sausages. Over this feast they linger a long while gossiping, till the Maid has burning cheeks and the Widow becomes indisputably drunk. She talks so broadly that the Vintner's boy laughs, and then she becomes extremely dignified, demanding an apology. In the end she patronises the Vintner, and makes him drink with them; and when at last her friends rise to go, she insists on paying the whole reckoning. It will be seen that the poem has no plot, and that the contents are very slight; but the workmanship is admirable, and the little realistic touches combine to form an interior as warm and full in colour as any painted by Brouwer or Ostade. It is one of the best studies of *genre* we possess in all Elizabethan literature. *'Tis Merry when Gossips Meet* went through at least seven editions before the end of the century.

Simultaneously with this humorous poem, Rowlands published, in 1602, a collection of prose stories of smart cheating and cozening under the title of *Greene's Ghost Haunting Coneycatchers*, adopting this popular name to attract public notice. As a catcher of rabbits, or conies, trades upon the stupidity of his victims, so it was represented by the pamphleteers of the day that

knaves took advantage of the credulity of simple
citizens, and hence the popularity of a title that Greene
had invented, but which found a score of imitators.
Rowlands' tales are lively, but for us the main interest
of the book centres in its preface and in its address to
the reader, in which Rowlands comes forward distinctly
as a pamphleteer, disclaiming any pretension to learning or an ambitious style. From this time forth he
appears solely as a caterer for the frivolous and casual
reader, and demands notice rather as a journalist than
as an author. His little books are what we should
now term social articles; they answer exactly to the
"middles" of our best weekly newspapers.

Our curiosity is excited by the lapses in his composition, and we wonder how such a man subsisted in
the intervals between the publication of his works.
His familiarity with the book-trade, and his cunning
way of adapting his titles and subjects to the exact
taste of the moment, suggest that he may have found
employment in one of the booksellers' shops. In this
connection we turn in hope of confirmation to the
imprints of his volumes, but in vain. He published
with a great variety of booksellers, and rarely more
than twice with the same. From 1600 to 1605 he was,
however, in business with William White, in Pope's
Head Alley, near the Exchange, and for ten years his
tracts were sold by George Loftus, in Bishopsgate
Street, near the Angel. As Loftus would seem to
have succeeded White, or to have removed from his
employment into a separate business, it is within the
bounds of legitimate speculation to guess that Row-

lands spent fifteen of his busiest years in the employment of these city booksellers.

In 1604 he published, under the sensational title of
Look to It, or I'll Stab You, a fresh collection of
satirical characters in verse, in form and substance
precisely like the epigrams in his *Letting of Humour's
Blood*. His style had by this time reached its highest
refinement and purity, without the slightest trace of
elevation. The character of the Curious Divine forms
a good example of his fluent and prosaic verse :—

> " Divines, that are together by the ears,
>   Puffed up, high-minded, seedsmen of dissension,
> Striking until Christ's seamless garment tears,
>   Making the Scripture follow your invention,
> Neglecting that whereon the soul should feed,
> Employed in that whereof souls have no need ;

> " Curious in things you need not stir about,
>   Such as concern not matter of salvation,
> Giving offence to them that are without,
>   Upon whose weakness you should have compassion,
> Causing the good to grieve, the bad rejoice,—
> Yet you, with Martha, make the worser choice,—
>   I'll stab you ! "

From this time forward every year saw one, at least,
of his facile productions. In 1605 it was *Hell's Broke
Loose*, one of the poorest things he ever wrote, a mean
kind of epic poem in his favourite six-line stanza, on
the life and death of John of Leyden. In the same
year he returned to his first love, and published *A
Theatre of Divine Recreation*, a collection of religious
poems, founded on the Old Testament. This book,

which was in existence as late as 1812, has disappeared.

The best of all Rowlands' works, from a literary point of view, is the rarest also. *A Terrible Battle between Time and Death* exists only in a single copy, which has been bound in such a way that the imprint and date are lost. There is little doubt, however, that the latter was 1606. The dedication is odd; Rowlands inscribes his book to a Mr. George Gaywood, whom he does not personally know, but who has shown more than fatherly kindness to a friend of the author's. We wonder if the "friend" may have been the author's wife, by a concealment not unprecedented in that age, and Mr. Gaywood her godfather or patron. At any rate, some singular chain of circumstances seems hinted at in this very cryptic dedication. The poem itself contains the best things that Rowlands has left behind him. It opens in a most solemn and noble strain, with a closer echo of the august music of the tragic Elizabethans than Rowlands attains anywhere else :—

> " Dread potent Monster, mighty from thy birth,
>   Giant of strength against all mortal power,
>   God's great Earl Marshal over all the earth,
>   Taking account of each man's dying hour,
>   Landlord of graves and tombs of marble stones,
>   Lord Treasurer of rotten dead men's bones."

Thus Time addresses Death, whom he has met wandering over the world on his dread mission. But Death cannot stay to talk with him; he has to mow down proud kings and tender women, gluttons and atheists and swaggering bullies, all who live without God, and take no thought of the morrow. Yet Time beguiles him to stay awhile, since, without Time, Death has no lawful right or power, and so they agree to converse together while half the sand runs through the hour-glass of Time. Their conversation deals with the obvious moralities, the frivolity of man, the solemnity of eternity, the various modes in which persons of different casts of character meet the advent of death. The dialogue is dignified, even where it is most quaint, and the reader is reminded of the devotional poetry of a later time, sometimes of Herbert, more often of Quarles. But Rowlands has not the strength of wing needed for these moral flights; his poem becomes tedious and then grotesque. At the close of Time's pleasant conversation with Death, they fall out, and the latter, who prides himself on his personal beauty, is extremely disconcerted at the rudeness with which Time compares his arm and hand to a gardener's rake, and his head to a dry empty oil-jar. After these amenities the reader prepares for that "terrible bloody battle" promised on the title-page, but he is disappointed, for the pair make up their quarrel immediately, and proceed together to their mortuary labours.

The year 1607 was one of great literary activity with Rowlands. He published no fewer than three books, though, singularly enough, we possess the first edition of but one of these. A work of 1607, of which the first edition has been lost, is *Doctor Merryman*, a series of bright sallies in verse, describing and ridiculing the popular affectations or "humours" of the day. In this book a slight change of tone is apparent; the fun becomes broader, the style more liquid, and Rowlands reminds us of a writer the very opposite of an ordinary Elizabethan, namely, Peter Pindar, and sometimes of the younger Colman. That the smartness and voluble wit have not entirely evaporated yet accounts for the immense popularity enjoyed by such a work as this when it was new; yet such writing can hardly be admitted to a place in literature. Another humorous volume of 1607, *Six London Gossips*, has absolutely disappeared, and the only first edition of that prolific year which we still possess is *Diogenes' Lanthorn*. In 1591 Lodge had used the name of Diogenes for the title of a prose satire, and Rowlands' is but a feeble copy of that quaint and witty book. Lodge brings out the venom of Diogenes in a dialogue; Rowlands makes him soliloquise, and after his cynical monologue in the streets of Athens, abruptly drops his hero, and closes the volume with a series of fables, put into easy popular verse with his customary facility.

In *The Famous History of Guy, Earl of Warwick*, he showed very plainly the limitation of his powers. This poem, printed in 1608, as if in heroic couplets, but really in the six-line stanza, was spoken of by Mr. Utterson as a travesty, intended to bring chivalric literature into ridicule; but this was entirely a mistake. Nothing could be more serious than the twelve heavy cantos of Rowlands' tedious romance, which seems to have been written in imitation or emulation of Fairfax's *Tasso*, published a few years earlier.

The year 1608 also saw the publication of *Humour's Looking-Glass*, a collection precisely similar in character to *The Letting of Humour's Blood*. As before, we find no spark of poetic fancy, but plenty of rhetorical skill, a picturesque and direct style, and much descriptive *verve*. The boastful traveller was a frequent and favourite subject with the poets of Elizabeth; he was a product of their showy and grandiloquent age, and, while they laughed at his bravado, they were half inclined to like him for his impudence. But not one of them has drawn his portrait better than Rowlands has in *Humour's Looking-Glass* :—

> Come, my brave Gallant, come, uncase, uncase!
> Ne'er shall oblivion your great acts deface :
> He has been there where never man came yet,
> An unknown country, ay, I'll warrant it ;
> Whence he could ballast a good ship in hold
> With rubies, sapphires, diamonds and gold,
> Great orient pearls esteemed no more than notes,
> Sold by the peck, as chandlers measure oats ;
> I marvel, then, we have no trade from thence?
> 'Oh! 'tis too far, it will not bear expense.'
> 'Twere far, indeed, a good way from our main,
> If charges eat up such excessive gain.
>
> . . . . . .
>
> I heard him swear that he,—'twas in his mirth,—
> Had been in all the corners of the earth ;
> Let all his wonders be together stitched ;
> He threw the bar that great Alcides pitched ;
> Yet he that saw the Ocean's farthest strands,
> You pose him if you ask where Dover stands."

It would be difficult to quote a more favourable example of Rowlands' versification, and there are couplets in this passage which Waller would not have disdained to use. The instances of such smoothness of heroic verse early in the century are commoner than has

been supposed, although they were rarely sustained
This, as well as all other branches of the universal art
of poetry, was understood by the great Elizabethan
masters; and if they did not frequently employ it,
it was because they left to such humbler writers
as Rowlands an instrument incapable of those noble
and audacious harmonies on which they chiefly prided
themselves.

In 1609, unless I am wrong in my conjecture that
the *Whole Crew of Kind Gossips* of that year was but
a new edition of the *Six London Gossips* of 1607,
Rowlands confined himself to the reprinting of several
of his tracts, and to this fact we owe the possession
of one or two of the earlier books already described.
His first book of satires, which had been condemned
to be burned in 1600, he now brought out anew, under
the title of *The Knave of Clubs*, and as in this later
form it contains nothing which could reasonably give
offence, it is to be supposed that the peccant passages
had been expunged. It is not a very clever perform-
mance, rather dull and ribald, and inferior in vivacity
to the fables at the close of *Diogenes' Lanthorn*.

The *Whole Crew of Kind Gossips* is a fairly diverting description of six citizens' wives, who meet in
council to denounce their husbands, the latter presently
entering to address the public, and turn the tables on
their wives. This humble sort of *Ecclesiazusæ* has
nothing very Aristophanic about it; it is, indeed, one
of Rowlands' failures. Seldom has he secured a
subject so well suited to his genius for low humour,
and never has he more completely missed the point of

the situation. The writing shows traces of rapid and careless composition, the speeches of the wives are wanting in variety and character, and those of the husbands are dragged on without rhyme or reason, unannounced and unexplained. The language, however, is admirably clear and modern. It is to be feared that our poet had fallen upon troublous days, for his works about this time are the merest catchpenny things, thrown off without care or self-respect. *Martin Mark-all*, his contribution to 1610, is an arrant piece of book-making. It professes to be an historical account of the rise and progress of roguery up to the reign of Henry VIII., as stated to the Bellman of London by the Beadle of Bridewell. It has this special interest to modern students, that it contains a very curious dictionary of canting terms, preceding by more than half a century that in the *English Rogue.* Moreover, buried in a great deal of trash, it includes some valuable biographical notes about famous highwaymen and thieves of the sixteenth century. It is entirely in prose, except some queer Gipsy songs. The wrath of Dekker, it is supposed, was roused by a charge of plagiarism brought against some author unknown in this book, and he appears to attack Rowlands in his *Lanthorn and Candlelight.* This very slight encounter is the only incident that associates Rowlands with any of his contemporaries, and even this might fairly be disputed on the ground of dates.

The success of the *Knave of Clubs* induced Rowlands to repeat his venture with the *Knave of Hearts* in 1612, and *The Knaves of Spades and Diamonds* in

1613. These works are in no way to be distinguished from those that preceded them; their author was perhaps growing a little coarser, a little heavier, but for the rest there is the same low and trivial view of life, the same easy satire, the same fluency and lucidity of language. The increasing heaviness of his style is still more plainly seen in his next work, *A Fool's Bolt is soon Shot*, though this is far from being the worst of his productions. In this volume, sure of a large body of readers, he disdains the artifice of a dedication, and simply inscribes his poem "To Rash Judgment, Tom Fool and his fellows." It consists of a series of tales, in heroic verse, concerning the practical blunders of all sorts of foolish people, and these stories happen to be particularly rich in those personal details that make the works of Rowlands so valuable to antiquaries.

By far the best written and most important of his late works is the *Melancholy Knight* of 1615. The title-page of this pamphlet is adorned by a most curious woodcut, faithfully rendered in facsimile in the reprint of the Hunterian Club. This represents a gentleman, apparelled in the richest gala-dress of that period, with his hat pulled over his eyes, and his head deeply sunken in his capacious ruff of point-lace. His arms are folded before him, and he lounges on, lost in melancholy reverie. It is he who is supposed to indite the poems. He says:

> " I have a melancholy skull,
>   That's almost fractured, 'tis so full !
>   To ease the same these lines I write ;
>   Tobacco, boy ! a pipe ! some light !'

His reflections upon the follies and knaveries of the age, its vices, its affectations, and its impertinencies, are full of bright and delightful reading, but especially when it is found that the Knight is a bookworm, and spends his time in devouring old folio romances and chivalric tales "of ladies fair and lovely knights,' like any Don Quixote; and most of all when he ventures to recite a very touching ballad of his own about Sir Eglamour and the Dragon. No doubt the fame of Cervantes' masterpiece, published just ten years before, had reached the English pamphleteer, and he had certainly seen *The Knight of the Burning Pestle* performed in 1611. Rowlands was never original, but he was very quick in adopting a new idea. In some of the descriptions of oddity in the *Melancholy Knight* he shows a greater richness in expression than in his early works. He had probably read the satires of Donne.

The remaining works of Rowlands need not detain us very long. In 1617 he published a poem called *The Bride*, but it is lost. In 1618 he brought out *A Sacred Memory of the Miracles of Christ*, remarkable only for the preface, in which he exhorts "all faithful Christians," with such confident unction as to suggest that he may possibly by this time have found a sphere for his energies within the Church of England. In the poems themselves there is nothing important; they present all the features of conventionality and effete piety which are to be met with in English poems on sacred narrative subjects before the days of Quarles. With *The Night Raven*, in 1620, and *Good News and*

G

Bad News, in 1622, the long series of Rowlands'
humoristic studies closes.   These two books, exactly
like one another in style, consist of the usual chain of
stories, less ably told than before, but still occupied,
as ever, with knavery and simplicity, the endless joke,
now repeated to satiety, at the ease with which dulness is gulled by roguery.   According to all probable
computation, Rowlands by this time was at least fifty
years of age ; and after producing this sort of homely
poetry for more than a quarter of a century, he
possibly found that the public he once addressed had
abandoned him.   At all events, *Good News and Bad
News* is the last of his comic writings.

Six years later there appeared a little duodecimo
volume of sacred verse and prose, entitled *Heaven's
Glory, Seek it; Earth's Vanity, Fly it ; Hell's Horror,
Fear it.*   Under this affected title a writer who signs
himself Samuel Rowland issues a collection of sufficiently tedious homilies, interspersed with divine poems.
That this book was written by Samuel Rowlands has
been freely affirmed, and as freely denied ; but I do
not think that any doubt on the subject can remain on
the mind of any one who carefully reads it.   The prose
pages, it is true, have all the dogged insipidity and
absolute colourlessness of style which mark the minor
theological literature of the seventeenth century, but
the poems are not so undecipherable.   They are
printed in a delusive way, so as to seem to be in a
short ballad metre ; but they are really, in all cases,
composed in that identical six-line stanza which Rowlands affected throughout his life.   Nor is there more

similarity to his authentic poems in the form than in
the style of these religious pieces.   There is precisely
the same fluid versification, the same easy and sensible
mediocrity, and the same want of elevation and originality.   At the end of this hortatory work there is found
a collection of Prayers for use in Godly Families, and
appended to these latter a collection of poems entitled
Common Calls, Cries and Sounds of the Bellman, con-
sisting of religious posies and epigrams, very poorly
written, but still distinctly recognisable as the work of
Rowlands.   I do not think there can be the slightest
doubt that this miscellaneous volume is rightly included
among his veritable works.

From this year (1628) he passes out of our sight,
having kept the booksellers busily engaged for exactly
thirty years.   His books continued to find a sale for
another half-century, and were reprinted at least as
late as 1675.   But they were considered as scarcely
above the rank of chapbooks, and Rowlands is included among the English poets in not one of the lists
of contemporary or former authors.   In 1630 he wrote
a few verses of congratulation to his loving friend John
Taylor, the Water Poet, and in earlier life he had paid
the same compliment to two still more obscure writers.
In 1612, W. Parkes, of whom absolutely nothing is
known, quoted a short poem by Rowlands in his
Curtain - Drawer of the World.   Such, and such
alone, are the minute points of connection with his
contemporaries which the most patient scholarship has
succeeded in discovering, and they show a literary
isolation which would be astounding in so fertile an

author if we were not to consider the undignified and ephemeral nature of Rowlands' writings, which the passage of time has made interesting to us, but which to his cultivated contemporaries must have scarcely seemed to belong to literature at all.

In an age when newspapers were unknown and when poetry was still the favourite channel for popular thought, such pamphlets as those of Samuel Rowlands formed the chief intellectual pabulum of the apprentice and of his master's wife, of the city shopkeeper and of his less genteel customers. When we consider the class addressed, and the general license of those times, we shall be rather inclined to admire the reticence of the author than to blame his occasional coarseness. Rowlands is never immoral, he is rarely indecent; his attitude towards vice of all sorts is rather indifferent, and he assumes the judicial air of a satirist with small success. He has neither the integrity nor the savagery that is required to write satire; he neither indulges in the sensual rage of Donne, nor the clerical indignation of Hall; he is always too much amused at vice to be thoroughly angry with it. His favourite subject of contemplation is a sharper; to his essentially bourgeois mind nothing seems so irresistibly funny as the trick by which a shrewd rascal becomes possessed of the purse or the good name of an honest fool; and no doubt it was this that peculiarly endeared his muse to the apprentice and to the serving-maid.

As a purely literary figure Rowlands has little importance save what he owes to those details which were commonplace in his own time, but which are of antiquarian importance to us. Yet however accidental the merit may be, we cannot refuse to him the praise of having made the London of Shakespeare more vivid to us than almost any other author has done. In his earlier works, and especially in his *'Tis Merry when Gossips Meet*, he has displayed the existence in him of a comic vein which he neglected to work, but which would have assured him a brilliant success if he had had the happy thought of writing for the stage. In comedy those bright and facile qualities of style which are wasted in the frivolous repetitions of his later tales and satires, might have ripened into a veritable dramatic talent. As it is, he is a kind of small non-political Defoe, a pamphleteer in verse whose talents were never put into exercise except when their possessor was pressed for means, and a poet of considerable talent without one spark or glimmer of genius.

1880.

In 1880 I had the privilege of editing for the first time the complete works of Rowlands, in three volumes, for the Hunterian Club. At that time my attention had not been drawn to a quarto pamphlet existing in a unique example in the library of Mr. Henry Huth. This was the poem of *Ave Cæsar: God Save the King*, an address of welcome to James I., printed in 1603, but not entered at Stationers' Hall. Although this tract is anonymous, I am convinced that it was written by Samuel Rowlands, and in 1888 the

Hunterian Club was persuaded to issue a separate reprint of it.   There is inserted in the text of the original an elegy on Queen Elizabeth, signed S. R., but the whole is obviously by the same hand.   The poem was sold by George Loftus, whom we have seen to have acted as Rowlands' publisher at that date, and, in short, both internal and external evidence unite in pointing to his certain authorship.

CAPTAIN DOVER'S COTSWOLD
GAMES

IN the extreme north of Gloucestershire there lies a
district which, even now, in these hurrying days
when the romance of geography has almost disappeared, preserves a certain isolation of speech and
custom. The Cotswold Hills, running north-west
through the length of the county from one Avon to
another, culminate in their broadest and loftiest form
just as they are about to disappear in the great central
plain. The elevated plateau they form is bounded on
one side by the Stour and the Vale of Evesham, on the
other by the Evenlode and the Windrush—rivers of
melodious name that hurry past Woodstock and past
Witney to feed the waters of the still crystal Thames.
The inhabitants of the Cotswold, if we may believe the
late Mr. R. W. Huntley, who employed his immense
experience of the district in forming a glossary of the
dialect, still speak an idiom so full of pure Saxon
forms that an acquaintance with their daily speech
greatly facilitates the study of old Robert of Gloucester,
many passages in whose long-winded chronicle are to
be recognised as good Cotswold of to-day. Even now
no railway traverses a district which is one of the
most isolated in England, though near the heart of

our populous country. From time immemorial the rounded hills and open wolds of this grassy desolation were perceived to be specially adapted for athletic and public games. On such an expanse of upland a vast concourse of persons might be massed without confusion and without disturbance to public business. It is not certain when first Cotswold became celebrated for its public sports ; but certainly in the middle of the sixteenth century we find John Heywood, the epigrammatist, talking familiarly of one who was as fierce "as a lion of Cotswold," and it is understood that this allusion is to the leonine youths who fought and raced in the fine bracing air of North Gloucestershire. But, however this may be, in the early manhood of Shakespeare these irregular sports were publicly recognised and formulated in a very curious way; and this forgotten chapter in old English life provides a curious little passage in the history of seventeenth century poetry.

Captain Robert Dover, born in Norfolk towards the end of the sixteenth century, was, at the time of the accession of James I., an attorney at Barton-on-the-Heath in Warwickshire. It is amusing to consider that he was within an easy walk of Stratford, but not very instructive, since there is not the slightest reason to suppose that Shakespeare ever took advantage of the fact to visit his neighbour. This is, perhaps, unfortunate ; for Dover was a man of charming presence, full of those qualities which attract the friendship of great minds—easy and genial, stirring, yet without ambition. There exists in the British Museum a unique copy of verses in his honour, which, after celebrating the virtues of—

> " Dover, that his knowledge not employs
> To increase his neighbours' quarrels but their joys,"

adds, in a prose note, " he was bred an attorney, who never tried but two causes, always made up the difference." All the contemporary notices of him agree in giving him credit for a generous and public spirit and great personal geniality. We seem to see before us, in contemplating him, a fine type of the manly English burgher of the period, an independent but loyal subject, ready to take his own part, but easily convinced and appeased, a stalwart person coloured with the brisk air of the wolds, nimble in all physical exercises, and most at home in the saddle. It would seem that he possessed a fortune at least sufficient to allow him to use his legal experience simply for the benefit of his townsfolk, and that he had plenty of leisure for the out-of-door employments that he loved. We do not know whether his revival of the Cotswold Games preceded or followed his change of residence, but it seems certain that early in the seventeenth century he left Barton and settled at " Wickham," by which is probably meant Winchcombe. He seems to have built himself a house at Stanway, near the latter town, in the heart of Cotswold, and here he lived and here he died.

We all know that no sooner had James ascended the vacant throne of Elizabeth than Puritans of every type, depending upon the new king's Presbyterian antecedents, buzzed round him demanding every species of privilege. We know also that the wily serpent turned a deaf ear to all their charming. A few trumpery concessions from the House of Commons were all they obtained, and these were made the excuse for granting no more. It became clear to James that kingly prerogative, and his other darling doctrines, ran much less fear of opposition from easy-going gentlemen loyal to the Establishment than from feverish devotees of religious fanaticism. The comfortable classes were on the side of the King, and though himself so neurotic and morbid, he was a mighty hunter, and always prepared to encourage genial enjoyments that helped to prop up royalism and the English Church. It is not likely that Captain Robert Dover entered at all into the stirring politics of the hour; he was not the man to perceive the budding liberty of England under the harsh husk of a truculent Puritanism. But he disliked, in the true spirit of a cheerful English gentleman, the fretful suspicion of athletic sports which has always been a symptom of a gravely theological habit of mind, and he determined to have none of it in the Cotswold.

Anthony à Wood, engaged long afterwards in the tiresome biography of Clement Barksdale, turned aside to gossip with his readers about a much more entertaining Cotswold personage; and it is to this happy accident that we learn what follows. Dover determined to give an official character to the games he proposed to celebrate, and consequently, about the year 1604 we may conjecture, he obtained leave from the King to select a place on the Cotswold Hills on which to act these sports. The spot he ultimately fixed upon was some distance eastward from his house at Stanway, and close to Chipping Campden, a little Italianated borough, now quite decayed, that lies on the open country-side almost midway between Evesham and Stow-in-the-Wold. From the scene of the games a brook runs through Campden into the Stour, and so at last into the Avon a mile below Stratford. Here on the wide downs, around a little acclivity that has ever since borne the title of Dover's Hill, the genial Captain inaugurated his sports in solemn state.

There were other places celebrated for public races and games in the reign of Elizabeth. Young sparks from Cambridge, with a taste for horseflesh, divided their patronage between Royston and Newmarket; at Brackley, in Northamptonshire, and at Banstead, in Surrey, there were public games, famous in their kind and day; on Salisbury Plain sports had long been instituted. But Captain Dover determined that the fame of all these should be as nothing beside the glory of Cotswold. In this scheme he received practical help from a romantic friend at court. Endymion Porter, afterwards Groom of the Bed-Chamber to his Majesty Charles I., was one of those successful men of the world, who, with a taste for art and letters, are conscious of being themselves without the power to excel; and who give themselves the pleasure, not being the rose, of cultivating and patronising that flower wherever they have the good fortune to find it. Endymion Porter enjoyed the title of "Patron of Poets," and by his uniform good nature went far to deserve it. He found them positions, honours, gifts, and they in return immortalised him in *encomiums* and *pareneticons*, where the known passion of the Moon for an individual of his name was always ingeniously and monotonously dwelt upon. Porter was precisely the person most fitted to help Dover in his games, and we find that he entered into the scheme with alacrity.

It is not stated, but we may well imagine, that it was the florid fancy of Endymion which suggested what would hardly have occurred to plain Captain Dover, that the games should be dubbed "Olympick," and an antique dignity to be lent to the trials of skill upon Cotswold. Whoever it was to whom the hint was due, it was extremely successful. The faded humanism of the taste of the day was charmed to think that England was to possess its classic playground for heroes, with Stour for its Alpheus and little Chipping Campden for its Pisa. It gave literary importance to the proceedings, and in the course of time—as the poetasters strove to outdo one another—honest Captain Dover became finally styled, by the most gushing of them all, "the great Inventor and Champion of the English Olympicks, Pythycks, Nemicks, and Isthmicks." These be brave words for a little merriment in Whitsun-week, but the poets must always be allowed their grain of salt. It is rather to be wondered at that no pedantic rhymster of them all remembered the special patronage of "Pythycks" by Phœbus Apollo, or

> "Prima Jovi magno celebrantur Olympia Pisæ,
> Parnassus Clario sacravit Pythia Phœbo,"

hexameters in which Ausonius lifted up a voice worthy of their own Alabaster.

Endymion Porter was himself a native of Gloucestershire, and he carried his interest in Dover so far as to beg for him some cast-off robes of the King's, with the royal hat, feather, and ruff, in which to open the ceremonies with great grace and dignity. A contemporary print gives us a rough picture of the brave Captain thus adorned, his plump person arrayed in what seems to be a slashed satin doublet, and with the plumes of borrowed majesty in a wide-brimmed Cavalier hat. On the hill that bore his name there was set up a rather grotesque erection known as Dover Castle, a portable fortress provided with ordnance and artillery, and turning, apparently, on a huge pivot. It had a little portcullis and two side bastions, each bastion provided with two real guns, which fired away at proper intervals to keep up the flagging spirit of the athletes. These "cannons roaring on the wold, which from thy castle rattle to the skies," impressed the contemporary imagination very much, and Dover was playfully exhorted to protect Cotswold against the King's enemies.

It was at Whitsuntide that the gentry assembled at Campden to be present at the Cotswold revels. A yellow flag was unfurled on the battlements of the portable castle, and a bugle was blown to summon the quality to the games. Captain Dover himself rode out on his palfrey to survey the scene, wearing a yellow favour in his hunting-cap. He seems to have rivalled the Chinese in his partiality for the colour yellow. At the foot of the hill and along the courses there were arranged tents, where food and drink were served, and where public contests at chess were fought out. There is some discrepancy in the accounts of the order of the sports; there was, perhaps no very strict arrangement maintained from year to year. According to a certain Robert Griffin, however, it was usual, after the bugle had blown, to open the ceremonies with horse-racing. The country-side outdid itself in adorning the animals which were to run with ribands and flowers. A poet who met such a palfrey going to be run at Cotswold, declared that if Europa had seen him so garlanded and pranked, she would never have cast eyes upon the Bull. The racecourse was some miles long, and remained in existence until our own time, when it was ploughed up by order of Lord Harrowby.

The horse-racing was not so original a sport as what followed next, the coursing of "silver-footed greyhounds." For this pastime Cotswold became specially famous, and it received the honour of mention from Shakespeare. In the very opening scene of *The Merry Wives of Windsor*, Slander says to Page, "How does your fallow greyhound, sir? I heard say he was outrun on Cotsall." The phrase, "I heard say he was *outrun*," can obviously only refer to a competitive coursing, in which Page's greyhound failed to win the first prize. It is remarkable that this passage does not occur in the quartos, and rests on the authority of the first folio; but it would be very rash to argue from this fact, as has been done, however, that the Cotswold games began between 1619 and 1623. There can be no doubt that at the latter date they had the notoriety which follows twenty years of success. It was made a great point by the humane Dover that not the killing of the hare, but the winning of the prize, should be the aim men set before them in competing. He desired to supersede hunting as much as possible by instituting these games of skill.

The next exercise was so curious and so characteristic of the times that I must give leave to the above-named Robert Griffin to describe it in his own words:—

> "This done, a virgin crew of matchless choice
> Nimbly set forth, attended with a noise
> Of music sweet, excelling that of spheres,
> Whose well-kept diapason ravished their's,"

meaning the spheres',

> "Of all that's sensitive. These nymphs advance
> Themselves with such a comely grace to dance,
> Each with her gallant paired, that all who see
> Their cunning motion and agility
> Are struck with admiration."

We imagine such a classic dance of loose-robed girls, girdled and garlanded with flowers, as Herrick was so fond of fancying, but the engraving to which we have referred destroys these fair illusions. There are no soft outlines of drapery, such as the pupils of Raffaelle loved — nothing antique or pseudo-antique. Three substantial nymphs are represented dancing conscientiously a country dance, in stiff gowns of unmistakable print, rather high in the waist, and adorned by nothing more fantastic than a large white apron and a ruff. Their tresses may be luxuriant, but they are modestly concealed beneath smooth muslin caps. The sweet music, excelling the diapason of the spheres, proceeds from a person seated on the ground, who vigorously blows the bagpipes. The gallants are not seen, the particular dance being apparently a *pas seul*, undertaken by each girl in competition with the others.

When the virgins had finished their elegant pastime, the character of the sports became more general. In one part of the course the indispensable quintain was put up, in one of its many forms. It is curious that what was at that time the most characteristic and universal English game should now require explanation; but quintain died in the days of the Commonwealth, never to revive. The essence of the sport was to run a tilt against an object so balanced, that if you failed to hit it at the exact point, some punishment or other fell upon you. The simple childish form of the game was a tub of water poised in such a way that if the cowering naked schoolboy who attacked it did not manage to strike it in the centre, it gave him a sudden douche of the most depressing kind. The most elaborate form was an armed figure, turning on a pivot, against which a man rode with a lance, and which, in case he failed to hit a certain mark on the forehead of the figure, swung round and banged him behind with a swinging bag of sand. Between these extremes, there existed many varieties of quintain, all of them rather violent specimens of good old English horse-play; Strutt's *Sports and Pastimes* may be referred to for further particulars.

Another game in favour at Cotswold was balloon, a kind of hand-ball played with a large leather ball like the modern football, driven through the air from person to person, struck by a bracer of wood, fastened round the hand and wrist for protection, a game still to be seen played by French boys in the gardens of the Tuileries.   In another part of the ground cudgel-players strove to break in one another's heads.   Men ran races, variously bound or handicapped; others were wrestling, leaping, casting the sledge-hammer, throwing the bar.   Everywhere athletic exercises of all sorts were encouraged and developed, and all under the personal guidance of Captain Robert Dover.   Prizes were abundantly given, to the number, it would seem, of five hundred, since it is recorded that so many gen-tlemen carried about with them for a twelvemonth the Dover favour of yellow.

For nearly forty years these games were held every year in Whitsun-week, and at the same place, till they became more famous than any sports of a similar kind held elsewhere.   The gentry crowded to them in a vast concourse from a radius of sixty miles.   Yet so ephemeral is the memory of these events, that we should know nothing about them but a faint rumour, and absolutely nothing about their founder, if it had not been for Captain Dover's personal charm of character and his friendships with a variety of literary men.   In 1636 there was published a little volume of verse, entitled *Annalia Dubrensia, or Celebration of Captain Robert Dover's Cotswold Games*.   This is one of the rarest books of that period, and was long practically inaccessible to students.   The Rev. A. B. Grosart, whose zeal for our early literature is un-

H

bounded, has increased the heavy debt which lovers of old English poetry already owe him, by reprinting for a select number of subscribers this fascinating little book, thereby preserving it from all chance of destruction. It is adorned with the rude frontispiece to which I have referred. At the top of this woodcut we see Dover Castle, with two of its cannon in the act of "rattling to the skies ;" on the left of this the virgins are dancing, while to the right cudgel-playing, leaping, and wrestling are represented. Below this are the tents, and a square *plaque*, which I take to be a facsimile of Dover's yellow favour. In the centre of the cut, persons of quality are feasting at a long table. Then follow the horse-racing and the coursing, while the foreground is occupied by Dover himself on his palfrey, in all his borrowed glory, with some men throwing the bar on his left, and the sledge-hammer on his right.

The letterpress of the volume has a mournful, half-posthumous air. It was published a little too late, and when the poets sing the glories of the games, we are inclined to murmur "Ichabod." For the merry days of royalism were over, and in the neighbouring county of Buckinghamshire, a sturdy gentleman, Mr. Hampden, was refusing that ship-money upon which rested so vast a fabric in the future. King Charles had played his game of quintain; he had tilted recklessly and missed, and now the creaking engine of the State was swinging round to smite him ignominiously. The days of hock-feasts and barley-breaks were over, and in the very heart of the growing uneasiness and discontent here appeared this cheerful little book of eulogies, manifestly born after due time. But in another sense it was late in appearing. It was the work, as far as we can judge by those writers whose names are familiar to us, of poets of the olden school, now all dead or aged. To describe its contents more exactly, the *Annalia Dubrensia* is an anthology of original verses by thirty-three hands, all to the honour and glory of Captain Robert Dover. In the list of authors we find some names of the highest eminence — Ben Jonson, Michael Drayton, Thomas Randolph, and Thomas Heywood; names of accomplished writers such as Owen Feltham, William Basse, Sir John Mennis, and Shackerley Marmion. One poem is anonymous, and another signed by initials; the others bear the names of unknown persons manifestly amateurs. The whole is edited by a Mr. Mat. Walbancke.

Drayton leads off with some thirty lines of good sound verse, "to his noble friend Mr. Robert Dover on his brave annual assemblies upon Cotswold." He congratulates England on having succeeded to the glories of Greece, compares the Cotswold with the Olympic Games, and foretells that coming generations will count their years from the former, just as Greece,

"Nurse of all arts and of all famous men,"

counted hers by Olympiads. It is plain that these lines had long circulated in MS.; several of the other writers refer to them, and besides, when the *Annalia Dubrensia* was published, Drayton had been at rest in Poet's Corner for nearly five years. It was natural that Dover should be specially delighted at a tribute from the heroic muse of Drayton. The latter had not been a popular or successful poet, in a worldly sense, but the force and dignity of his writing, and his position a little aloof from and above the warring of the wits, gave him a sort of pre-eminence. The sweet and courtly Daniel had held the same kind of poetical kingship, but he had died soon, and Drayton seems to have succeeded him in a sort of non-official laureate-ship. From the character of the verse in this little eulogy, I hazard the conjecture that it was written in the last period of his life, when he was the honoured guest of the Earl of Dorset.

A still greater man than Drayton contributes a brief poem to this charming little "Amulet" or "Keepsake." If we recollect the circumstances of Ben Jonson in the year 1636, the melancholy significance of these bluff lines, evidently written years before, will be very apparent. He had ceased in 1636 to care about Captain Dover or his Olympic games, and indeed a hard life was fast drawing to its painful close. Stricken with palsy, he had long struggled against poverty by the painful composition of entertainments and pageants, but now even his last labour of love, *The Sad Shepherd*, dropped unfinished from his hands. In a few months England was to pause in the midst of her civic troubles to discuss the news of the great poet's death. Jonson's lines are brief, and have an air of compulsion. Perhaps Captain Dover teased the old man for a contribution to his "garland;" at all events, the verses, the last production of the author's printed in his lifetime, have more growling than singing in them.   He declines in the outset to follow Drayton in his airy parallels between Chipping Campden and Pisa in Elis :—

> "I cannot bring my Musë to drop vies *
> 'Twixt Cotswold and the Olympic exercise,"

but he hopes that Church and State may flourish and be advanced, in spite of hypocrites, and that Dover may have a share in this good work.

By far the most admirable poem in the collection, from a literary point of view, is Randolph's contribution.   This also had the melancholy fortune to be posthumous, for the poet, cut off by we know not what accident in the flower of his youth, had died at the house of a friend a few months before.   It was a deplorable loss to English literature.   The stars must have erred in casting his horoscope, for Randolph had none of that precocious ripeness which seems so often to be the presage of, and the consolation for, an early death.   His genius, which had something resolute and sturdy about it, was one that would certainly have raised him, at least, to an honourable place in the second rank of poets.   His six plays and his thin collection of lyrics were but the infant motions of a wing that meant to strike hard and wide into the empyrean of poetry.

---

* Great difficulty has been found in the measure and meaning of this line.   To me there seems to be none if we take "Musë" to be a dissyllable, as "statuë" was a trisyllable (in Habington and elsewhere), and if we understand "vie" to be a noun equivalent to "comparison."

There is nothing hectic or hysterical in what remains to us of Randolph; no attractive weakness or dolphin colour of approaching death. Had he lived he might have bridged over, with a strong popular poetry, the abyss between the old romantic and the new didactic schools, for he had a little of the spirit of each. As it is, he holds a better place in English literature than Dryden, or Gray, or Massinger would have held had they died before they were thirty. His "Eclogue on the Palilia and noble Assemblies revived on Cotswold Hills" is charming. Two shepherds, Collen and Thenot, converse about the degeneracy of the English swains. Collen is exceedingly afflicted to find his compeers so boorish, and Thenot replies that it cannot be for want of ability, since nowhere in the world can you find men so vast in stature, so sinewy and so supple, as the swains of England. Collen explains that the Puritans are to blame for this boorishness. In early times there were joyous games, in which the English athletes contended and grew skilful and graceful. In those days, he continues, in a charming vein of pastoral—

> "Early in May up got the jolly rout,
>   Called by the lark, and spread the fields about;
>   One, for to breathe himself, would coursing be
>   From this same beech to yonder mulberry;
>   A second leaped, his supple nerves to try;
>   A third was practising his melody;
>   This a new foot was jigging; others were
>   Busy at wrestling or to throw the bar,
>   Ambitious which should bear the bell away,
>   *And kiss the nut-brown Lady of the May.*

This stirred them up !   A jolly swain was he
Whom Peg and Susan, after victory,
Crowned with a garland they had made, beset
With daisies, pinks, and many a violet,
Cowslip, and gilliflower.   Rewards, though small,
Encourage virtue ; but if none at all
Meet her, she languisheth and dies, as now,
Where worth's denied the honour of a bough."

Thenot deplores the decline of these merry sports, and
Collen informs him that it is the work of certain
splenetic persons, given up to extreme piety.

"These teach that dancing is a Jezebel,
And barley-break the ready way to hell ;
The morrice, idols ; Whitsun-ales can be
But profane relics of a jubilee ;
These, in a zeal to express how much they do
The organs hate, have silenced bagpipes too ;
And harmless maypoles all are railed upon,
As if they were the towers of Babylon."

Thenot, crying out against these deluded bigots, longs
for the time to come when such innocent pleasures
may thrive again.   Collen, at this, can no longer refrain from telling him that his prayer is heard, and
that "Pan hath approved dancing shall be this year
holy as is the motion of a sphere."   Thenot cannot
believe this good news, and begs for an explanation.
He is told that Collen has just met a handsome fellow
spurring a spirited steed over the plain towards Cotswold ; and begging him to explain whither he went so
blythe and so gaily decked, he told him to the Hill,
where horses, fleet as sons of the wind, competed for

prizes, and where the hounds went coursing with such musical, full cries, that Orion leaned out of heaven and wished his dog might be there to join in the races. Thenot rejoices again, and desires to know at whose bidding these noble games have recommenced. He is told that it is jovial Dover's deed, and Collen closes by calling the nymphs around, and bidding them do honour to that great man.

> "Go, maids, and lilies get,
> To make him up a glorious coronet ;
> Swains, keep his holiday, and each man swear
> To saint him in the Shepherd's Calendar.

It is a most ingenious, pretty poem, one of the best eclogues we possess in English.

Thomas Heywood comes in at the end of the book with a kind of appendix. After having read all the eulogies by the thirty-three poets, he professes himself at a loss to know what new thing to say. But the veteran who had already had a main finger in more than two hundred plays, and who was ready, as a satire falsely attributed to Cowley assures us, to write on any subject for the smallest pay, was not likely to be really at a loss for words. At the most reasonable computation, Heywood must at this time have been nearly seventy years of age, and the chirruping cheerfulness of his lines is very consoling. The author of the "Panegerick" may have been old and poor, but he cannot have been very unhappy. His poem possesses no other significance than its joviality. Ben Jonson had declined to "drop vies" between Olympus and

Cotswold, but Heywood does not object to do, not this only, but to compare Dover with Hercules. The old poet being hard of hearing, we may whisper, confidentially, that his poem is, in truth, very dull and silly.

The second-rate poets need not detain us long. Owen Feltham, so honourably known as the author of the *Resolves*, was an exception to the general rule of the book, for he was still young, and to live for forty years more. His poem is in good supple verse, but obscure and affected to the last degree, like his prose in all but its best passages. Shackerley Marmion, author of the graceful epic poem of *Cupid and Psyche* and of several creditable plays, contributes one of the most readable and sensible pieces in the volume, congratulating Dover on his good work without ridiculous extravagance. Marmion was soon after to die miserably of a sickness brought on by marching as a soldier in Sir John Suckling's troop on the ill-starred expedition to Scotland. "A goodly, proper gentleman," as Anthony à Wood calls him, to whose merits posterity has scarcely been just. Finally, in return for all the kind wishes expressed, Robert Dover himself essays "A Congratulatory Poem to my Poetical and Learned Friends, Compilers of this Book," in which, with considerable humour, he defends his love of athletic sports against the Puritans, who are so ready to see "wicked, horrid sin" in every kind of innocent pastime. Such are the contents of a volume of unusual interest, adorned with many illustrious names, and destined to preserve the memory of an interesting public movement, which, but for the existence of these verses, we should scarcely have heard of; for it was the accident of Anthony à Wood's possession of the book in his library that led him to turn aside into pleasant gossip about the person celebrated in it.

Captain Robert Dover did not long survive the apotheosis and the destruction of his games. The one occurred in 1636, the other probably in 1638, and in 1641 he died at Stanway. He had a nephew or a grandson, who became a small dramatist during the Restoration. The scenes of the Cotswold games were left intact, and, according to a manuscript in the possession of the late Sir Thomas Winnington, the sports themselves were revived in the reign of Charles II. It was probably very soon after this second revival that their neighbourhood was the scene of a most lurid and mysterious event, which I may be permitted to recount as a foil to the joviality of the games themselves. Mr. William Harrison, the steward of a wealthy lady of Chipping Campden, riding out from home one day in 1676 to collect the rents of his mistress at Charringworth, did not return at night. A servant of the house, John Perry, was sent to search for him in the morning, and when he returned without any news, a general examination of the neighbourhood began. In a lonely spot there were found a hat, a band, and a comb, which were recognised as having belonged to Mr. Harrison, and which were covered with blood. The body itself was not discovered, but the trial for murder began, and suspicion fell upon John Perry. This was increased by his confusion, and at last, cross-examined before the magistrates, he confessed that his mother and his brother had murdered Mr. Harrison, after robbing him of his effects. Circumstantial evidence was so strong against the prisoners, that, although the dead body had not been discovered, the Perrys were found guilty of the murder and all three were hanged, John Perry protesting with his last breath that he had made a mistake, or been deluded by his fancy. Every one in the district, however, was satisfied with the justice of the sentence, when, after two years were passed, one day Mr. Harrison came quietly riding into Chipping Campden, with the story that he had been met on the wold by a party of men, who, after a violent struggle, had secured him, had ridden hard with him to the sea, had sailed to Turkey with him, and had sold him as a slave to a Moslem physician. He declared that in the course of time he had escaped and fled on board a vessel bound for Portugal, whence he had found his way home again. What part of this romantic tale was true we know not; the horrible circumstance is the execution of the family of the Perrys on the strength of an hallucination.

The Cotswold games, in a hueless and debased form, continued to be celebrated during Whitsun-week almost all through the last century; but they were vulgarised, and all the charming air of distinction that Captain Dover had given them vanished with his death. Yet in their original form they were well worthy to be remembered. These humane and innocent sports, with their graceful mingling of antique revival with plain, homely English merriment, are characteristic of the very best side of the Royalist party in the seventeenth century, and they are not unimportant in helping us to realise the every-day life of gentry and peasantry in distant country places.

1881.

ROBERT HERRICK

IT is told of Mahommed that when the political economists of the day provoked him by the narrowness of their utilitarian schemes, he was wont to silence them with these words: "If a man has two loaves of bread, let him exchange one for some flowers of the narcissus; for bread only nourishes the body, but to look on the narcissus feeds the soul." Robert Herrick was one of the few who have been content to carry out this precept, and to walk through life with a little bread in the one hand, and in the other a bunch of golden flowers. With an old serving-woman in a tumble-down country parsonage, his life passed merrily among such dreams as Oriental sultans wear themselves out to realise, and his figure stands out in front of the shining ranks of his contemporaries as that around which most vividly of all there flashes the peculiar light of imagination. He may be well contrasted with a man whose native genius was probably exceedingly like his own, but whose life was as brilliant and eventful as Herrick's was retired, namely, Sir John Suckling. The wit, fire, and exuberant imagination that interpenetrated both found scope in the life of one and in the works of the other. Suckling's poems are strangely inadequate to represent his genius and fame; Herrick, on the other hand, may be taken almost as the typical poet, the man who, if not a lyrist, would be nothing —the birdlike creature whose only function was to sing in a cage of trammelling flesh.

There are many features in his career, besides the actual excellence of his verse, which make him an object of peculiar interest. Among the pure poets he occupies the most prominent position in the school that flourished after Ben Jonson and before Milton, and though his life was of immense duration—he was born before Marlowe died, and died after the birth of Addison—his actual period of production covers the comparatively small space occupied by the reign of Charles I. This period was one of great lyrical ability; the drama was declining under Cartwright and Shirley, and all the young generation of poets, brought up at the feet of Jonson and Fletcher, were much more capable of writing songs than plays. Indeed, no one can at this time determine what degree of technical perfection English literature might not have attained if the Royalist lyrists had been allowed to sun themselves unmolested about the fountains of Whitehall, and, untroubled by the grave questions of national welfare, had been able to give their whole attention to the polishing of their verses. In fact, however, it will be noticed that only one of the whole school was undisturbed by the political crisis. The weaker ones, like Lovelace, were completely broken by it; the stronger, like Suckling, threw themselves into public affairs with a zeal and intensity that supplied the place of the artificial excitements of poetry so completely as to put a stop to their writing altogether. Herrick alone, with imperturbable serenity, continued to pipe out his pastoral ditties, and crown his head with daffodils, when England was torn to pieces with the most momentous struggle for liberty in her annals. To the poetic student he is, therefore, of especial interest, as a genuine specimen, of an artist pure and simple. Herrick brought out the *Hesperides* a few months before the King was beheaded, and people were invited to listen to little madrigals upon Julia's stomacher at the singularly inopportune moment when the eyes of the whole nation were bent on the unprecedented phenomenon of the proclamation of an English republic. To find a parallel to such unconsciousness we must come down to our own time, and recollect that Théophile Gautier took occasion of the siege of Paris to revise and republish his *Emaux et Camées.*

Herrick was born in London, in " the golden Cheapside," and baptized on the 23rd of August 1591. His father died in the course of the next year, from a fall from an upper window, which was attributed to suicide. All we can guess about the poet's childhood is to be picked up in one of his own confidential pieces about himself, where he speaks with intense delight of his early life by the river-side, going to bathe in the " summer's sweeter evenings " with crowds of other youths, or gliding with pomp in a barge, with the young ladies of the period, " soft-smooth virgins," up as far as Richmond, Kingston, and Hampton Court. In the same poem he speaks of his " beloved Westminster," from which allusion it has been illogically imagined that he was at school there. The first certain fact in his life is that in 1607 he was apprenticed to his uncle, the rich goldsmith of Wood Street, with whom one may presume that he remained until 1615, when we find him entered as fellow-commoner of St. John's College, Cambridge. His London life, therefore, closed when his age was twenty-four, and his acquaintance with literary life in the metropolis must have come to rapid development within the eight years of his apprenticeship. Speculation in this case is not so vain as usual. If any fact about Herrick be certain, it is that he sat at the feet of Ben Jonson ; the poems of rapturous admiration and reverence that abound in the *Hesperides* set this beyond question. In one piece, it will be remembered, he speaks, with passion unusual to him, of the old days when Ben Jonson's plays were brought out at the London theatres, and gives us an important date by describing the unfavourable reception of the *Alchemist*, much as a poet of the Romanticism would have described the reception of *Hernani* for the first time at the Théâtre Français. But the *Alchemist* was brought out in 1610, when our poet was nineteen years old, and it was received with great excitement as an innovation. We may well believe that the young apprentice, fired with enthusiasm for the great poet, distinguished himself by the loudness and truculence of his applause, and claimed the privilege of laying his homage afterwards at the author's feet. Nineteen years later exactly the same thing was done by a younger generation, when Carew, Randolph, and Cleaveland made a riot at the damning of the *New Inn*, and then laid their lyric worship at the grand old poet's feet.

Jonson loved to receive such homage, and to pose as the poet of the age; in fact, we cannot be too often reminded that to the intellectual public of that day he took exactly the same regal position among his contemporaries that we now unanimously accord to Shakespeare. Taking for granted that Herrick became a familiar member of Jonson's circle about 1610, we must suppose him to have witnessed in succession the first performances of *Catiline* and of *Bartholomew Fair*, and to have known the poet of the "mountain belly and the rocky face" at the very height of his creative power. More important for us, however, as being far more in unison with the tastes and genius of Herrick, are the masques upon which Jonson was engaged at this time. It is very strange that no writer upon the poetry of that age has noticed what an extraordinary influence the masques of Ben Jonson had upon Herrick. We have seen that he must have become acquainted with that poet in 1610. It is more than remarkable to notice that it was in this year that Jonson produced *Oberon the Fairy Prince*, a beautiful masque that contains the germs of many of Herrick's most fantastic fairy-fancies. *The Masque of Queens*, brought out some months earlier, is full of Herrick-like passages about hags and witches; and we might pursue the parallel much further, did space permit, showing how largely Jonson, on the milder and more lyrical side of his genius, inspired the young enthusiast and pointed out to him the poetic path that he should take

I

We cannot with equal certainty say that Herrick was acquainted with any other of the great poets. Shakespeare was settled at Stratford, and in London only briefly and at distant intervals; he died at the end of Herrick's first year at Cambridge. Herrick writes of Fletcher thirty years later as though he had known him slightly, and speaks of the power of the *Maid's Tragedy* to make "young men swoon," as though he had seen it at the first performance in 1611. He must have known Jonson's jolly friend Bishop Corbet, who was also a lover of fairy-lore, and he may have known Browne, whose poetry Jonson approved of, and who was then studying in the Inner Temple, and beginning to publish *Britannia's Pastorals*. It was probably at this time, and through Ben Jonson, that he became acquainted with Selden, for whose prodigious learning and wit he preserved an extravagant admiration through life. This is as far as we dare to go in speculation. If Herrick, so fond of writing about himself, had found time for a few more words about his contemporaries, we might discover that he had dealings with other interesting men during this period of apprenticeship, but probably his circle was pretty much limited to the personal and intimate friends of Jonson.

In 1615, as we have said, he took up his abode at Cambridge as a fellow-commoner of St. John's, and here and at Trinity Hall he seems to have remained till 1629, when his mother died. How these fourteen years or early manhood were spent it is now impossible to conjecture. That he became Master of Arts in 1620 is not so important an item of history as that he was certainly very poor, and in the habit of making a piteous annual appeal to his rich uncle for ten pounds to buy books with. Fourteen of these appeals exist, written in a florid, excited style, with a good many Latin quotations and old-fashioned references to " Apelles ye painter," in the manner of *Euphues*. It is amusing to note that he manages to spell his own surname in six different ways, and not one of them that which is now adopted on the authority of the title-page of the *Hesperides*. There can be no doubt that he began writing in London ; it is certain that he was known as a poet at Cambridge. One of the few dates in the *Hesperides* is 1627, two years before the exodus into Devonshire, and in "Lacrime" he says that before he went into exile into the loathed west

> " He could rehearse
> A lyric verse,
> And speak it with the best."

The *Hesperides*, in its present state, offers no assistance to us in trying to discover what was written early or late, for nothing is more obvious than that the verses were thrown together without the slightest regard to the chronology of their composition. However, on the 2nd of October 1629, he succeeded Potter, Bishop of Carlisle, in the living of Dean Prior, under Dartmoor, in South Devon, and there he remained in quiet retirement until 1648, when he was ejected by the Puritans.

Such is the modest biography of this poet up to the time of the publication of the two books which caused and have retained his great reputation. Fortunately he has himself left copious materials for autobiography in the gossipy pages of his own confidential poems. Glancing down the index to the *Hesperides*, one is constantly struck by such titles as "On Himself," "To His Muse," and "His Farewell to Sack," and one is not disappointed in turning to these to collect an impression of the author's individuality.   Indeed, few writers of that age appear more vividly in relief than Herrick; the careful student of his poems learns to know him at last as a familiar friend, and every feature of body and mind stands out clearly before the eye of the imagination.   He was physically a somewhat gross person, as far as his portrait will enable one to judge, with great quantities of waving or curling black hair, and a slight black moustache; the eyebrows distinct and well arched, the upper lip short, the nose massive and Roman.   In the weighty points of the face, especially in the square and massive under-jaw, there is much of the voluptuous force of the best type among the Roman emperors; and bearing these features well in mind, it becomes easy to understand how it was that Herrick came to write so much that an English gentleman, not to say clergyman, had better have left unsaid.   His temperament was scarcely clerical:—

> " I fear no earthly powers,
>   But care for crowns of flowers ;
>   And love to have my beard
>   With wine and oil besmeared.
>   This day I'll drown all sorrow ;
>   Who knows to live to-morrow ?"

This was his philosophy, and it is not to be dis-

tinguished from that of Anacreon or Horace. One
knows not how the old pagan dared to be so outspoken
in his dreary Devonshire vicarage, with no wild friends
to egg him on or to applaud his fine frenzy.

His Epicureanism was plainly a matter of conviction, and though he wrote *Noble Numbers*, preached
sermons, and went through all the perfunctory duties
of his office, it is not in these that he lives and has his
pleasure, but in half-classical dreams about Favonius
and Isis, and in flowery mazes of sweet thoughts
about fair, half-imaginary women. It matters little
to him what divinity he worships, if he may wind
daffodils into the god's bright hair. In one hand he
brings a garland of yellow flowers for the amorous
head of Bacchus, with the other he decks the osier-
cradle of Jesus with roses and Lent-lilies. He has
no sense of irreverence in this rococo devotion. It
is the attribute, and not the deity he worships. There
is an airy frivolity, an easy-going callousness of soul,
that makes it impossible for him to feel very deeply.

There is a total want of passion in Herrick's language
about women. The nearest approach to it, perhaps,
is in the wonderful song "To Anthea," where the
lark-like freshness of the ascending melody closely
simulates intense emotion. With all his warmth of
fancy and luxurious animalism, he thinks more of the
pretty eccentricities of dress than of the charms the
garments contain. He is enraptured with the way in
which the Countess of Carlisle wears a riband of black
silk twisted round her arm ; he palpitates with pleasure
when Mistress Katherine Bradshaw puts a crown of

laurel on his head, falling on one knee, we may believe, and clasping his hands as he receives it. He sees his loves through the medium of shoe-strings and pomander bracelets, and is alive, as no poet has been before or since, to the picturesqueness of dress. Everybody knows his exquisite lines about the "tempestuous petticoat," and his poems are full of little touches no less delicate than this.

Only two things make him really serious: one is his desire of poetic fame. Every lyric he writes he considers valuable enough to be left as a special legacy to some prime friend. He is eager to die before the world; to pass away, like Pindar, garlanded, and clasped in the arms of love, while the theatre resounds with plaudits. His thirst for fame is insatiable, and his confidence of gaining it intense. His poesy is "his hope and his pyramides," a living pillar "ne'er to be thrown down by envious Time," and it shall be the honour of great musicians to set his pieces to music when he is dead. When he is dead! That has a saddening sound! Life was meant to last for ever, and it makes him angry to think of death. He rings his head about with roses, clasps Julia to his arms, and will defy death. Yet, if death should come, as he sometimes feels it must, he is not unmindful of what his end should be. No thoughts of a sad funeral or the effrontery of a Christian burial oppress him; he cannot even think of dismal plumes or of a hearse. He will be wound in one white robe, and borne to a quiet garden-corner, where the overblown roses may shower petals on his head, and where, when the first primrose blossoms, Perilla may remember him, and come to weep over his dust :—

> " Then shall my ghost not walk about, but keep
> Still in the cool and silent shades of sleep."

He was never married; he explains over and over again that he values his liberty far too highly to give it into any woman's hands, and lived in the country, as it would seem, with no company save that of an excellent old servant, Prudence Baldwin.

In many sweet and sincere verses he gives us a charming picture of the quiet life he led in the Devonshire parsonage that he affected to loathe so much. The village had its rural and semi-pagan customs, that pleased him thoroughly. He loved to see the brown lads and lovely girls, crowned with daffodils and daisies, dancing in the summer evenings in a comely country round; he delighted in the maypole, ribanded and garlanded like a thyrsus, reminding his florid fancy of Bacchus and the garden god. There were morris dances at Dean Prior, wakes and quintels; mummers, too, at Christmas, and quaint revellings on Twelfth Night, with wassail bowls and nut-brown mirth; and we can imagine with what zeal the good old pagan would encourage these rites against the objections of any roundhead Puritan who might come down with his newfangled Methodistical notions to trouble the sylvan quiet of Dean Prior. For Herrick the dignity of episcopal authorship had no charm, and the thunders of Nonconformity no terror. Graver minds were at this moment occupied with *Holy Living and Holy Dying*, and thrilled with the Sermons of Calamy. It is delightful to think of Herrick, blissfully unconscious of the tumult of tongues and all the windy war, more occupied with morris dances and barley-breaks than with prayer-book or psalter. The Revolution must indeed have come upon him unaware.

Herrick allowed himself to write a great deal of nonsense about his many mistresses. It was the false Anacreontic spirit of the day; and a worse offender was in the field, even Abraham Cowley, who, never having had the courage to speak of love to a single woman, was about to publish, in 1648, a circumstantial account of his affairs with more than one-and-twenty mistresses. It is not easy to determine how much of Herrick's gallantry is as imaginary as this. We may dismiss Perilla, Silvia, Anthea, and the rest at once, as airy nothings, whom the poet created ror the sake of hanging pretty amorous fancies on their names; but Julia is not so ephemeral or so easily disposed of. She may well be supposed to have died or passed away before Herrick left Cambridge. All the poet's commentators seem to have forgotten how old he was before he retired to that country vicarage where they rightly enough perceive that the presence of a Julia was impossible. When we recollect that he did not enter holy orders till he was thirty-eight, we may well believe that Julia ruled his youth, and yet admit his distinct statement with regard to his clerical life, that

" Jocund his muse was, but his life was chaste."

We have a minute chronicle of Julia's looks and ways in the *Hesperides*, and they bear a remarkable air of truth about them. She is presented to us as a buxom person, with black eyes, a double chin, and a strawberry-cream complexion. Her attire, as described by our milliner-poet, is in strict accordance with the natural tastes of a woman of this physical nature. She delights in rich silks and deep-coloured satins; on one occasion she wears a dark blue petticoat, starred with gold, on other she ravishes her poet-lover by the glitter and vibration of her silks as she takes her stately walks abroad. Her hair, despite her dark eyes, is bright and dewy, and the poet takes a fantastic pleasure in tiring and braiding it. An easy, kindly woman, we picture her ready to submit to the fancies of her lyric lover; pleased to have roses on her head, still more pleased to perfume herself with storax, spikenard, galbanum, and all the other rich gums he loved to smell; dowered with so much refinement of mind as was required to play fairly on the lute, and to govern a wayward poet with tact; not so modest or so sensitive as to resent the grossness of his fancy, yet respectable enough and determined enough to curb his license at times. She bore him one daughter, it seems, to whom he addressed one of his latest poems and one of his tamest.

But it is time to turn from the poet to his work, from Julia to the *Hesperides* that she inspired. They are songs, children of the West, brought forth, if not conceived, in the soft, sweet air of Devonshire. And

the poet strikes a keynote with wonderful sureness
in the opening couplets of the opening poem :—

> " I sing of brooks, of blossoms, birds and bowers,
>   Of April, May, of June and July flowers ;
>   I sing of maypoles, hock-carts, wassails, wakes,
>   Of bridegrooms, brides, and of their bridal-cakes."

It would not have been easy to describe more
correctly what he does sing of. The book is full of
all those pleasant things of spring and summer, full of
young love, happy nature, and the joy of mere existence. As far as flowers are concerned, the atmo-
sphere is full of them. We are pelted with roses and
daffodils from every page, and no one dares enter the
sacred precincts without a crown of blossoms on his
hair. Herrick's muse might be that Venus of Botticelli
who rises, pale and dewy, from a sparkling sea, blown
at by the little laughing winds, and showered upon
with violets and lilies of no earthly growth. He tells
us that for years and years his muse was content to
stay at home, or straying from village to village, to
pipe to handsome young shepherds and girls of flower-
sweet breath, but that at last she became ambitious to
try her skill at Court, and so came into print in London.
In other words, these little poems circulated widely in
manuscript long before they were published. They are
not all of the bird and blossom kind, unhappily ; the
book is fashioned, as we shall presently see, closely
upon the model of the Epigrams of Martial ; and as
there the most delicate and jewel-like piece of sentiment rubs shoulders with a coarse and acrid quatrain

of satire, so has Herrick shuffled up odes, epithalamia, epigrams, occasional verses and canzonets, in glorious confusion, without the slightest regard to subject, form, or propriety. There are no less than one thousand two hundred and thirty-one distinct poems in the book, many of them, of course, only two lines long. There are too many "epigrams," as he called them, scraps of impersonal satire, in the composition of which he followed Ben Jonson, who had followed Martial. These little couplets and quatrains are generally very gross, very ugly, and very pointless; they have, sometimes, a kind of broad Pantagruelist humour about them which has its merit, but it must be confessed even of these that they greatly spoil the general complexion of the book.

More worthy of attention in every way are the erotic lyrical pieces, which fortunately abound, and which are unrivalled in our literature for their freshness and tender beauty. They are interpenetrated with strong neo-pagan emotion; had they been written a century earlier, they would be called the truest English expression of the passion of the Renaissance. This is, however, what they really are. Late in the day as they made their appearance, they were as truly an expression of the delirious return to the freedom of classical life and enjoyment as the Italian paintings of the fifteenth or the French poetry of the sixteenth century. The tone of the best things in the *Hesperides* is precisely the same as that which permeates the wonderful designs of the *Hypnerotomachia*. In Herrick's poems, as in that mysterious and beautiful romance, the sun

shines on a world re-arisen to the duty of pleasure;
Bacchus rides through the valleys, with his leopards
and his maidens and his ivy-rods; loose-draped nymphs,
playing on the lyre, bound about their foreheads with
vervain and the cool stalks of parsley, fill the silent
woods with their melodies and dances; this poet sings
of a land where all the men are young and strong, and
all the women lovely, where life is only a dream of
sweet delights of the bodily senses. The *Hesperides*
is an astounding production when one considers when
it was written, and how intensely grave the temper
of the age had become. But Herrick hated sobriety
and gravity, and distinguished very keenly between
the earnestness of art and the austerity of religion.
Here he lays down his own canons :—

> " In sober mornings, do not thou rehearse
> The holy incantation of a verse ;
> But when that men have both well drunk and fed,
> Let my enchantments then be sung or read.
> When laurel spirts in the fire, and when the hearth
> Smiles to itself, and gilds the roof with mirth,
> When up the thyrse is raised, and when the sound
> Of sacred orgies flies around, around,
> When the rose reigns, and locks with ointment shine,
> Let rigid Cato read these lines of mine."

At such moments as these Herrick is inspired above
a mortal pitch, and listens to the great lyre of Apollo
with the rapture of a prophet. From a very interesting poem, called " The Apparition of his Mistress
calling him to Elysium," we quote a few lines that
exemplify at the same moment his most ideal condition

of fancy and the habitual oddities of his style. This
is the landscape of the Hesperides, the golden isles of
Herrick's imagination :—

> " Here in green meadows sits eternal May,
>   Purpling the margents, while perpetual day
>   So doubly gilds the air, as that no night
>   Can ever rust the enamel of the light.
>   Here naked younglings, handsome striplings, run
>   Their goals for maidens' kisses, which when done,
>   Then unto dancing forth the learned round
>   Commixt they meet, with endless roses crowned ;
>   And here we'll sit on primrose-banks, and see
>   Love's chorus led by Cupid."

But although he lived in this ideal scenery, he was not
entirely unconscious of what actually lay around him.
He was the earliest English poet to see the picturesqueness of homely country life, and all his little landscapes
are exquisitely delicate. No one has ever known better
than Herrick how to seize, without effort and yet to
absolute perfection, the pretty points of modern pastoral life. Of all these poems of his, none surpasses
"Corinna's going a-Maying," which has something of
Wordsworth's faultless instinct and clear perception.
The picture given here of the slim boys and the girls
in green gowns going out singing into the corridors
of blossoming whitethorn, when the morning sun is
radiant in all its " fresh-quilted colours," is ravishing,
and can only be compared for its peculiar charm with
that other where the maidens are seen at sunset, with
silvery naked feet and dishevelled hair crowned with
honeysuckle, bearing cowslips home in wicker-baskets.

Whoever will cast his eye over the pages of the
Hesperides, will meet with myriads of original and
charming passages of this kind :—

> " Like to a solemn sober stream
>   Bankt all with lilies, and the cream
>   Of sweetest cowslips filling them,"

the "cream of cowslips" being the rich yellow anthers
of the water-lilies.   Or this, comparing a bride's breath
to the faint, sweet odour of the earth :—

> " A savour like unto a blessed field,
>   When the bedabbled morn
>   Washes the golden ears of corn."

Or this, a sketched interior :—

> " Yet can thy humble roof maintain a choir
>   Of singing crickets by the fire,
> And the brisk mouse may feed herself with crumbs,
>   Till that the green-eyed kitling comes."

Nor did the homeliest details of the household escape
him.   At Dean Prior his clerical establishment consisted of Prudence Baldwin, his ancient maid, of a
cock and hen, a goose, a tame lamb, a cat, a spaniel,
and a pet pig, learned enough to drink out of a tankard;
and not only did the genial vicar divide his loving
attention between the various members of this happy
family, but he was wont, a little wantonly, one fears,
to gad about to wakes and wassailings and to increase
his popular reputation by showing off his marvellous
learning in old rites and ceremonies.   These he has
described with loving minuteness, and not these only,

but even the little arts of cookery do not escape him. Of all his household poems, not one is more character- istic and complete than the "Bride-cake," which we remember having had recited to us years ago with immense gusto, at the making of a great pound-cake, by a friend since widely known as a charming follower of Herrick's poetic craft :—

> "This day, my Julia, thou must make
> For Mistress Bride the wedding-cake :
> Knead but the dough, and it will be
> To paste of almonds turned by thee,
> Or kiss it, thou, but once or twice,
> And for the bride-cake there'll be spice."

There is one very curious omission in all his de- scriptions of nature, in that his landscapes are without background ; he is photographically minute in giving us the features of the brook at our feet, the farmyard and its inmates, the open fireplace and the chimney corner, but there is no trace of anything beyond, and the beautiful distances of Devonshire, the rocky tors, the rugged line of Dartmoor, the glens in the hills—of all these there is not a trace. In this he contrasts curiously with his contemporary William Browne, another Devonshire poet, whose pictures are infinitely vaguer and poorer than Herrick's, but who has more distance, and who succeeds in giving a real notion of Devonian rock and moor, which Herrick never so much as suggests. In short, it may be said that Herrick made for himself an Arcadian world, in the centre of which the ordinary daily life of a country parish went contentedly on, surrounded by an imagi-

nary land of pastoral peace and plenty, such as England
can hardly have been then in the eyes of any other
mortal, unless in those of the French poet St. Amant,
who came over to the court at Whitehall just before
the Rebellion broke out, while Herrick was piping at
Dean Prior, and who on his return wrote a wonderfully fulsome ode to their serenest majesties Charles
and Mary, in which he took precisely the same view of
our island as Herrick did :—

> " Oui, c'est ce pays bienheureux
> Qu'avec des regards amoureux
> Le reste du monde contemple ;
> C'est cette île fameuse où tant d'aventuriers
> Et tant de beautés sans exemple
> Joignirent autrefois les myrtes aux lauriers ! "

St. Amant lived to alter his opinion, and hurl curses
at the unconscious Albion ; but to Herrick the change
came too late, and when the sunshine ceased to warm
him, he simply ceased to sing, as we shall see.

The personal epithalamium is a form of verse which
had a very brief period of existence in England, and
which has long been completely extinct.   Its theme
and manner gave too much opportunity to lavish adulation on the one hand, and unseemly innuendo on
the other, to suit the preciser manners of our more
reticent age ; but it flourished for the brief period
contained between 1600 and 1650, and produced
some exquisite masterpieces.   The *Epithalamion* and
Prothalamion of Spenser struck the keynote of a
fashion that Drayton, Ben Jonson, and others adorned,
and of which Herrick was the last and far from the

least ardent votary. His confidential muse was delighted at being asked in to arrange the ceremonies of a nuptial feast, and described the bride and her surroundings with a world of pretty extravagance. Every admirer of Herrick should read the " Nuptial Ode on Sir Clipseby Crew and his Lady." It is admirably fanciful, and put together with consummate skill. It opens with a choral outburst of greeting to the bride :—

> " What's that we see from far ? the spring of day
> Bloom'd from the east, or fair enjewelled May
> Blown out of April ? or some new
> Star filled with glory to our view
> Reaching at Heaven,
> To add a nobler planet to the seven ? "

Less and less dazzled, he declares her to be some goddess floating out of Elysium in a cloud of tiffany. She leaves the church treading upon scarlet and amber, and spicing the chafed air with fumes of Paradise. Then they watch her coming towards them down the shining street, whose very pavement breathes out spikenard. But who is this that meets her ? Hymen, with his fair white feet, and head with marjoram crowned, who lifts his torch, and, behold, by his side the bridegroom stands, flushed and ardent. Then the maids shower them with shamrock and roses, and so the dreamy verses totter under their load of perfumed words, till they close with a benediction over the new-married couple, and a peal of maiden laughter over love and its flower-like mysteries.

Once more, before we turn to more general matters,

there is one section of the *Hesperides* that demands
a moment's attention—that, namely, devoted to descriptions of Fairyland and its inhabitants.   We have
seen that it was probably the performance of Ben
Jonson's pretty masque of *Oberon* that set Herrick
dreaming about that misty land where elves sit eating butterflies' horns round little mushroom tables,
or quaff draughts

> " Of pure seed-pearl of morning dew,
>   Brought and besweetened in a blue
>   And pregnant violet."

And with him the poetic literature of Fairyland ended.
He was its last laureate, for the Puritans thought its
rites, though so shadowy, superstitious, and frowned
upon their celebration, while the whole temper of the
Restoration, gross and dandified at the same time, was
foreign to such pure play of the imagination.   But some
of the greatest names of the great period had entered
its sacred bounds and sung its praises.   Shakespeare
had done it eternal honour in *A Midsummer-Night's
Dream*, and Drayton had written an elaborate romance,
The Court of Faerie.   Jonson's friend Bishop Corbet
had composed fairy ballads that had much of Herrick's
lightness about them.   It was these literary traditions
that Herrick carried with him into the west; it does
not seem that he collected any fresh information about
the mushroom world in Devonshire ; we read nothing
of river-wraiths or pixies in his poems.   He adds,
however, a great deal of ingenious fancy to the stores
he received from his elders ; and his fairy-poems, all

written in octosyllabic verse, as though forming parts
of one projected work, may be read with great interest
as a kind of final compendium of all that the poets of
the seventeenth century imagined about fairies.

Appended to the *Hesperides*, but bearing date one
year earlier, is a little book of poems, similar to these
in outward form, but dealing with sacred subjects.
Here our pagan priest is seen, despoiled of his vine-
wreath and his thyrsus, doing penance in a white
sheet and with a candle in his hand. That rubicund
visage, with its sly eye and prodigious jowl, looks
ludicrously out of place in the penitential surplice;
but he is evidently sincere, though not very deep,
in his repentance, and sings hymns of faultless ortho-
doxy, with a loud and lusty voice to the old pagan
airs. Yet they are not inspiriting reading, save where
they are least Christian; there is none of the religious passion of Crashaw, burning the weak heart
away in a flame of adoration, none of the sweet and
sober devotion of Herbert—nothing, indeed, from an
ecclesiastical point of view, so good as the best of
Vaughan, the Silurist. Where the *Noble Numbers*
are most readable is where they are most secular.
One sees the same spirit here as throughout the
worldly poems. In a charming little "Ode to Jesus"
he wishes the Saviour to be crowned with roses and
daffodils, and laid in a neat white osier cradle; in
"The Present," he will take a rose to Christ and,
sticking it in His stomacher, beg for one mellifluous
kiss." The epigrams of the earlier volume are re-
placed in the *Noble Numbers* by a series of couplets,

attempting to define the nature of God, of which none
equals in neatness this, which is the last :—

> " Of all the good things whatsoe'er we do,
>   God is the 'Αρχὴ and the Τέλος too."

As might be expected, his religion is as grossly an-
thropomorphic as it is possible to be. He almost surpasses in indiscretion those mediæval priests of Picardy
who brought such waxen images to the Madonna's
shrine as no altar had seen since pagan days; and
certain verses on the circumcision are more revolting
in their grossness than any of those erotic poems—

> " unbaptized rhymes
> Writ in my wild unhallowed times "—

for which he so ostentatiously demands absolution.

It is pleasant to turn from these to the three or
four pieces that are in every way worthy of his
genius. Of these, the tenderest is the " Thanks-
giving," where he is delightfully confidential about his
food, thus :—

> " Lord, I confess, too, when I dine
>   The pulse is Thine,
>   And all those other bits that be
>   Placed there by Thee,—
>   The worts, the purslain, and the mess
>   Of water-cress.
> .   .   .   .   .
> 'Tis Thou that crown'st my glittering hearth
>   With guiltless mirth,
>   And giv'st me wassail-bowls to drink,
>   Spiced to the brink."

And about his house :—

> " Like as my parlour, so my hall
> And kitchen's small,
> A little buttery, and therein
> A little bin."

The wild and spirited " Litany " is too well known
to be quoted here, but there are two very fine odes in
the *Noble Numbers* that are hardly so familiar. One
is the " Dirge of Jephthah's Daughter," written in a
wonderfully musical and pathetic measure, and full of
fine passages, of which this is a fair sample :—

> " May no wolf howl, or screech-owl stir
> A wing about thy sepulchre !
> No boisterous winds or storms come hither
> To starve or wither
> Thy soft sweet earth, but, like a spring,
> Love keep it ever flourishing."

But beyond question the cleverest and at the
same time the most odd poem in the *Noble Numbers*
is " The Widows' Tears; or, Dirge of Dorcas," a
lyrical chorus supposed to be wailed out by the
widows over the death-bed of Tabitha. The bereaved
ladies disgrace themselves, unfortunately, by the greedi-
ness of their regrets, dwelling on the loss to them of
the bread—" ay ! and the flesh and the fish "—that
Dorcas was wont to give them; but the poem has
stanzas of marvellous grace and delicacy, and the
metre in which it is written is peculiarly sweet. But
truly Herrick's forte did not lie in hymn-writing, nor
was he able to refrain from egregious errors of taste,
whenever he attempted to reduce his laughing features

to a proper clerical gravity.   Of all his solecisms, how-
ever, none is so monstrous as one almost incredible poem
"To God," in which he gravely encourages the Divine
Being to read his secular poems, assuring Him that—

> "Thou, my God, may'st on this impure look,
> Yet take no tincture from my sinful book."

For unconscious impiety this rivals the famous
passage in which Robert Montgomery exhorted God
to "pause and think."

We have now rapidly considered the two volumes
on which Herrick claims his place among the best
English lyrical poets.   Had he written twenty instead
of two, he could not have impressed his strong poetic
individuality more powerfully on our literature than
he has done in the *Hesperides*.   It is a storehouse of
lovely things, full of tiny beauties of varied kind and
workmanship; like a box full of all sorts of jewels—
ropes of seed-pearl, opals set in old-fashioned shifting
settings, antique gilt trifles sadly tarnished by time;
here a ruby, here an amethyst, and there a stray
diamond, priceless and luminous, flashing light from all
its facets, and dulling the faded jewellery with which it
is so promiscuously huddled.   What gives a special
value to the book is the originality and versatility of
the versification.   There is nothing too fantastic for
the author to attempt, at least; there is one poem
written in rhyming triplet, each line having only *two*
syllables.   There are clear little trills of sudden song,
like the lines to the "Lark;" there are chance
melodies that seem like mere wantonings of the air

upon a wind-harp ; there are such harmonious endings
as this, " To Music " :—

> " Fall on me like a silent dew,
>   Or like those maiden showers
> Which by the peep of day do strew
> A baptism o'er the flowers.
>   Melt, melt my pains
>   With thy soft strains,
> That, having ease me given,
>   With full delight
>   I leave this light
>   And take my flight
>   For heaven."

With such poems as these, and with the delicious
songs of so many of Herrick's predecessors and compeers before them, it is inexplicable upon what possible grounds the critics of the eighteenth century
can have founded their astonishing dogma that the
first master of English versification was Edmund
Waller, whose poems, appearing some fifteen years
after the *Hesperides*, are chiefly remarkable for their
stiff and pedantic movement, and the brazen clang, as
of stage armour, of the dreary heroic couplets in which
they strut. Where Waller is not stilted, he owes his
excellence to the very source from which the earlier
lyrists took theirs—a study of nature and a free but
not licentious use of pure English. But not one of his
songs, except " Go, Lovely Rose," is worth the slightest
of those delicate warbles that Herrick piped out when
the sun shone on him and the flowers were fresh.

It is an interesting speculation to consider from what
antique sources Herrick, athirst for the pure springs of

pagan beauty, drank the deep draughts of his inspiration. Ben Jonson it was, beyond doubt, who first introduced him to the classics, but his mode of accepting the ideas he found there was wholly his own. In the first place, one must contradict a statement that all the editors of Herrick have repeated, sheep-like, from one another, namely, that Catullus was his great example and model. In all the editions of the *Hesperides* we find the same old blunder: "There is no collection of poetry in our language which more nearly resembles the *Carmina* of Catullus." In reality, it would be difficult to name a lyric poet with whom he has less in common than with the Veronese, whose eagle-flights into the very noonday depths of passion, swifter than Shelley's, as flaming as Sappho's, have no sort of fellowship with the pipings of our gentle and luxurious babbler by the flowery brooks. In one of his poems, "To Live Merrily," where he addresses the various classical poets, and where, by the way, he tries to work himself into a great exaltation about Catullus, he does not even mention the one from whom he really took most of form and colour. No one carefully reading the *Hesperides* can fail to be struck with the extraordinary similarity they bear to the *Epigrams* of Martial; and the parallel will be found to run throughout the writings of the two poets, for good and for bad, the difference being that Herrick is much the more religious pagan of the two, and that he is as much a rural as Martial an urban poet. But in the incessant references to himself and his book, the fondness for gums and spices, the delight in the picturesqueness of private life, the art of making a complete and gemlike poem in the fewest possible lines, the curious mixture of sensitiveness and utter want of sensibility, the trick of writing confidential little poems to all sorts of friends, the tastelessness that mixes up obscene couplets with delicate odes " De Hortis Martialis " or " To Anthea "—in all these and many more qualities one can hardly tell where to look for a literary parallel more complete. As far as I know, Herrick mentions Martial but once, and then very slightly. He was fond of talking about the old poets in his verse, but never with any critical cleverness. The best thing he says about any of them is said of Ovid in a pretty couplet. In a dream he sees Ovid lying at the feet of Corinna, who presses

> " With ivory wrists his laureat head, and sleeps
> His eyes in dew of kisses while he sleeps."

How much further Herrick's learning proceeded it is difficult to tell. Doubtless he knew some Greek; he mentions Homer and translates from the spurious Anacreon. The English poets of that age, learned as many of them were, do not seem to have gone much further than Rome for their inspiration. Chapman is, of course, a great exception. But none of them, as all the great French poets of the Renaissance did, went directly to the Anthology, Theocritus and Anacreon. Perhaps Herrick had read the Planudian Anthology; the little piece called " Leander's Obsequies " seems as though it must be a translation of the epigram of Antipater of Thessalonica.

It is curious to reflect that at the very time that the

Hesperides was printed, Salmasius, soon to be hunted to death by the implacable hatred of Milton, was carrying about with him in his restless wanderings the manuscript of his great discovery, the inestimable Anthology of Constantine Cephalas. One imagines with what sympathetic brotherliness the Vicar of Dean Prior would have gossiped and glowed over the new storehouse of Greek song. That the French poets of the century before were known to Herrick is to me extremely doubtful. One feels how much there was in such a book as *La Bergerie* of Remy Belleau, in which our poet would have felt the most unfeigned delight, but I find no distinct traces of their style in his; and unless the Parisian editions of the classics influenced him, I cannot think that he brought any honey, poisonous or other, from France. His inspiration was Latin; that of Ronsard and Jodelle essentially Greek. It was the publication of the Anthology in 1531, and of Henri Estienne's *Anacreon* in 1554, that really set the Pleiad in movement, and founded *l'école gallo-grecque*. It was rather the translation of Ovid, Lucan, Seneca, and Virgil that gave English Elizabethan poetry the start-word.

To return to Herrick, there is not much more to say. He had sung all the songs he had to sing in 1648, being then fifty-seven years of age. He came up to London when the Puritans ejected him from his living, and seems to have been sprightly enough at first over the pleasant change to London life. Soon, however, bad times came. So many friends were gone; Jonson was dead, and Fletcher; Selden was very old and in disgrace. It was poor work solacing himself with Sir John Denham, and patronising that precocious lad Charles Cotton; and by-and-by the Puritans cut off his fifths, and poor old Herrick is vaguely visible to us in poor lodgings somewhere in Westminster, supported by the charity of relations. In August 1662, some one or other graciously recollected him, and he was sent back in his seventy-second year to that once detested vicarage in "rocky Devonshire," which must now have seemed a kind asylum for his old age.

The latest verses of his which seem to have been preserved are these, carved on the tomb of two of his parishioners in the south aisle of Dean Prior Church—

> " No trust to metals nor to marbles, when
> These have their fate and wear away as men ;
> Times, titles, trophies may be lost and spent,
> But virtue rears the eternal monument.
> What more than these can tombs or tombstones pay ?
> But here's the sunset of a tedious day :
> These two asleep are : I'll but be undress'd
> And so to bed : pray wish us all good rest."

There is something extremely pathetic in the complete obscurity of the poet's last days. In those troublesome times his poetry, after a slight success, passed completely out of all men's minds. The idiotic Winstanley, in his *Lives of the Most Famous English Poets*, written shortly after Herrick's death, says that "but for the interruption of trivial passages, he might have made up none of the worst poetic landscapes." This is the last word spoken, as I think, on Herrick, till Mr. Nichols revived his fame in 1796. All we know of his latest years is summed up in one short extract from the church register of Dean Prior: "Robert Herrick, vicker, was buried ye 15th day of October 1674." By that time a whole new world was formed in poetry. Milton was dead; Wycherley and Dryden were the fashionable poets; Addison and Swift were lately born; next year the *Pilgrim's Progress* was to appear; all things were preparing for that bewigged and bepowdered eighteenth century, with its mob of gentlemen who wrote with ease, its Augustan self-sufficiency, and its horror of nature; and what wonder that no one cared whether Herrick were alive or dead?

1875.

RICHARD CRASHAW

NO sketch of the English literature of the middle
of the seventeenth century can pretend to be
complete if it does not tell us something of that
serried throng of poets militant who gave in their
allegiance to Laud, and became ornaments and then
martyrs of the High Church party. Their piety was
much more articulate and objective than that which
had inspired the hymn-writers and various divine
songsters of an earlier age; an element of political
conviction, of anger and apprehension, gave ardour
and tension to their song. They were conservative
and passive, but not oblivious to the tendencies of the
time, and the gathering flood of Puritanism forced
them, to use an image that they would not themselves
have disdained, to climb on to the very altar-step of
ritualism, or even in extreme instances to take wing
for the mystic heights of Rome itself.

It is from such extreme instances as the latter that
we learn to gauge their emotion and their desperation,
and it is therefore Crashaw rather than Herbert whom
we select for the consideration of a typical specimen
of the High Church poets. Nor is it only the hysterical
intensity of Crashaw's convictions which marks him
out for our present purpose; his position in history,

his manhood spent in the last years of the reign of "Thorough," and in the very forefront of the crisis, give him a greater claim upon us than Herbert, who died before Laud succeeded to the Primacy, or Vaughan, who was still a boy when Strafford was executed. There are many other points of view from which Crashaw is of special interest; his works present the only important contribution to English literature made by a pronounced Catholic, embodying Catholic doctrine, during the whole of the seventeenth century, while as a poet, although extremely unequal, he rises, at his best, to a mounting fervour which is quite electrical, and hardly rivalled in its kind before or since. Nor is the story of his life, brief and vague though its outline may be, unworthy of having inspired, as it has evidently done, that noble romance of *John Inglesant* which all the world has been reading with so much curiosity and delight.

It has remained for Dr. Grosart to discover that Crashaw, who has hitherto been supposed to have been born in 1616, must really have seen the light in 1612. His father, the Rev. William Crashaw, Vicar of Whitechapel and preacher at the Temple, was a notable Puritan divine. Forty years of age when his son was born, William Crashaw had grown up within the vehement and instant fear of Papal aggression, and had but become fiercer in his love for a simple Protestantism under the irritating pressure of James the First's decisions. His numerous tracts and sermons are almost entirely devoted to an exposure of what he conceived to be the fatal errors of Rome, and their titles and contents have often been referred to in order to emphasise the difference between their study Protestantism and his son's adoring Mysticism. The suggestive title-page of the *Bespotted Jesuit*, however, is now proved to have been added by a zealous hand after his death; it is quite plain, at the same time, that he would not have shrunk from saying "bespotted," or something far worse, if it had occurred to him so to distinguish a Jesuit, a monk, or a friar. This vigorous personage was the intimate friend of Usher, who is said to have baptized Richard Crashaw, and to have buried a second Mrs. Crashaw, stepmother to the poet, who died at the age of twenty-four in 1620. It is pleasant to read the great divine's praise of "her singular motherly affection to the child of her predecessor." We learn also that she was a gentlewoman of considerable beauty and accomplishment, a good singer and dancer, and that she gave up the vanities of the world to marry a clergyman who may have been grim and who was certainly elderly. But of Crashaw's own mother we hear not a word, and even her Christian name is missing.

The boy was admitted to the Charterhouse. In October 1626 his father died, leaving him an orphan at fourteen. His childhood is an absolute blank, until we find him elected, at the rather advanced age of nineteen, to be a scholar of Pembroke Hall, Cambridge, on July 6, 1631. He became a matriculated pensioner of Pembroke on March 26, 1632, a Bachelor of Arts in 1634, was transferred to Peterhouse on November 26, 1636, was elected a Fellow of that college in 1637, and became a Master of Arts in 1638, on the same day with his younger friend and enthusiastic admirer, Joseph Beaumont, afterwards Master of Peterhouse. He was finally ejected, in company with a large number of other Royalist gentlemen, by the Earl of Manchester, on June 11, 1644. These barren statements give us but little power of realising the poet's life at Cambridge during thirteen years of residence, but it is possible to supplement them with certain facts and illustrations which enable us to see the progress of this delicate spirit through a rough and perilous age.

The Master of Pembroke, Dr. Benjamin Lany, was an old friend of Crashaw's father, and there can be little doubt that the boy was sent to that college to be under his personal protection. Lany, as far as we can collect an impression of his views, was a stout Protestant, whose opinions had at one time coincided with those of the author of the *Bespotted Jesuit*, but who now was leaning more and more in a Laudian direction, and to whom neither ritual nor a flowery poetical diction was distasteful. We really know Dr. Lany almost entirely through a copy of English verses addressed by him to the elder Crashaw, and through another copy of Latin verses addressed to him by the younger Crashaw. In the latter he is spoken of as one around whom young poets throng with their tributes of verse, as "the dear guardian of the Pierian flock," and as one whose habit it is to encourage and guide the children of the Muses. It is, therefore, not unlikely that the transition between the grim Puritanism of his father's household and the fervid

Anglicanism of Cambridge was made easy to the youth by the personal character and guidance of Dr. Benjamin Lany.

It would be interesting to know whether or not Crashaw had begun to compose poetry before going up to the University. It is at all events certain that he was busy versifying almost immediately on his arrival. He was stimulated into the production, or I am afraid we must say the manufacture, of an extraordinary number of exercises, in English and Latin, by the death of William Herries, a promising undergraduate of his own college, who seems to have died rather suddenly in October 1631, when Crashaw had been at Cambridge only three months. Four of these elegies on a single person pleased their author sufficiently to be retained by him for a prominent position in his *Delights of the Muses* fifteen years afterwards, and others exist and have been printed. Genuine grief does not bewail itself with this fluency, or upon so many stops, and indeed all these pieces seem to be dictated rather by an official than a personal regret. It is interesting, however, to find in them that at the age of twenty Crashaw already possessed the germ of that fine metrical skill and coloured fancy which afterwards distinguished him. The extreme vehemence of praise, the laudation of this youth for wit, learning, piety, and physical beauty, was not calculated to startle any one in the seventeenth century, and was probably accepted by the entire college, from Dr. Lany downwards, as being the proper and becoming, and indeed the only possible tone for a young poet to adopt on a

L

melancholy occasion of the kind.   The alternations of
life and death are dwelt upon in flowing numbers :—

> " For the laurel in his verse,
>   The sullen cypress o'er his hearse ;
> For a silver-crownèd head,
>   A dirty pillow in death's bed ;
> For so dear, so deep a trust,
>   Sad requital, so much dust ! "

These verses belong to the school of Ben Jonson,
but with a difference ; there is an indefinable touch
of brightness and colour about them, which may have
suggested to Crashaw's college friends the advent of
a new poet.   Moreover, these elegies on Herries are
valuable to us as belonging certainly to the year 1631,
when neither Donne, Herbert, nor Habington, although
well known in private circles, had been brought before
the world as poets.   It is very important to observe
that Crashaw had already formed the foundation of
his lyrical style at a time when it is exceedingly
improbable that he can have read a line of Donne's
manuscripts.   Certain tendencies were in the air, and
poets in various provinces sounded the same note
simultaneously and with unconscious unanimity.

Crashaw's first public appearance was made in a
little Latin anthology prepared in 1632 to congratulate
Charles I. on the preservation of his health.   Re-
peatedly, through his college career, he was called
upon to contribute to those learned garlands of respectful song which were all remembered against the
University when that " nest of serpents " fell into the
hands of the Puritans.   In 1634 Crashaw published

a little volume of his Latin verses, entitled *Epigrammatum Sacrorum Liber*, following a fashion which was already antiquated, and of which John Owen's famous collection had been a typical example. One of these epigrams contains the celebrated conceit on the miracle of the water turned into wine, *Lympha pudica Deum vidit et erubuit*, which has been very felicitously translated—

"The conscious water saw its God and blushed."

It would be very interesting, but it is unfortunately impossible, to trace the gradual transformation which the religious nature of Crashaw underwent. He found a very fervid piety maintained by certain young men at Cambridge, and he adopted their doctrines while surpassing them in zeal. He had already, we cannot doubt, passed far from the narrow rigour of his father's faith when he came under the influence of the saintly Nicholas Ferrar, whose famous community at Little Gidding gave a final stamp to his character. It is to be lamented that when John Ferrar wrote his deeply interesting life of his brother, it did not occur to him to give us fuller particulars of Crashaw; we must, however, be grateful for what he has given. The family of Ferrars and Colletts retired to their lonely manor-house of Little Gidding, in Huntingdonshire, in 1625. Nicholas, already thirty-four years of age, and weary of a career of action, had determined to abandon the world and to adopt a life of pious retirement. The "Protestant Nunnery," a name given to it in malice by the Puritans, was an establishment conducted on purely unaffected principles, and took its peculiar colouring slowly and unconsciously, as these grave persons, all of one mind, and unopposed in their country solitude, found more and more opportunity of following the natural bent of their inclinations. Until the beauty of their books and the report of their singular devotion had attracted the personal notice of the King, the colony at Little Gidding seems to have been but little distracted by visitors or perturbed by injudicious praise or blame. But the King passed on to Cambridge inflamed with the holy loyalty of these gentle people, and his subjects in the University woke up to the importance of the ritual and the monastic seclusion practised at Little Gidding. Those who were like-minded contended for the honour of following Nicholas Ferrar from the oratory to the church, and from the church to the hospital, in that round of devotion and benefaction which made life busy in the Protestant Nunnery.

But it was when Mrs. Ferrar died, in 1635, that the saintly life at Gidding reached its final ecstasy and fervour. The old lady had watched over the physical welfare of the community, and had preserved sufficient authority over her son Nicholas to prevent him from entirely neglecting what the body craves in sleep and food. But her death released him from all such obligation, and after the day of her funeral he never slept in a bed again, but for the rest of his life wrapped himself in a bearskin and lay upon the floor, when nature overwhelmed him, and obliged him to take brief snatches of sleep between his long prayers

and vigils. He became more exalted, more unearthly,
and of course more attractive than ever to those young
ascetics who, like Crashaw, tried to imitate him in the
churches and chapels of Cambridge, and who took
every opportunity of riding over to Little Gidding to
refresh their faith and passion by intercourse with the
saintly household. We know that Crashaw was one
of these, that he was in constant communion with
Nicholas Ferrar until the death of the latter in the
winter of 1637, and that, when he could not join in
the midnight functions at Little Gidding, he would
emulate the vigils of his teacher by nightly watches
in the Church of Little St. Mary's, which was close to
his new College of Peterhouse.

If the Civil War had never broken out, it is probable that Crashaw would never have left the Anglican
communion.   Nicholas Ferrar, who had sympathies
for the ritual and even for the dogmas of Rome, such
as had been unheard of a generation earlier, stayed his
foot very firmly outside the Papal precincts. He died
deliberately satisfied with the English forms of faith.
He had never taken priest's orders, and, what is still
more strange, it seems that Crashaw never did; but
the latter took the warmest interest in ecclesiastical
affairs, and was one of those who clamoured most
importunately for the restoration of the college chapel
of Peterhouse, which was performed during his fellowship.   And when no longer he was forced at midnight
to cross the college bounds and enter the neighbouring
chancel of Little St. Mary's, there can be no doubt
that he spent more hours than ever in prayer under

the shadow of the great gold angels of Peterhouse
Chapel, and among the hundred saints and cherubs,
with "God the Father in a chair, holding a glass in
His hand," which formed part of the ancient ornament
of this splendid building.

There, in a trance of orison, with the rich notes of
the organ pouring upon him and the light from the
antique windows surrounding him, the Puritan Commission found him unaware.   On December 21, 1643,
Mr. Horscot and his soldiers sacked the chapel of
Peterhouse, pulling down the images and breaking the
windows.   This was but a local realisation of the
universal fact that the reign of Laudian ceremonial
was over.   Laud himself was executed a year later,
and the very foundations of Episcopacy in England
were shaken.   Cambridge formed a helpless island in
a sea of Puritan counties, and in the summer of 1644
the Earl of Manchester, on his way to the siege of
York, lingered in the eastern University long enough
to hold out the alternative of the Covenant or of ejection
to every Master and Fellow.   On June 11 five Fellows
of Peterhouse, Crashaw and Beaumont being two of
them, were forcibly driven out, and five Puritans
appointed in their place.

The Fellows were scattered in all directions.   Beaumont, even then engaged upon his High Church epic
of *Psyche*, lamented, in a passage which Dr. Grosart
was the first to point out, that his friend was not by
his side to revise it.   It seems probable that Crashaw
proceeded at once to Oxford, where the King was still
for a few months undisturbed.   It is at least natural

that he should have done so, since in 1641 he had been incorporated a member of the sister University, and had been that year in residence at Oxford. It may even be conjectured that the events which followed the execution of Strafford so terrified the timid scholar that he removed to the western and more loyal University, and was ejected from Peterhouse during his absence. However this may be, his position must have become desperate soon after 1644, and he may even have been concealed at Newnham Paddox by his friends, the Earl and Countess of Denbigh, until the defeat at Naseby finally overwhelmed the Royalist party in ruin. It was at this time that the poet seemed to have entered the Catholic Church. His religious nature possessed what Milton calls "a fugitive and cloistered virtue;" to him it must have seemed that the English ritual was destroyed, its bishops scattered, its creed disused, and its authority ridiculed; and from the face of anarchy this shrinking soul fled to the staunch and conservative arms of Rome. He had long been meditating the possibility of this step, although very probably it was forced upon him at last harshly and suddenly. Cowley, who was always a sincere Anglican, refers to his friend's conversion to Rome with a charming tact and delicacy :—

> " Pardon, my mother Church, if I consent
> That angels led him when from thee he went ;
> For even in error sure no danger is
> When joined with so much piety as his.
> Ah ! mighty God, with shame I speak't, and grief ;
> Ah ! that our greatest faults were in belief ! "

Regarding the sanctity and single-heartedness of the unfortunate Crashaw there is but one testimony. The only dissentient voice is that of the harsh and ribald Prynne, whose accusation is a eulogy. And now, having attempted to conduct the sacred poet to the great crises of his life, let us leave him there for a while, and consider those poems which his first editor tells us were written beneath the wings of God, when Crashaw lodged under "Tertullian's roof of angels at Peterhouse, where he made his nest more gladly than David's swallow near the house of God, and, like a primitive saint, offered more prayers in the night than others usually offer in the day."

Crashaw's English poems were first published in 1646, soon after his arrival in Paris. He was at that time in his thirty-fourth year, and the volume contains his best and most mature as well as his crudest pieces. It is, indeed, a collection of juvenile and manly verses thrown together with scarcely a hint of arrangement, the uncriticised labour of fifteen years. The title is *Steps to the Temple, Sacred Poems, with other delights of the Muses*. The sacred poems are so styled by his anonymous editor because they are "steps for happy souls to climb heaven by;" the *Delights of the Muses* are entirely secular, and the two divisions of the book, therefore, reverse the order of Herrick's similarly edited *Hesperides* and *Noble Numbers*. The *Steps to the Temple* are distinguished at once from the collection with which it is most natural to compare them, the *Temple* of Herbert, to which their title refers with a characteristic touch of modesty, by the fact that they are not poems of experience, but of ecstasy—not of meditation, but of devotion. Herbert, and with him most of the sacred poets of the age, are autobiographical; they analyse their emotions, they take themselves to task, they record their struggles, their defeats, their consolation.

But if the azure cherubim of introspection are the dominant muses of English sacred verse, the flame-coloured seraph of worship reigns in that of Crashaw. He has made himself familiar with all the amorous phraseology of the Catholic metaphysicians; he has read the passionate canticles of St. John of the Cross, the books of the Carmelite nun, St. Teresa, and all the other rosy and fiery contributions to ecclesiastical literature laid by Spain at the feet of the Pope during the closing decades of the sixteenth century. The virginal courage and ardour of St. Teresa inspire Crashaw with his loveliest and most faultless verses. We need not share nor even sympathise with the sentiment of such lines as these to acknowledge that they belong to the highest order of lyric writing :—

> " Thou art Love's victim, and must die
> A death more mystical and high ;
> Into Love's arms thou shalt let fall
> A still-surviving funeral.
> His is the dart must make thy death,
> Whose stroke will taste thy hallowed breath—
> A dart thrice dipped in that rich flame
> Which writes thy spouse's radiant name
> Upon the roof of heaven, where aye
> It shines and with a sovereign ray
> Beats bright upon the burning faces
> Of souls which in that name's sweet graces

Find everlasting smiles.   So rare,
So spiritual, pure, and fair,
Must be the immortal instrument
Upon whose choice point shall be spent
A life so loved ; and that there be
Fit executioners for thee,
The fairest first-born sons of fire,
Blest seraphim, shall leave their choir,
And turn Love's soldiers, upon thee
To exercise their archery."

Nor in the poem from which these lines are quoted does this melodious rapture flag during nearly two hundred verses.   But such a sustained flight is rare, as in the similar poem of "The Flaming Heart," also addressed to St. Teresa, where, after a long prelude of frigid and tuneless conceits, it is only at the very close that the poet suddenly strikes upon this golden chord of ecstasy :—

"Let all thy scattered shafts of light, that play
Among the leaves of thy large books of day,
Combined against this breast at once break in,
And take away from me myself and sin ;
This gracious robbery shall thy bounty be,
And my best fortunes such fair spoils of me.
O thou undaunted daughter of desires !
    By all thy dower of lights and fires,
    By all the eagle in thee, all the dove,
    By all thy lives and deaths of love.
    By thy large draughts of intellectual day,
And by thy thirsts of love more large than they,
By all thy brim-filled bowls of fierce desire,
By thy last morning's draught of liquid fire,
By the full kingdom of that final kiss
That seized thy parting soul and sealed thee His ;

> By all the heaven thou hast in Him,
> Fair sister of the seraphim !
> By all of thine we have in thee—
> Leave nothing of myself in me ;
> Let me so read thy life that I
> Unto all life of mine may die."

If Crashaw had left us nothing more than these two fragments, we should be able to distinguish him by them among English poets. He is the solitary representative of the poetry of Catholic psychology which England possessed until our own days ; and Germany has one no less unique in Friedrich Spe. I do not know that any critic has compared Spe and Crashaw, but they throw lights upon the genius of one another which may seasonably detain us for a while. The great Catholic poet of Germany during the seventeenth century was born in 1591. Like Crashaw, he was set in motion by the Spanish Mystics ; like him, he stood on the verge of a great poetical revolution without being in the least affected by it. To Waller and to Opitz, with their new dry systems of precise prosody, Crashaw and Spe owed nothing; they were purely romantic and emotional in style. Spe was born a Catholic, spent all his life among the Jesuits, and died, worn out with good works and immortalised by an heroic struggle against the system of persecution for witchcraft, in the hospital of Trèves in 1635, just when Crashaw was becoming enthralled by the delicious mysteries of Little Gidding. Both of them wrote Jesuit eclogues. In Spe the shepherd winds his five best roses into a garland for the infant

Jesus; in Crashaw he entertains the "starry stranger"
with conceits about his diamond eyes and the red
leaves of his lips.   In each poet there is an hysterical
delight in blood and in the details of martyrdom, in
each a shrill and frantic falsetto that jars on the
modern ear, in each a sweetness of diction and purity
of fancy that redeem a hundred faults.[1]   The poems
of Spe, entitled *Trutz-Nachtigal*, were first printed in
1649, the year that Crashaw died.

The chief distinction between Spe and Crashaw is,
in the first place, that Crashaw is by far the greater
and more varied of the two as regards poetical gifts,
and, secondly, that while Spe was inspired by the
national *Volkslied*, and introduced its effects into his
song, Crashaw was an adept in every refinement of
metrical structure which had been invented by the
poet-artists of England, Spain, and Italy.   The progress of our poetical literature in the seventeenth
century will never be thoroughly explained until some
competent scholar shall examine the influence of

---

[1] As an illustration of almost all these qualities, and as a specimen
of Spe's metrical gifts, I give one stanza from the *Trutz-Nachtigal*:—

> " Aus der Seiten
> Lan sich leiten
>   Rote Strahlen wie Korall ;
> Aus der Seiten
> Lan sich leiten
>   Weisse Wässer wie Krystal !
> O du reines,
> Hübsch und feines
>   Bächlein von Korall und Glas,
> Nit noch weiche,
> Nit entschleiche,
>   O Rubin und Perlengass !"

Spanish poetry upon our own. This influence seems
to be particularly strong in the case of Donne, and in
the next generation in that of Crashaw. I am not
sufficiently familiar with Spanish poetry to give an
opinion on this subject which is of much value;
but as I write I have open before me the works of
Gongora, and I find in the general disposition of
his *Octavas Sacras* and in the style of his *Canciones*
resemblances to the staves introduced to us by
Crashaw which can scarcely be accidental.

Mr. Shorthouse reminds me that Ferrar was much
in Spain; we know that Crashaw "was excellent in
Italian and Spanish," and we are thus led on to
consider the more obvious debt which he owed to the
contemporary poetry of Italy. One of the largest
pieces of work which he undertook was the translation
of the first canto of the *Strage degli Innocenti*, or
"Massacre of the Innocents," a famous poem by the
Neapolitan Cavaliere Marini, who had died in 1625.
Crashaw has thrown a great deal of dignity and fancy
into this version, which, however, outdoes the original
in ingenious illustration, as the true Marinists, such
as Achillini, outdid Marini in their conceited sonnets.
Crashaw, in fact, is a genuine Marinist, the happiest
specimen which we possess in English, for he preserves a high level of fantastic foppery, and seldom,
at his worst, sinks to those crude animal imagings—
illustrations from food, for instance—which occasionally make such writers as Habington and Carew not
merely ridiculous but repulsive.

In criticising with severity the piece on Mary

Magdalene which stands in the forefront of Crashaw's poems, and bears the title of "The Weeper," I have the misfortune to find myself at variance with most of his admirers. I cannot, however, avoid the conviction that the obtrusion of this eccentric piece on the threshold of his shrine has driven away from it many a would-be worshipper. If language be ever liable to abuse in the hands of a clever poet, it is surely outraged here. Every extravagant and inappropriate image is dragged to do serviee to this small idea— namely, that the Magdalen is for ever weeping. Her eyes, therefore, are sister springs, parents of rills, thawing crystal, hills of snow, heavens of ever-falling stars, eternal breakfasts for brisk cherubs, sweating boughs of balsam, nests of milky doves, a voluntary mint of silver, and Heaven knows how many more incongruous objects, from one to another of which the labouring fancy flits in despair and bewilderment. In this poem all is resigned to ingenuity; we are not moved or softened, we are merely startled, and the irritated reader is at last appeased for the fatigues he has endured by a frank guffaw, when he sees the poet, at his wits' end for a simile, plunge into the abyss of absurdity, and style the eyes of the Magdalen

> "Two walking baths, two weeping motions,
> Portable and compendious oceans."

These are the worst lines in Crashaw. They are perhaps the worst in all English poetry, but they must not be omitted here, since they indicate to us the

principal danger to which not he only but most of his
compeers were liable. It was from the tendency to
call a pair of eyes "portable and compendious oceans"
that Waller and Dryden, after both of them stumbling
on the same stone in their youth, finally delivered us.
It is useless to linger with indulgence over the stanzas
of a poem like "The Weeper," simply because many
of the images are in themselves pretty. The system
upon which these juvenile pieces of Crashaw are
written is in itself indefensible, and is founded upon
what Mr. Matthew Arnold calls an "incurable defect
of style."

Crashaw, however, possesses style, or he would not
deserve the eminent place he holds among our poets.
The ode in praise of Teresa, written while the author
was still among the Protestants, and therefore probably about 1642, has already been cited here. It is
an exquisite composition, full of real vision, music of
the most delicate order, and imagery which, although
very profuse and ornate, is always subordinated to
the moral meaning and to the progress of the poem.
The "Shepherd's Hymn," too, is truly ingenious and
graceful, with its pretty pastoral tenderness. "On
Mr. G. Herbert's Book sent to a Gentleman" evidently
belongs to the St. Teresa period, and contains the
same charm. The lyrical epistle persuading the
Countess of Denbigh to join the Roman communion
contains extraordinary felicities, and seems throbbing
with tenderness and passion. We have already drawn
attention to the splendid close of "The Flaming Heart."
There is perhaps no other of the sacred poems in the

volume of 1646 which can be commended in its entirety.   Hardly one but contains felicities ; the dullest is brightened by such flashes of genius as—

> " Lo, how the thirsty lands
> Gasp for the golden showers with long-stretch'd hands ! '

But the poems are hard, dull, and laborious, the exercises of a saint indeed, but untouched by inspiration, human or divine.   We have to return to the incomparable " Hymn to St. Teresa " to remind ourselves of what heights this poet was capable.

There can be very little doubt that Crashaw regarded the second section of his book, the secular *Delights of the Muses*, as far inferior in value and importance to the *Steps to the Temple*.   That is not, however, a view in which the modern reader can coincide, and it is rather the ingenuity of his human poems than the passion of his divine which has given him a prominent place among poets.   The *Delights* open with the celebrated piece called the " Muse's Duel," paraphrased from the Latin of Strada.   As one frequently sees a reference to the " Latin poet Strada," it may be worth while to remark that Famianus Strada was not a poet at all, but a lecturer in the Jesuit colleges.   He belonged to Crashaw's own age, having been born in 1572, and dying in the year of the English poet's death, 1649.   The piece on the rivalry of the musician and the nightingale was published first at Rome in 1617, in a volume of *Prolusiones* on rhetoric and poetry, and occurs in the sixth lecture of the second course on poetic style.   The Jesuit rhetorician has been trying to familiarise his pupils with the style of the great classic poets by reciting to them passages in imitation of Ovid, Lucretius, Lucan, and the rest, and at last he comes to Claudian. This, he says, is an imitation of the style of Claudian, and so he gives us the lines which have become so famous. That a single fragment in a school-book should suddenly take root and blossom in European literature, when all else that its voluminous author wrote and said was promptly forgotten, is very curious, but not un-precedented.

In England the first person who adopted or adapted Strada's exercise was John Ford, in his play of *The Lover's Melancholy*, in 1629. Dr. Grosart found another early version among the Lansdowne MSS., and Ambrose Phillips a century later essayed it. There are numerous references to it in other litera-tures than ours, and in the present age M. François Coppée has introduced it with charming effect into his pretty comedy of *Le Luthier de Crémone*. Thus the schoolmaster's task, set as a guide to the manner of Claudian, has achieved, by an odd irony of for-tune, a far more general and lasting success than any of the actual verses of that elegant writer. With regard to the comparative merits of Ford's version, which is in blank verse, and of Crashaw's, which is in rhyme, a confident opinion has generally been expressed in favour of the particular poet under consideration at the moment; nor is Lamb him-self superior to this amiable partiality. He denies that Crashaw's version " can at all compare for

M

harmony and grace with this blank verse of Ford's."
But my own view coincides much rather with that of
Mr. Swinburne, who says that "between the two
beautiful versions of Strada's pretty fable by Ford
and Crashaw, there will always be a diversity of judgment among readers; some must naturally prefer the
tender fluency and limpid sweetness of Ford, others
the dazzling intricacy and affluence in refinements, the
supple and cunning implication, the choiceness and
subtlety of Crashaw." Mr. Shorthouse, on the other
hand, suggests to me that "Crashaw's poem is surely
so much more full and elaborate, that it must be
acknowledged to be the more important effort." There
can be no doubt that it presents us with the most
brilliant and unique attempt which has been made in
our language to express the very quality and variety
of musical notation in words. It may be added that
the only reference made by Crashaw in any part of
his writings to any of the dramatists his contemporaries
is found in a couplet addressed to Ford :—

> "Thou cheat'st us, Ford, mak'st one seem two by art ;
> What is *love's sacrifice* but *the broken heart?*"

After "Music's Duel," the best-known poem of
Crashaw's is his "Wishes to his Supposed Mistress,"
a piece in forty-two stanzas, which Mr. Palgrave
reduced to twenty-one in his *Golden Treasury*. He
neglected to mention the "sweet theft," and accordingly most readers know the poem only as he reduced and rearranged it. The act was bold, perhaps,
but I think that it was judicious. As Crashaw left

it, the poem extends beyond the limits of a lyric, tediously repeats its sentiments, and gains neither in force nor charm by its extreme length. In Mr. Palgrave's selection it challenges comparison with the loveliest and most original pieces of the century. It never, I think, rises to the thrilling tenderness which Donne is capable of on similar occasions. Crashaw never pants out a line and a half which leave us faint and throbbing, as if the heart of humanity itself had been revealed to us for a moment; with all his flying colour and lambent flame, Crashaw is not Donne. But the " Wishes " is more than a charming, it is a fascinating poem, the pure dream of the visionary poet, who liked to reflect that he too might marry if he would, and choose a godly bride. He calls upon her—

> " Whoe'er she be
> That not impossible She
> That shall command my heart and me ;
>
> Where'er she lie
> Locked up from mortal eye
> In shady leaves of destiny "—

to receive the embassy of his wishes, bound to instruct her in that higher beauty of the spirit which his soul demands—

> " Something more than
> Taffata or tissue can,
> Or rampant feather, or rich fan."

But what he requires is not spiritual adornment alone;

he will have her courteous and accomplished in the
world's ways also, the possessor of

> " Sydneian showers
>   Of sweet discourse, whose powers
>   Can crown old Winter's head with flowers ; "

and finally,

> " Life, that dares send
>   A challenge to his end,
>   And when it comes say, ' Welcome, friend.'
>
>   I wish her store
>   Of worth may leave her poor
>   Of wishes ; and I wish—no more."

The same refined and tender spirit animates the
" Epitaph upon Husband and Wife, who died and
were buried together."   The lovely rambling verses
of "To the Morning, in satisfaction for Sleep," are
perhaps more in the early manner of Keats than any
other English lines.   In some of those sacred poems
which we have lately been considering, he reminds us
no less vividly of Shelley, and there are not a few
passages of Crashaw which it would require a very
quick ear to distinguish from Mr. Swinburne.   We
may safely conjecture that the latter poet's " Song in
Season " was written in deliberate rivalry of that song
of Crashaw's which runs—

> " O deliver
>   Love his quiver ;
> From thine eyes he shoots his arrows,
>   Where Apollo
>   Cannot follow,
> Feathered with his mother's sparrows."

But perhaps the sweetest and most modern of all Crashaw's secular lyrics is that entitled *Love's Horoscope*. The phraseology of the black art was never used with so sweet and picturesque an ingenuity, and the piece contains some of the most delicately musical cadences to be found in the poetry of the age :—

> "Thou know'st a face in whose each look
> Beauty lays ope Love's fortune-book,
> On whose fair revolutions wait
> The obsequious motions of Love's fate.
> Ah ! my heart ! her eyes and she
> Have taught thee new astrology.
> Howe'er Love's native hours were set,
> Whatever starry synod met,
> 'Tis in the mercy of her eye
> If poor Love shall live or die."

It is probable from internal and from external evidence also that all these secular poems belong to Crashaw's early years at Cambridge. The pretty lines "On Two Green Apricocks sent to Cowley by Sir Crashaw" evidently date from 1633; the various elegies and poems of compliment can be traced to years ranging from 1631 to 1634. It is doubtful whether the "Wishes" themselves are at all later than this. Even regarding him as a finished poet ten years before the publication of his book, however, he comes late in the list of seventeenth century lyrists, and has no claims to be considered as an innovator. He owed all the basis of his style, as has been already hinted, to Donne and to Ben Jonson. His originality was one of treatment and technique; he forged a more rapid and brilliant short line than any of his predecessors had done, and for brief intervals and along sudden paths of his own he carried English prosody to a higher refinement, a more glittering felicity, than it had ever achieved.   Thus, in spite of his conceits and his romantic colouring, he points the way for Pope, who did not disdain to borrow from him freely.

It is unfortunate that Crashaw is so unequal as to be positively delusive; he baffles analysis by his uncertain hold upon style, and in spite of his charm and his genius is perhaps most interesting to us because of the faults he shares with purely modern poets.   It would scarcely be unjust to say that Crashaw was the first real poet who allowed himself to use a splendid phrase when a simple one would have better expressed his meaning; and in an age when all but the best poetry was apt to be obscure, crabbed, and rugged, he introduces a new fault, that of being visionary and diffuse, with a deliberate intention not only, as the others did, to deck Nature out in false ornament, but to represent her actual condition as being something more " starry " and " seraphical " than it really is.   His style has hectic beauties that delight us, but evade us also, and colours that fade as promptly as the scarlet and the amber in a sunset sky.   We can describe him best in negatives; he is not so warm and real as Herrick, nor so drily intellectual as the other hymnists, nor coldly and respectably virile like Cowley.   To use an odd simile of Shelley's, he sells us gin when the other poets offer us legs of mutton, or at all events baskets of bread and vegetables.

Crashaw now disappeared from the circle of his

friends. Joseph Beaumont, preparing his epic for the press in his retirement at Hadleigh, knew not where to turn for advice, and sighed to think how

> " Fair had my *Psyche* been had she at first
> By thy judicious hand been dressed and nursed."

But to us the movements of this spiritual luminary are somewhat more obvious.

After the birth of the future Duchess of Orleans in 1644, Queen Henrietta Maria fled to Paris, and held a kind of court there for the benefit of her husband's cause. The poet Cowley was her secretary, and seems to have introduced Crashaw to her. Tradition says that the younger poet found the elder in great poverty in Paris, and that his good offices with the Queen enabled him to secure for Crashaw one of the last fragments of preferment yet clinging about exiled majesty. To a fellow-Catholic Henrietta Maria could still offer an introduction to Roman society, and it is said that she gave the poet a letter to Cardinal J. B. Pallotta, then the Governor of Rome, a post to which he had been raised, in the flower of his age, by Pope Urban VIII. Pallotta was a man of force and ambition, feared as much as honoured for the extreme severity of his morals. His influence over Innocent X. was so considerable and so salutary that he was himself talked of as a possible successor to the tiara. This man, as Canon Bargrave recounts in his *Pope and College of Cardinals* in 1660, offered Crashaw the post of private secretary to himself, which the poet seems to have held for about two years.

In the vivid pages of the close of *John Inglesant*
the reader will find a very correct and stirring picture
of the condition of the Holy City some six years after
Crashaw's departure from it. He will easily realise,
from that description, that although Rome had purged
itself from its most crying scandals of a hundred years
before, its society was far from being calculated to
soothe or delight the soul of a chaste mystic, who had
seen no ruder side of life than was to be found in the
quiet hall of Peterhouse or the saintly society of Little
Gidding. His soul burned within him because of the
wickedness of the servants of the Cardinal, and at
last, like Joseph, he felt constrained to bring their
evil report to his father in God. We hear from Bargrave, who was in Rome at the time, in common with
several of the exiled Fellows of Peterhouse, that Pallotta
took the hint and chastised his followers, whereupon
they in revenge threatened to take Crashaw's life.
The Cardinal, who came from Ancona, bethought him
of the neighbouring sanctuary of Loreto, of which he
was himself the patron, and on April 24, 1649, he
procured for the poet a small benefice in the famous
Basilica Church of Our Lady.

We can imagine with what feelings of rapture and
content the world-worn poet crossed the Apennines
and descended to the dry little town above the shores
of the Adriatic, in which he doubtless pictured to
himself a haunt of peace and prayer till his life's
end. As he ascended the last hill, and saw before
him the magnificent basilica which Bramante had built
as a shelter for the Holy House, he would feel that

his feet were indeed upon the threshold of his rest.
With what joy, with what a beating heart, he would
long to see that very Santa Casa, the cottage built
of brick, which angels lifted from Nazareth out of
the black hands of the Saracen, and gently dropped
among the nightingales in the forest of Loreto on
that mystic night of the year 1294! There, like a
child's bare body wrapped in the velvets and naperies
of a princely cradle, the humble Casa lay in the marble
enclosure which Sansovino had made for it, and there
through the barbaric brickwork window in the Holy
Chimney he could see, in a trance of wonder, the
gilded head of Madonna's cedarn image that St. Luke
the Evangelist had carved with his own hands. Here
indeed a delicious life seemed planned for Crashaw—
to minister all day in the rich incense; to touch the
very raiment of Our Lady, stiff with pearls and rubies
to the feet; to trim the golden lamps, the offerings
of the kings of the whole Catholic world; to pass
in and out between the golden cherubim and brazen
seraphim; to cleanse the mosaics of lapis-lazuli, and
to polish the silver bas-reliefs till they shouted the
story of the magic flight from Nazareth. There, in
the very house of Jesus, to hear the noise and mutter
of the officiating priest, the bustle of canons, chaplains,
monks, and deacons, the shrill sweet voices of the
acolytes singing all day long—this must have seemed
the very end of life and beginning of heaven to the
mystical and sensuous Crashaw.

It appears, however, that his joys were brief. In
August 1649, four months after his appointment, his

benefice had passed into other hands, and we learn from Bargrave that he died a few weeks after he arrived at Loreto, not without suspicion of having been poisoned by those whom he had denounced to Cardinal Pallotta.   He seems to have been in his thirty-seventh year.   Cowley composed a lovely elegy for his funeral, promising him an immortality which he has in some sort achieved.   He was a good man and a gentleman, an extreme instance of a remarkable type, and the only one of all the English divine poets of the century whose temperament drove him actually within the precincts of Rome.

1882.

Too often it is with regret, or with a grudged esteem, that we hail newly-discovered works by standard authors.   The best writing generally takes care of itself, and is remembered and preserved, whatever may be lost.   The first sprightly running is commonly the best, and editors scarcely earn our thanks by troubling the lees for us.   For once we have an exception before us.   The pamphlet of newly-discovered poems by Crashaw which Dr. Grosart forwarded to his subscribers in 1888 contains some things which, even in the congested condition of our national literature, are never likely to be obscured again.   The British Museum bought from a bookseller, who had picked it up as an odd lot at Sotheby's or Puttick & Simpson's, a MS. volume of Crashaw's poems, indubitably, as would appear, in his own, previously untraced, handwriting. Dr. Grosart gives us an example of the latter in fac-simile, selecting the page which contains the well-known epigram on " The Water being made Wine."

We turn at once to the poems which are entirely new. Here is one apparently intended to form the dedication to a gift-volume of the poet's *Steps to the Temple* :—

> " At the ivory tribunal of your hand,
> Fair one, these tender leaves do trembling stand,
> Knowing 'tis in the doom of your sweet eye
> Whether the Muse they clothe shall live or die ·
> Live she or die to Fame, each leaf you meet
> Is her life's wing, or else her winding-sheet."

We could swear this was Crashaw if we picked it up anonymous on Pitcairn's Island. Moreover, something very like the second couplet is to be found already in *Love's Horoscope* :—

> " 'Tis in the mercy of her eye
> If poor Love shall live or die."

It is very pretty. But this, a nameless lyric, is more than pretty; it is exquisite, and in Crashaw's most transcendental manner :—

> " Though now 'tis neither May nor June,
> And nightingales are out of tune,
> Yet in these leaves, fair One, there lies
> (Sworn servant to your sweetest eyes)
> A nightingale, who, may she spread
> In your white bosom her chaste bed,
> Spite of all the maiden snow
> Those pure untrodden paths can show,

> You straight shall see her wake and rise,
> Taking fresh life from your fair eyes,
> And with claspt wings proclaim a spring,
> Where Love and she shall sit and sing ;
> For lodged so near your sweetest throat
> What nightingale can lose her note?
> Nor let her kindred birds complain
> Because she breaks the year's old reign ;
> For let them know she's none of those
> Hedge-quiristers whose music owes
> Only such strains as serve to keep
> Sad shades, and sing dull night asleep.
> No, she's a priestess of that grove,
> The holy chapel of chaste love,
> Your virgin bosom.   Then whate'er
> Poor laws divide the public year,
> Whose revolutions wait upon
> The wild turns of the wanton sun,
> Be you the Lady of Love's year,
> Where your eyes shine his suns appear,
> There all the year is Love's long Spring,
> > There all the year
> Love's nightingales shall sit and sing."

The break in the penultimate verse is a charming
addition to the melody, and I am very much mistaken
if this lyric does not take its place among the best of
Charles I.'s reign.

The remainder of the new poems are religious, and
they are not in Crashaw's very finest manner.   " To
Pontius, Washing his Blood-stained Hands," is a typical
example of the monstrous chains of conceits which these
most unequal poets were at any moment liable to produce.   The face of Pilate was originally a nymph—

> " The daughter of a fair and well-famed fountain
> As ever silver-tipped the side of shady mountain,"—

(in itself a charming image); this nymph has suffered the fate of Philomela from this new Tereus, the hand of Pilate, and "appears nothing but tears." A paraphrase of Grotius gives us a first version of the well-known verse on the Eucharist :—

> " The water blushed and started into wine."

We trace the great Crashaw of the fiery surprises but seldom in this long, tame, and somewhat crabbed poem; but he asserts himself in a few such phrases as this :—

> " Before the infant shrine
> Of my weak feet, the Persian Magi lay,
> And left their mithra for my star ; "

and this, which well describes the condition of Crashaw's muse :—

> " A sweet inebriated ecstasy."

The new readings of old poems which the MS. gives are neither, it would seem, very numerous nor very important. "The Weeper" is such a distressing, indeed such a humiliating poem, that we receive a new stanza of it with indifference ; we may note one novelty,—this string of preposterous conceits on the tears of the Magdalen must in future close with a conceit that swallows up all the rest :—

> " Of such fair floods as this
> Heaven the crystal ocean is."

Dr. Grosart takes this opportunity of recording an interesting little discovery. Crashaw's important Latin poem "Bulla" is found to have made its first appearance in a very rare Cambridge volume, the *Crepundia Siliana* of Heynsius, in 1646, two years after the poet's ejection from his Fellowship. It appeared the same year in the *Delights of the Muses*, with a considerable number of variations of the text. It is a pity that Crashaw did not write "Bulla" in English, for it is full of the characteristics of his style.

ABRAHAM COWLEY

THE period of English poetry which lies between the decline of Ben Jonson and the rise of Dryden was ruled with undisputed sway by a man whose works are now as little read as those of any fifth-rate Elizabethan dramatist. During the whole lifetime of Milton, the fame of that glorious poet was obscured and dwarfed by the exaggerated reputation of this writer; and so general and so unshaken was the belief in the lyrist of the day, that a Royalist gentleman of Cambridge or an exiled courtier at Paris in the year 1650 would have laughed in your face had you suggested that time could ever wither the deathless laurels of Mr. Cowley, or untune the harmonies of his majestic numbers. Yet in a very short space this work of destruction was most thoroughly done. The generation of Dryden admired his genius passionately, but not without criticism. The generation of Pope praised him coldly, but without reading him, and within fifty years of his own decease this nonpareil of the Restoration fell into total disfavour and oblivion. With the revival of naturalistic poetry, the lyrists and dramatists of the reign of Charles I. came once more into favour. Crashaw, Quarles, Lovelace, martyrs, pietists, and rakes, all the true children of the Muses, whatever their mode or matter, were restored and reprinted.

Not these only, but some very small and unattractive talents have lately been presented anew to the public; but Cowley, the one representative genius of the age, as his contemporaries supposed, still lacked an editor who would collect his scattered works and give him the chance of a new lease of life, until in 1881 the Rev. A. B. Grosart issued his privately printed edition in two 4to volumes, one of the best of his many valuable publications. Cowley's prose essays, it must be acknowledged, have held their ground in our literature, but as a poet he is a dead name, or living only in depreciation and ridicule. We hope to show that, however great his faults, this depreciation is unjust and this ridicule absurd, and in doing so it will be necessary to solve two questions—why Cowley ever attained so immense a poetic reputation, and why, having once gained it, he has so completely lost it.

A wealthy citizen of London, stationer or grocer, dying in the summer of 1618, left, besides ample provision for his widow, a sum of £1000 to be divided among his six children and one other not yet born. In the autumn of the year this latter heir appeared, and was christened Abraham Cowley. We, looking back upon the history of the time, see that it was a period of rapid poetic decadence into which this baby was born. Shakespeare was dead; Jonson and the philosophic poets, to whom the newly awakened brain was to be so intimately indebted, were already past

middle life. The years directly after the birth of
Cowley were to be darkened by the deaths of many
poets, but none were to be born, except Marvell,
Vaughan, and, much later, Dryden, for nearly forty
years. Of his immediate compeers, Milton was ten
years of age, Denham three, Suckling nine years, and
Lovelace only a few weeks older than himself.

We know nothing of his early childhood but what
he has himself told us with a charming simplicity—
namely that his mother's parlour was full of works of
devotion, among which he was so fortunate as to find
a copy of the *Faery Queen*. This became his con-
tinual reading, and, without much understanding of
the matter, he became so interpenetrated with the
delicious recurrence of the rhyme and rhythm that he
insensibly was made a poet. Before he was twelve
years old he had read the entire works of Spenser.
So much he himself tells us, but there can be no doubt
to those who study his earliest writings that the magic
of another name was added to the charm that woke
him into verse. At ten years of age, the child composed an epical romance of *Pyramus and Thisbe*, which
is one of the most extraordinary instances of precocity
in the whole annals of literature. Indeed, to find a
parallel to it, we must leave the art of poetry altogether, and note what was done by Mozart in music,
or Lucas van Leyden in engraving. But this was
but the prelude to fresh infantine exertions. The
precocious boy was very early sent to Westminster
School, and his intense interest in versification and
the grace and charm of his manners won him many

N

friends and patrons. To his schoolfellows he might well seem the prodigy that we know they considered him; and the masters of the school, with a gentleness unusual in those austerer times, encouraged his continued production of verses. In 1630, two years after composing *Pyramus and Thisbe*, he attempted a bolder flight in his little epic of *Constantia and Philetus*, being then twelve years of age, and by the year 1633 he had accumulated such a store of poems that his friends determined to hide the treasure no longer from the world.

The first edition of the *Poetical Blossoms, by A. C.,* is a charming little quarto of thirty-two leaves. It is now one of the chief prizes of book-hunters, and a great bibliographical rarity. It ought to possess, what is often lost, a large portrait of the author at the age of thirteen, as the frontispiece. Referring to this volume in after-life, Cowley spoke of it as published at the age of thirteen, in all probability recollecting and being misled by this portrait; and his error has been repeated ever since. As a matter of fact, however, he was in his fifteenth year. It opens with a pompous little invocation to the Muse Melpomene, and is then introduced to the public, after the fashion of the day, by commendatory verses signed by two schoolfellows. One of these, Robert Meade, became a man of some note, and, twenty years after this, a candidate himself for poetic honours in his comedy of *The Combat between Friendship and Love*. Cowley's contributions are five in number—" Constantia and Philetus," " Pyramus and Thisbe," " Elegy on the

Death of Dudley, Lord Carlton," " Elegy on Mr. Richard Clark," and " A Dream of Elysium."

Let any reader of *Pyramus and Thisbe* consider how naïve, artless, and infantine are the writings of the very cleverest child of ten that he has ever known when compared with this first work of Cowley's. After more than two hundred years it remains still readable —much more readable, in fact, than many of its author's more elaborate poems of maturity. The story of that " palpable-gross play " that well beguiled Theseus and Hippolyta to laughter, is here told in all tragic seriousness, but not without several signs, such as " the sucking of odoriferous breath," that show Cowley to have been familiar with the drama so unsuccessfully produced at Athens with Bottom for the hero. The boy-poet has been ambitious enough to invent a new stanza, and a rather good one too, as will be acknowledged from this example. Thisbe finds Pyramus dead, and after tearing her golden hair—

" She blames all-powerful Jove, and strives to take
　　His bleeding body from the moistened ground ;
　She kisses his pale face till she doth make
　It red with kissing, and then seeks to wake
　　His parting soul with mournful words, his wound
　　Washes with tears that her sweet voice confound."

Pyramus and Thisbe is a work which few of the adult poets of that day would have been ashamed of writing. It contains mistakes of rhyme and grammar that might be so easily corrected that they form an interesting proof that the poem was not touched up for the press by older hands ; but in other respects it

is smooth and singularly mature. The heroic verse
in which it is written is nerveless, but correct, and
the story is told in a straightforward way, and with a
regular progress, that are extraordinary in so young
a child.   It was dedicated to the head-master of Westminster, Lambert Osbalston.

The amazing promise of *Pyramus and Thisbe* is
hardly justified by the cleverness of the poem written
two years later, *Constantia and Philetus*.   There is
here hardly any sign at all of immaturity, but a far
worse fault than childishness has stepped in.   Instead
of being like the puerile poem of a little boy, it is like
the correct and tedious work of some man that never
can be famous.   In point of grammar and rhyme there
is a great advance apparent, and we see the justice of
the pretty phrase Cowley afterwards used in speaking
of these juvenile pieces, "that even so far backward
there remain yet some traces of me in the little foot-
steps of a child;" for the language has already begun
to take the same ingenious turns and involutions that
characterise *The Mistress* and the *Odes*.   It is, indeed,
singular that, at the age of twelve, the child should be
so much the father of the man as to produce this most
Cowleyan stanza, illustrative of the author's high-flown
rhetoric, as much as those I have just referred to are
of his ingenuity :—

> "Oh ! mighty Cupid ! whose unbounded sway
>   Hath often ruled the Olympian Thunderer,
> Whom all celestial deities obey,
>   Whom men and gods both reverence and fear !
> Oh, force Constantia's heart to yield to Love,
> *Of all thy works the Masterpiece 'twill prove.*"

Constantia and Philetus is an extremely tragical tale, not so briefly or so simply told as *Pyramus and Thisbe*, and is padded out by "songs" and "letters" to the extent of nearly seven hundred lines, an extraordinary feat, of course, for so young a child. Of the other pieces in the volume, the "Elegy on Dudley, Lord Carlton," an imitation of Ben Jonson, must date from the year of that statesman's death, 1631; "A Dream of Elysium" is almost a very charming reverie on the poets of old and the dreams of neo-pagan romance: we say "almost," for something of the essence of poetry is wanting.

While Cowley was posing as the child-genius at Westminster, a youth ten years his senior was about to retire to a solitude at Horton which was to enrich English poetry with some of its most exquisite and most perfect treasures. It is possible that the fame of Cowley's precocity had reached the ears of Milton when he lamented, in his earliest sonnet, now the seventh, that no bud or blossom adorned his late spring, such as endued "more timely-happy spirits." However this may be, we have no reason to prefer to the slow maturity of such a manhood as his the exhausting precocity of Cowley's marvellous boyhood. His contemporaries, however, thought otherwise, and when the *Poetical Blossoms* appeared in 1633 it enjoyed an immediate popularity. A few months earlier, Milton's first printed English verses, the lines on Shakespeare, had appeared in front of the Second Folio. Whether Ben Jonson, now bed-ridden and almost blind, but still eager in poetic matters, expressed any favour for the verses of Cowley, is not known. But various signs in the writings of the latter tend to show that he was increasingly influenced by the style of Jonson, and anxious to write like one of his poetic "sons." The very year that the public career of Cowley commenced, that of Jonson virtually closed in the publication of *The Tale of a Tub*. But Randolph, that admirable writer and dramatic poet, whose early death cut short a career that promised great things in literature, was continuing the traditions of the school with the utmost brilliance. There can be no doubt that in longing to go to Cambridge, as we know that Cowley did, the desire of associating with Randolph was not the least inducement. His *Love's Riddle* proves that he was familiar with *The Jealous Lovers*, printed in 1632. But we shall presently return to this.

Just as Cowley was leaving Westminster to go to Cambridge, in 1636, a second edition of *Poetical Blossoms* was called for, and appeared in a smaller form, much augmented. Among the additions was an ode containing these fine and thoughtful verses written at the age of thirteen :—

> " This only grant me, that my means may lie
> Too low for envy, for contempt too high ;
>   Some honour I would have,
>   Not from great deeds, but good alone ;
>   Th' unknown are better than ill-known.
>   Rumour can ope the grave :
> Acquaintance I would have, but when 't depends
> Not on the number, but the choice of friends.
>
> Books should, not business, entertain the light,
> And sleep, as undisturbed as death, the night.

> My house a cottage, more
> Than palace, and should fitting be
> For all my use, no luxury.
> My garden painted o'er
> With nature's hand, not art's ; and pleasures yield
> Horace might envy in his Sabine field."

It was for strains of this elevated morality that Cowley won the enthusiastic praise of such later didactic writers as Denham and Roscommon, and in a certain sense originated a school. As an example of another class of gifts, we may read with pleasure the amusing piece called *The Poetical Revenge*, the story of which may be here told in prose. Cowley, having made an appointment with a young companion to meet him in Westminster Hall at a certain hour, waited in vain, till he despaired of his friend, and out of curiosity went into one of the courts. Here he found a vacant seat, and made himself at home, when a fellow in a satin suit came and pushed him out. Whereupon Cowley expostulated so loudly that a barrister, "a neat man in a ruff," rose and said, "Boy, get you gone; this is no school!" To which Master Impudence replied, "Oh no! for if it were, all you gowned men would go up for false Latin!" At this

> "The young man
> Aforesaid, in the satin suit, began
> To strike me ; doubtless there had been a fray
> Had I not providently skipped away,
> Without replying,"

but not without inwardly murmuring this curse:

> "May he
> Be by his father in his study took
> At Shakespeare's Plays, instead of my Lord Coke."

The additional poems are all far better than the first
infantine verses.   There is more eloquence, more
enthusiasm, more power, and some of the odes are
fully worthy, at least in extract, of a place in all collections of English poetry.   They breathe a great pride
in the art of poesy, great desire for and confidence of
fame, and a scholastic turn of mind.

> " 'Tis not a pyramid of marble stone,
>   Though high as our ambition ;
> 'Tis not a tomb cut out in brass, which can
>   Give life to the ashes of a man,
> But verses only."

Throughout Cowley's life, however occupied with
courtly intrigue or with public duty, he never failed
to be true to this boyish declaration of faith.

He was entered a scholar of Trinity College, Cambridge, and proceeded thither with the manuscript of
his pastoral drama of *Love's Riddle*, written about the
age of sixteen, in his pocket.   Though Randolph was
unhappily dead, there were others who would welcome
the boy-genius to the banks of the Cam.   Suckling,
Cleveland, Fanshawe, Beaumont, and Crashaw were
all at Cambridge; and with the last of these, at any
rate, he struck up an immediate friendship.   It is probable also that the needy and forlorn Butler, in some
obscure corner of a college, was picking up such odd
scraps of learning as vary the pages of *Hudibras*.
Cowley, with a different fate, came into port with
flowing sails, and lost no time in winning a position.
In 1637 a third edition of the *Poetical Blossoms* was
published, and in 1638 his pastoral comedy of *Love's*

Riddle. This made what was then considered a very dainty little volume, adorned with a portrait of the young author, pretty but pertly smiling, while a florid angel descends from heaven with a great quill pen in one hand, and in the other a garland of laurel that he lays on the flowing silky locks. A prologue to Sir Kenelm Digby apologises that

> " The style is low, such as you'll easily take
> For what a swain might say or a boy make."

This boyish drama is one of the most readable things that Cowley ever executed, and is in distinct following, without imitation, of Randolph's *Jealous Lovers.* It is written in good blank verse, with considerable sprightliness of dialogue, and with several threads of intrigues that are held well in hand, and drawn skilfully together at last. Callidora, the heroine, flies from her father's court, and Act I. describes her arrival and welcome by some vulgar but amusing shepherds; the next act shows how anguished at her loss every one at her father's court is, but especially her lover Philistes; and the rest of the action, of course, records the vicissitudes that prevent their reunion until the fifth act. I have no space to quote, but may in passing be permitted to refer to the last scene of the second act, as containing a passage of genuine and delightful humour. In *Love's Riddle* there is much, as I have said, to praise; but there is an absence of many qualities that Cowley never possessed, and which are essential to pastoral poetry. There is no genuine passion, no knowledge of the phenomena of nature, no observant love of birds or flowers or the beauties of country life. All the exquisite touches that illuminate *The Faithful Shepherdess* are eminently absent; nor have we in the precocious humour of the world-wise boy any equivalent for the sweet garrulous music of Chalkhill or Browne.

In February of the same year, 1638, was published, but not translated until by Charles Johnson in 1705, a five-act Latin comedy, *Naufragium Joculare*, in prose and verse, the scene laid at Dunkirk, but the style and persons strictly imitative of Plautus. In emulation of the *Miles Gloriosus*, there is a loud boasting soldier named Bombardomachides! Later on in 1638, Cowley completed his twentieth year. At the age when youths of talent are usually beginning to dream of future enterprise, he found himself an admired and popular poet, author of three successful works, and highly esteemed as a rising scholar. With long fair hair falling on his shoulders, and with a fresh, intelligent face, he must without doubt have been an elegant youth in the fashion of the day, even if with none of the superlative beauty of John Milton, "the Lady of Christ's." With all the adulation which he received, his sensible young head does not seem to have been turned. Past all the praises of the present, he looked wistfully forward into the future; and with some inkling, perhaps, that his fine talents could not promise the lasting crown he sought for, he set himself the memorable enigma with which his *Miscellanies* open:—

> "What shall I do to be for ever known
> And make the age to come my own?"

With these same *Miscellanies* and with the preparation
of the volume called *The Mistress* he seems to have
been quietly and happily occupied until the breaking
out of the Civil War. We can at all events affix dates
to the elegies on Sir Henry Wootton (1639) and Sir
Anthony Vandyke (1641), each displaying increased
facility in skilful employment of the heroic couplet.

The visit of Prince Charles to Cambridge in 1641
gave occasion to the production of a more bulky work.
In a great hurry Cowley was called upon to write a
comedy, and *The Guardian*, an ill-digested, unrevised
performance, was acted before His Royal Highness on
March 12. The prologue fiercely satirised the Round-
heads, and sneered at Prynne, who had just published
his ridiculous Jersey poem of *Mont-Orgueil*. The
farcical part of the piece is in prose, but the grand
personages, Lucia and her lover Trueman Junior, talk
in blank verse. The part of a poet, Doggrell, is
amusing, but insisted on too much. One sentence put
into the mouth of a girl, Aurelia, is worth recording :—

"I shall never hear my virginals when I play upon 'em, for
her daughter Tabitha's singing of psalms ; the first pious deed
will be to banish Shakespeare and Ben Jonson out of the
parlour, and to bring in their rooms Marprelate and Prynne's
works."

The Guardian was never included in the works of
Cowley, and underwent some curious vicissitudes. It
was not printed until 1650, when its author was in
exile in Paris, and this, apparently, unauthorised
edition is very rare. When Cowley returned to
England he entirely rewrote the play in the year 1658,

and it was brought out on the stage as *The Cutter of Coleman Street*, but proved a complete failure. Cowley finally tried the effect of his piece in print by publishing it in 1663, but again to receive the disapproval of the critics.

Happy in his work at the University, and in his newly attained fellowship, the young poet was busy on many literary schemes, and mainly on an epic, the *Davideis*, on the sorrows and victories of King David, when the great Civil War broke upon him like a wave. After the indecisive battle of Edgehill, Oxford became for a while the headquarters of the Royalists. Thither Crashaw had already gone, in 1641, and Cowley was now fain to follow. Cambridge was now no longer a bed of roses to a Royalist poet, and Cowley "was soon torn thence by that public violent storm which would suffer nothing to stand where it did, but rooted up every plant, even from the princely cedars to me, the hyssop. Yet I had as good fortune as could have befallen me in such a tempest, for I was cast by it into the favour of one of the best persons, and into the court of one of the best princesses of the world." These were Lord Falkland and Queen Henrietta Maria, to whom the sobriety and excellent fidelity of Cowley pointed him out as a fit staff to lean upon in such perilous times.

Yet it was not in him not to cling to scholarship, and for two years more, or somewhat less, he pursued his studies at Oxford with no less ardour than before at Cambridge. But Newbury shook and Naseby broke the hopes of the Cavaliers. The Queen fled to Paris, and Cowley followed her, leaving the Earl of Manchester and his Puritan divines to purge the University and eject the sixty-five fellows, of whom Crashaw was one. The melancholy mystic repaired, as we have seen in the last chapter, to Paris, where in 1646 Cowley found him in utter destitution, and, with characteristic warmth of heart, insisted on labouring for his relief.

In the meantime Cowley himself was on terms of confidential intimacy with the Queen and the heads of her party. All his time and thought were dedicated to delicate diplomacy, and he was despatched to various parts of Jersey, Scotland, Flanders, and Holland on private state business. But when the King was given up by the Scots into the custody of the Parliamentary Commissioners, in January 1647, Cowley was recalled to Paris to undertake a yet more onerous duty. To no one less trustworthy than himself would Henrietta Maria delegate the preparation of those letters in cipher by means of which she communicated with her husband till his execution in 1649. Cowley was next occupied in corresponding with the leaders of Royalist reaction in Scotland and Ireland. But when the young King Charles took refuge in Holland, and the Anglo-Parisian Court was in some measure broken up, it was suggested that Cowley should return to England, "and, under pretence of privacy and retirement, should take occasion of giving notice of the posture of things in this country." He was immediately caught, however, and imprisoned, apparently in the year 1655; nor did he regain his liberty on a less bail than of £1000.

At Cromwell's death in 1658 he ventured back into France, and remained there until the Restoration.

In the course of eighteen years of enforced inaction, much had occurred to literary men, though little to literature itself. Just before the Civil War broke out, a whole group of eminent dramatists, among whom may be named Jonson, Ford, Massinger, and Field, had passed away. The years of contention saw the deaths of Carew, Suckling, Cartwright, Quarles, and Drummond. In 1649 Cowley's dear friend and brother, Richard Crashaw, had breathed his last at the shrine of Loreto. A new generation had meanwhile been born—Shadwell, Wycherley, Southerne, and Otway. Even in the Civil War, moreover, poetry was read and published. In 1647, the year before the *Hesperides* was brought out, an edition, probably pirated, of Cowley's love-cycle, called *The Mistress*, was issued in England. From the last piece in this collection we learn, or are intended to believe, that Cowley wrote them in three years, during which time he was tormented with a love-passion that he saw at last to be hopeless. It is just possible that, like Waller, he was really devoted to some lady of rank beyond his reach, but the poems themselves breathe no ardour of tenderness, and such a supposition is directly at variance with his own singularly frank exposition of the genesis of the book. "Poets," he says, "are scarce thought freemen of their company, without paying some duties, and obliging themselves to be true to love. Sooner or later they must all pass through their trial, like some Mahometan monks that are bound by their order, once at least in their life, to make a pilgrimage to Mecca."

The Mistress was fated to become one of the most admired books of the age. It was a pocket compendium of the science of being ingenious in affairs of the heart; and its purity and scholastic phrase recommended it to many who were no judges of poetry, but very keen censors of morality. To us it is the most unreadable production of its author, dry and tedious, without tenderness, without melancholy, without music. Here and there we find a good rhetorical line, such as—

> " Love which is soul to body and soul of me ;"

and, what is very curious, almost all the pieces lead off with a sonorous and well-turned phrase. But scarcely one is readable throughout; scarcely one is even ridiculous enough for quotation. All are simply dull, overloaded with ingenious, prosaic fancy, and set to eccentric measures of the author's invention, that but serve to prove his metrical ineptitude.

It is not correct to say that these poems continue and cultivate to excess the over-ornate style of the philosophical poets of the generation before. When Habington loads his pages with tasteless conceits, he over-colours his style in the manner learned from Lyly, Marini, and Gongora. So Donne, in a more brilliant and masculine way, errs in the introduction of unsuitable and monstrous ornament. But Cowley is hardly ornamented at all, and his heresy is not so much that of Marini as that of the inflated, prosaic French poets of the class of Saint Amant. He seizes an idea, perhaps sensible, perhaps preposterous, but in no case beautiful; he clothes this idea with illustration drawn, not from external nature or objects of any kind, but from the supposed phenomena of the human mind.   I think we can trace all this pedantic ingenuity to the personal training and example of Dr. Henry More, who was the great oracle of English Platonism at Cambridge during Cowley's residence there, and whose extraordinary volume of *Philosophical Poems*, published in 1640, may, I think, be constantly found reflected in the lyrics of the younger poet.   And in considering why these poems of Cowley's were popular, we must not forget to note that the prose writings of More and others of his stamp were greatly delighted in by the seventeenth century, although now entirely unread.   The taste for these ingenuities and paradoxical turns of thought came like a disease, and passed away.   So Cowley, who confidently believed that time to come would admit him to have been "Love's last and *greatest* prophet," and who was quoted as having written what ensphered the whole world of love, is now justly denied the humblest place among the erotic poets.   One piece alone must be excepted in this sweeping condemnation.   The poem called "The Wish" is so simple, sincere, and fresh, that we are disposed to wonder at finding so delicious a well in such an arid desert.   Thus it begins:—

> " Well then, I now do plainly see
> This busy world and I shall ne'er agree ;
> The very honey of all earthly joy
> Does of all meats the soonest cloy,

> And they, methinks, deserve my pity,
> Who for it can endure the stings,
> The crowd, and buzz, and murmurings,
>   Of this great hive, the City.
>
> " Ah, yet, ere I descend to the grave,
> May I a small house and large garden have!
> And a few friends and many books, both true,
>   Both wise, and both delightful too!
>   And since Love ne'er will from me flee,
>   A mistress moderately fair,
>   And good as guardian-angels are,
>   Only beloved, and loving me."

The moral purity of Cowley's muse in so licentious a time must not pass without praise, if only to rebut the foolish and fanatic rage of such critics as the Rev. Edmund Elys, who sought, after his death, to persuade the public to the contrary. As a matter of fact, Cowley seldom forgot to write as became a gentleman.

In 1648 a very inferior satire, *The Four Ages of England*, and again a piece of doggerel called *A Satire against Separatists*, were printed, with the name of Abraham Cowley on the title-pages. With these productions he had nothing to do, nor with the printing of *The Guardian* in 1650. The increased demand for his unpublished writings and the fear of piracy determined him, so soon as he was released on bail, to set about revising his genuine writings for the press. The result was the appearance, in 1656, of a very important volume, the *Works of A. Cowley*, in small folio. This contained many things long ago written or imagined, and never before presented to the public.

o

The opening section of the book consisted of the *Miscellanies*, poems the composition of which had extended over many years. Among the most notable pieces are "The Motto," an admirable poem on his artistic aspirations and ambitions; "The Ode of Wit," which contains an odd reference to a *Bajazet* on the stage, which seems just too early to be Racine's, and may probably be Magnon's, which was brought out at Paris in 1648; a horrid "Ode to Dick, my Friend," which is worthy of study as a perfect summary of Cowley's sins of style; a prettily conceived poem called "Friendship in Absence," which is unhappily spoiled by an inherent wooden ingenuity that never ceases to obtrude itself; "The Chronicle," an amusing *jeu d'esprit*, in which he feigns to make for himself such a list of conquered hearts as Leporello quotes on his master's account in *Don Giovanni;* an epistle to Davenant from Jersey, complimenting him on the publication of *Gondibert*, and making fun of Prynne's absurd verses; and finally two really splendid elegies on William Harvey and on Richard Crashaw.

These two latter poems, as perhaps the finest wheat that the winnowing of criticism will finally leave on this wide granary-floor, we must examine more at leisure. William Harvey, who is not by any means to be confounded with the great physiologist, was a young friend and fellow-student of Cowley's, with whom he was on terms of sympathetic and affectionate intimacy. This excellent and gifted lad, like another Arthur Hallam, was taken away suddenly by fever in the midst of his hopes and labours. Cowley celebrated his memory in an elegy of unusual directness and tenderness :—

> " Ye fields of Cambridge, our dear Cambridge, say
>   Have ye not seen us walking every day ?
>   Was there a tree about, which did not know
>   The love betwixt us two ?
>   Henceforth, ye gentle trees, for ever fade,
>   Or your sad branches thicker join
>   And into darksome shades combine,
>   Dark as the grave wherein my friend is laid.

This seems to prophesy of that later lovely dirge of *Thyrsis* and the tree that knew the soul of the Scholar-Gipsy. Cowley was incapable of long sustaining these level flights, and the poem grows didactic and flat as it proceeds, but gathers fire and force in the last stanza :—

> " And if the glorious saints cease not to know
>   Their wretched friends who fight with life below,
>   Thy flame to me doth still the same abide,
>   Only more pure and rarified.
>   There whilst immortal hymns thou dost rehearse,
>   Thou dost with holy pity see
>   Our dull and earthly poesy
>   Where grief and misery can be joined with verse."

But the fine elegiac qualities of these memorial verses on Harvey are quickened into ardour, nay, we may almost say fired into rapture, in the lines on the death of Crashaw. In the first case, the poignant regret of an intimate and private sorrow inspired the poem ; in the second, the public loss of a poet whom Cowley might be well forgiven for fancying absolutely supreme, were combined with personal grief at the loss of a friend.

Friendship and poetry were the two subjects that alone set Cowley's peculiar gifts on flame. Languid or insincere on other subjects, on these two he never failed to be eloquent. In the elegy on Crashaw these combined to stimulate his lyric powers to their utmost, and the result was most brilliant. Crashaw, after suffering so much after his ejection from Cambridge, had been helped, as we have seen, by the noble exertions of Cowley. When the news of his death at Loreto was circulated, hardly a voice in England was raised to his honour save that of Cowley, who never failed in manly and courageous acts of fidelity. "Poet and saint," he begins, braving all criticism in the outset, thou art now in heaven, companion of the angels, who, when they call on thee for songs, can have no greater pleasure than to hear thine old earthly hymns. "Thy spotless muse," says Cowley, "like Mary, did contain the Godhead;" and did disdain to sing of any lower matter than eternity. In this strain he proceeds half through the elegy, and then in a sudden ecstasy of contemplation he cries:—

> " How well, blest Swan, did Fate contrive thy death,
>   And made thee render up thy tuneful breath
>   In thy great mistress' arms ! thou most divine
>   And richest offering of Loreto's shrine !
>   Where like some holy sacrifice to expire,
>   A fever burns thee, and Love lights the fire.
>   Angels, they say, brought the famed chapel there,
>   And bore the sacred load in triumph through the air,—
>   Tis surer much they brought thee there, and they
>   And thou, their charge, went singing all the way."

But he feels it needful to apologise to the Anglican

Church for saying that angels led Crashaw when from
her he went, and thus the elegy finally winds up :—

> ' His faith, perhaps, in some nice tenets might
>   Be wrong ; his life, I'm sure, was in the right,
>   And I myself a Catholic will be,
>   So far, at least, great Saint, to pray to thee.
>   Hail, Bard triumphant ! and some care bestow
>   On us, the poets militant below,
>   Opposed by our old enemy, adverse Chance,
>   Attacked by Envy and by Ignorance,
>   Enchained by Beauty, tortured by Desires,
>   Exposed by tyrant Love to savage beasts and fires.
>   Thou from low earth in nobler flames didst rise,
>   And, like Elijah, mount alive the skies,
>   Elisha-like (but with a wish much less
>   More fit thy greatness and my littleness)
>   Lo, here I beg,—I whom thou once didst prove
>   So humble to esteem, so good to love,—
>   Not that thy spirit might on me doubled be,
>   I ask but half thy mighty spirit for me,
>   And when my Muse soars with so strong a wing
>   'Twill learn of things divine, and first of thee to sing."

The reader will not need to be persuaded that these
are very exquisite and very brilliant lines. Had Cowley
written often in such a nervous strain as this, he had
needed no interpreter or apologist to-day ; nay, more—
Dryden, his occupation gone, would have had to pour
the vigour of his genius into some other channel. The
tenderness of the allusion to Crashaw's sufferings and
persecution, the tact and sweetness of the plea for his
saintship, the sudden passion of invocation, the modest
yet fervent prayer at the close,—all these are felicities
of the first order of rhetorical poetry.

At the close of the *Miscellanies* were printed, in the volume of 1656, twelve translations or imitations of the *Odes of Anacreon* done into octosyllabic verse, or rather into that iambic measure of either seven or eight syllables, but always of four cadences, which Milton used with such admirable effect in his minor poems and *Comus*.   Cowley, whose ear was certainly not sensitive, could ill afford to compete with Milton in melody, and made some sad discords with this delicate instrument.   Stanley, again, in 1651, had introduced this kind of writing to the public with a great deal more spirit.   Still, Cowley's *Anacreontics* are frequently pretty and sparkling, and they have been praised, even in our own time, at the expense of all his other writings.   In this judgment, however, I can by no means coincide.

The second division of the folio is occupied with the *Mistress*, reprinted from the edition of 1647.   This, again, is followed by the *Pindarique Odes*.   In publishing these odes Cowley performed a dangerous innovation; nothing at all like these pompous lyrics in *vers libres* had hitherto been attempted or suggested in English.   In his preface he acknowledged this with a proud humility characteristic of the man.   "I am in great doubt whether they will be understood by most readers, nay, even by very many who are well enough acquainted with the common roads and ordinary tracks of poesy.   The figures are unusual and bold even to temerity, and such as I durst not have to do withal in any other kind of poetry: the numbers are various and irregular, and sometimes, especially some of the long ones, seem harsh and uncouth, if the just measures and cadences be not observed in the pronunciation. So that almost all their sweetness and numerosity, which is to be found, if I mistake not, in the roughest, if rightly repeated, lies in a manner wholly at the mercy of the reader." The readers of the day were very merciful or very uncritical, for it was chiefly on the score of those raucous odes that so many sweet words were said about "the majestick numbers of Mr. Cowley." They became the rage, and founded a whole school of imitators. Bishop Sprat states in his *Life of Cowley* that the poet was set thinking on this style of poetry by finding himself with the works of Pindar in a place where there were no other books. It seems likely that this place was Jersey or some other temporary station of exile, while his headquarters were at Paris.

The writing of irregular inflated verse of a rhetorical character was just coming into fashion in France. Although condemned by Boileau, it was frequently practised by Corneille, and still more characteristically, long after Cowley's death, by Racine in *Esther* and *Athalie*. But to Cowley is due the praise of inventing or introducing a style of ode which was a new thing in modern literature, and which took firm hold of our poetry until, in Collins, it received its apotheosis and its death-blow. But though the chaster form of ode designed by Collins from a Greek model has ever since his day ruled in our poetic art, there has always been a tendency to return to the old standard of Cowley. So lately as our own day, Mr. Lowell's *Commemoration*

Ode is a specimen of the informal poem of unequal lines and broken stanzas supposed to be in the manner of Pindar, but truly the descendant of our Royalist poet's "majestick numbers." * Keats, Shelley, and Swinburne, on the other hand, have restored to the ode its harmony and shapeliness. Congreve attempted a diversion in favour of regularity, but in vain, and until the days of Collins and Gray, the ode modelled upon Cowley was not only the universal medium for congratulatory lyrics and pompous occasional pieces, but it was almost the only variety permitted to the melancholy generations over whom the heroic couplet reigned supreme. Dryden, whose *Song on St. Cecilia's Day* directly imitates Cowley's *Ode on the Resurrection*, used it with grand effect for his rolling organ-music. The forgotten lyrists of the Restoration found it a peculiarly convenient instrument in their bound and inflexible fingers. Pope only once seriously diverged from the inevitable couplet, and then to adopt the ode-form of Cowley. Yet so rapidly had the fame of the latter declined that Pope could ask, in 1737—

> "Who now reads Cowley? if he pleases yet,
>   His moral pleases, not his pointed wit ;
>   Forgot his Epic, nay, Pindaric art,
>   But still I love the language of his heart."

The language of the heart has not much to do with the *Odes* of 1656. They are fifteen in number, and open with two paraphrases of Pindar himself, the second

* See *Appendix*.

Olympic and the first Nemean.   Following these is a
praise of " Pindar's unnavigable Song," in imitation of
Horace.   The remaining twelve are supposed to be
original, but two are taken from the prophetic Scrip-
tures.   One on " Destiny " contains the following lines,
which form a favourable example of Cowley's style of
Pindarising and of the construction of his odes.   In
a series of grotesque and rather unseemly images, he
declares that he was taken from his mother's childbed
by the lyric Muse, and that she addressed him thus, as
he lay naked in her hands :—

> " ' Thou of my church shalt be ;
>   Hate and renounce,' said she,
>   ' Wealth, honour, pleasures, all the world for me.
>   Thou neither great at court, nor in the war,
>   Nor at the Exchange shalt be, nor at the wrangling bar.
>   Content thyself with the small barren praise
>   That neglected verse doth raise.'
>   She spake, and all my years to come
>   Took their unlucky doom.
>   Their several ways of life let others choose,
>   Their several pleasures let them use,
>   But I was born for love, and for a Muse.
>
>   " With fate what boots it to contend ?
>   Such I began, such am, and so must end.
>   The star that did my being frame
>   Was but a lambent flame,
>   And some small light it did dispense,
>   But neither heat nor influence.
>   No matter, Cowley, let proud Fortune see
>   That thou canst her despise no less than she does thee.
>   Let all her gifts the portion be
>   Of folly, lust, and flattery,
>   Fraud, extortion, calumny,

> Murder, infidelity,
>   Rebellion, and hypocrisy.
>   Do not thou grieve or blush to be
>   As all the inspirèd tuneful men,
> And all thy great forefathers were from Homer down to Ben."

With such a sonorous hyber-alexandrine he loves to wind his odes up in a stormy close. Else, in spite of much well and even nobly said, and in spite of occasional lines and couplets such as—

> " Whether some brave young man's untimely fate
>   In words worth dying for he celebrate,"

or,

> " Where never fish did fly
> And with short silver wings cut the low liquid sky,"

which linger in the memory, the grandiose language and the broken versification unite to weary the ear and defy the memory. Nor can the *Odes* ever again take a living place in literature. But to the student they are very interesting as the forerunners of a whole current of loud-mouthed lyric invocation not yet silent after more than two centuries.

The folio of 1656 closed with the sacred epic of the *Davideis*, on the sorrows and achievements of David. We have already seen that this poem was conceived, and in great part written, while Cowley was at Cambridge. It is in four books, and composed in the heroic couplet, varied with occasional alexandrines, another innovation introduced by Cowley and accepted by Dryden, but excluded from the rules of verse by Pope. The first book of the *Davideis* opens with an invocation, couched in language very similar to that employed in the Elegy on Crashaw, and bearing internal evidence of being of a later date than the rest of the piece. These lines may be quoted as exceptionally tuneful and earnest :—

> " Lo, with pure hands thy heavenly fires to take,
> My well-changed Muse I a chaste vestal make !
> From earth's vain joys, and love's soft witchcraft free,
> I consecrate my Magdalene to thee !
> Lo, this great work, a temple to thy praise,
> On polished pillars of strong verse I raise ! "

The action commences in hell, where the devil calls for a spirit who will tempt Saul. Envy replies, and her figure is described in lines of great power and realistic horror, which were evidently studied by Milton before he wrote his far finer description of Sin and Death. Envy flies up to Saul's palace, and whispers jealousy of David in his ear.

> " With that she takes
> One of her worst, her best-belovèd snakes :
> ' Softly, dear worm, soft and unseen,' said she,
> ' Into his bosom steal, and in it be
> My viceroy.' At that word she took her flight,
> And her loose shape dissolved into the night."

We are then transported to heaven, and into the presence of God Himself, who sends an angel to David. In consequence, David goes to play before Saul, and Saul in vain tries to kill him. The book closes with a lengthy description of the Prophets' College, which appears to have been closely modelled on the University of Cambridge. In certain passages, such as the pretty description of David and his wife walking among the lemon-trees, Cowley approaches nearer than usual to a naturalistic style in poetry. The other three books of this epic are tedious and redundant beyond all endurance. It is, in fact, the sort of poem with which, if you sit on the grass in a quiet place some summer afternoon, you cannot by any means fail to slumber soundly. This is indeed its only merit, save that of marking a distinct step in the process of the ossification of the English heroic couplet. I must not omit, however, to acknowledge that in the third book there is a serenade, "Awake, awake, my lyre," which ought to rank among Cowley's most accomplished lyrics. At the end was printed a translation, by the author, of the first book only, into Latin hexameters.

While the volume we have been examining in detail was being prepared for the press, Cowley's position was considered so equivocal, that he was urged, by way of diverting political suspicion, to study for some profession. He chose that of medicine, and although he was now forty years of age, worked like a young student at anatomy and *materia medica*. In December 1657, he passed a final examination at Oxford, but it does not appear to be recorded whether he ever practised as a physician. The principal consequence of this line of labour was to interest Cowley in botany, which henceforward became increasingly his favourite study.

At the death of Cromwell, as we have seen, he took occasion to slip back to his friends in France, and returned in 1660, only just in time to see through the

press an *Ode on his Majesty's Restoration and Return*,
a Pindaric poem of immense length, very bombastic
and rhetorical, but no doubt earnest enough, and, for
those fulsome times, not extremely grovelling in its
attitude to Royalty.   It was to be supposed that if
any man deserved reward, it was he who with so much
purity of purpose and devoted service had given the
best years of a flourishing youth to the despairing
cause of the King, and who, in spite of temptations,
had never wavered in his active fidelity.   But Cowley
was not the man to win honours in such a court as
that of Charles II.   Of austere life, a sincere and even
rigid religionist, an earnest lover of scholarship and
holy living, he was looked upon with suspicion by
the gay butterflies that flocked to Whitehall.   Charles
himself, who admired his genius and respected his
character, was prejudiced against him by spiteful
tongues, who pointed to certain pacific passages in
his writings, as if they proved his lukewarmness in
the Royalist cause.   Nothing could be more wantonly
unjust.   In point of fact, Charles was too ready to
embrace his enemies and let his friends shift for
themselves.

   The poets, however, managed to provide for their
own maintenance.   The easy turncoat, Waller, came
skipping back to court; Herrick regained his vicarage,
and Roscommon his wealth and influence.   " In that
year when manna rained on all, why should the Muse's
fleece only be dry?" lamented Cowley, who found
himself alone unwatered by the golden shower of
preferments.   In his despair, he had resolved to go to

America, and seems to have made arrangements for so doing, when he discovered that his fortunes were at so low an ebb that he had not money enough for the outward voyage. He possessed two faithful friends, however—Lord St. Albans and the young Duke of Buckingham, afterwards author of the *Rehearsal*. By the united efforts of these noblemen a generous provision was made for the poet, who was by these means relieved from anxiety, the world being all before him where to choose.

In the language of Bishop Sprat, "He was now weary of the vexations and formalities of an active condition. He had been perplexed with a long compliance to foreign manners. He was satiated with the arts of court, which sort of life, though his virtue had made innocent to him, yet nothing could make it quiet. Immediately he gave over all pursuit of honour and riches in a time when, if any ambitious or covetous thoughts had remained in his mind, he might justly have expected to have them readily satisfied. In his last seven or eight years he was concealed in his beloved obscurity, and possessed that solitude which from his very childhood he had always most passionately desired. Though he had frequent invitations to return into business, yet he never gave ear to any persuasions of profit or preferment. His visits to the city and court were very few; his stays in town were only as a passenger, not as an inhabitant. The places that he chose for the seats of his declining life were two or three villages on the banks of the Thames."

In 1661 he published *A Discourse by Way of Vision*

concerning the Government of Oliver Cromwell, one of
his finest prose works, containing several pieces of
verses, of no very striking merit; and in 1662 two
books of plants in Latin verse, the result of his
enthusiastic but somewhat pedantic studies in botany.
These "books" were printed after Cowley's death by
Nahum Tate, in an English translation by the latter,
by Mrs. Aphra Behn, a great imitator of the style,
though not the ethics, of Cowley, and by certain other
persons whose names are now forgotten. It must have
been about this time that he made the acquaintance of
"the matchless Orinda," Mrs. Katherine Philips, with
whom he corresponded at great length, and for whom
he seems to have shared the popular admiration.
Orinda was a poetess of the new school, who preferred
force of thinking in poetry before harmony or tenderness of style, and her verses were expressly modelled
upon those of Cowley. This remarkable young woman,
who was but twenty-nine years of age at the time of
the Restoration, had already a great reputation, and
Elys declares that Cowley was no less enamoured of
her poetry than impressed to a still more serious pietism
by her devotional austerity. When she died, still
young, in 1664, Cowley mourned her in an ode that
passes all bounds of discretion and moderation, in
which he sets her above Sappho, and, what is still
more funny, above Pope Joan!

In 1663 he reprinted some poems that had appeared
in his *Essays on Verse and Prose,* with other miscellaneous pieces. The publication of this volume, which
he entitled *Verses on Several Occasions,* was forced

upon him by the piratical printing of a volume of his inedited poems at Dublin. This small quarto contains fourteen copies of verses of an occasional kind. We find an ode on the death of Dr. William Harvey, the great anatomist; and an "Ode Sitting and Drinking in the Chair made out of the Relics of Sir Francis Drake's Ship," which is a capital instance of the author's fantastic wit. He further included a number of gracefully turned paraphrases from the Latin poets, particularly Horace, Martial, and Claudian. The solitude he had so long desired suited his body less than his mind, and about the time that this volume was published, when he was living at Barnes, he fell into a low fever, from which with great difficulty he recovered. He therefore removed, in 1666, to Chertsey, where he took the Porch House, towards the west end of that town, and bought some fields in the vicinity. He seems to have suffered again much during the one winter he spent there, but to have recovered in the spring; but through staying over long in the meadows one summer afternoon, superintending his labourers, he caught a cold, which he neglected. Within a fortnight he died, on July 28, 1667, not having quite completed his forty-eighth year.

With his death his glory flourished. King Charles declared that Mr. Cowley had not left a better man behind him. On August 3 he was laid in Westminster Abbey, beside the ashes of Chaucer and Spenser. The Earl of Orrery composed a funeral poem, and Sir John Denham, himself in a few months to die, wrote an elegy, beginning "Old Chaucer, like the morning star,"

which is quoted in every work on English literature.
All the poets of the day wrote "Pindarique Odes," in
imitation of the transcendent poet of that form of
verse, and his heroic couplet became the despair of all
gentlemen who wrote with ease.

> " He who would worthily adorn his hearse,
> Should write in his own way, in his immortal verse,"

said Thomas Higgins, who indited a very good Pindaric
ode to his memory.   His fame was more materially
served by Sprat, afterwards Bishop of Rochester, who
published in Latin in 1668, and then in English in
1669, a *Life of Cowley*, which is one of the very best
examples of memorial prose or elegiac monograph in
the language, being pure, elegant, and forcible in style,
and full of fine thought.   George, Duke of Buckingham,
raised a monument to his memory in Westminster
Abbey, and so, crowned with unusual honour, and
lighted by the funeral flambeaux of temporal and spiritual peers, this poet also, like his obscurer brethren,
went down into the place where all the incidental
advantages of life are as if they had not been.

If it be held that the two questions with which I
started have not been wholly answered, and that I
have still to show why Cowley once was the most
popular poet of his age, and why he is now forgotten,
a few words may, at all events, suffice to complete the
reply.   Every student of English poetry will admit
that two great opposite influences have alternately
ruled the writers of our verse.   Before the age of
Elizabeth, it is not quite so easy to mark the differ-

P

ence between the fresh and natural spirit of Chaucer and some of his Scottish followers, and the wholly didactic and scholastic spirit of Lydgate, Barclay, and Skelton; but at least from the *Mirror for Magistrates*, when poetry once more burst into sudden blossom, and every branch upon every tree rang with melodious voices, it is easy enough to trace down to Herrick the unbroken chain of objective and naturalistic poets, born to teach through singing, and not through rhetoric. With Cowley a wholly new influence came in. From Cowley to Darwin all the poets made oratorical effect take the place of the observation and inspired interpretation of nature. With Collins, through Cowper, and first fully in Wordsworth, there came that return to primal forms and primal feeling which still breathes in our latest poetry.

Cowley gave the reading public a new experience. Tired of the exotic and over-jewelled style of the religious and philosophical lyrists, tired of the romantic epic which had slipped from Shakespeare and Marlowe down into such hands as Chamberlayne's, tired of the Cavalier song-writers, who harped for ever on the same strained string, and with no ears or hearts for Milton's glorious revival, the public of the day rejoiced in Cowley as Parisian society of a generation before had welcomed Malherbe. Versification had lost all nerve and shape in the lax lips of the last slovenly dramatists. In France the great Corneille was making the stage resound with the harmonious cadences of his heroical couplets; why should not England also aspire to such sublime eloquence, to such chaste numbers?

Feeling, passion, romance, colour, all these had been poured out so lavishly that the public palate was cloyed with sweetness. The severity of Cowley's writings, their intellectual quality, their cold elevation and dry intelligence, were as charming as they were novel. But the charm was not to last. A far greater man, Dryden, with assimilative genius of the most marvellous kind, was to tarnish the glory of Cowley by sheer superiority of imitation. No form of verse that the elder poet cultivated, with the single exception of the Elegy, but was to be carried to far greater perfection in the same line by the younger. Even to the technicality of the occasional use of an alexandrine in heroic verse, Dryden was to illuminate the discoveries of Cowley, not to strike out new paths for himself.

Three writers of less influence than Cowley supported the new school, and strengthened the determination of Dryden. These were Davenant in his stilted, Gallicised dramas, Denham in his correct, but cold and measured descriptive poem of *Cooper's Hill*, and Waller in his smooth, emasculated lyrics. Neither of these had Cowley's genius or power, but they all had the tact to seize the turn of the tide to put out into new seas. Waller had been the first to employ the new versification, but Cowley earliest perceived its propriety for didactic uses. To him, and to him alone, belongs the doubtful honour of inaugurating the reign of didactic and rhetorical poetry in England.

It may be asked, why restore a memory so justly dishonoured, why recall to our attention a writer whose verses were but galvanised at the outset, and now are

long past all hope of revival? In the first place, if
the judgment of a whole generation has unanimously
set an unambitious man on a pedestal of supreme
reputation, I am more ready to doubt my own perception than to stigmatise so many cultivated persons with
folly. No poet universally admired in his own age can
be wholly without lasting merit. In the second place,
Cowley in particular, whether judged as a man or as
a *littérateur*, or even as a poet more or less malformed,
has qualities of positive and intrinsic merit. I trust
that my citations have at least proved so much. For
the rest, I confess that I find a particular fascination
in the study of these maimed and broken poets, these
well-strung instruments upon whose throbbing strings
Destiny has laid the pressure of her silencing fingers.
The masters of song instil me with a sort of awe. I
feel embarrassed when I write of Milton. But Cowley
has surely grown humble in the long years of his exile,
and he will not exact too much homage from the last
of his admirers.

1876.

THE MATCHLESS ORINDA

IT was not until the second half of the seventeenth century that women began to be considered competent to undertake literature as a profession. In the crowded galaxy of Elizabethan and Jacobean poets there is no female star even of the seventh magnitude. But with the Restoration, the wives and daughters, who had learned during the years of exile to act in political and diplomatic intrigue with independence and skill, took upon themselves to write independently too, and the last forty years of the century are crowded with the names of "celebrated scribbling women." Among all these the Matchless Orinda takes the foremost place—not exactly by merit, for Aphra Behn surpassed her in genius, Margaret, Duchess of Newcastle, in versatility, and Catherine Trotter in professional zeal; but by the moral eminence which she attained through her elevated public career, and which she sealed by her tragical death. When the seventeenth century thought of a poetess, it naturally thought of Orinda; her figure overtopped those of her literary sisters; she was more dignified, more regal in her attitude to the public, than they were; and, in fine, she presents us with the best type we possess of the woman of letters in the seventeenth century.

Yet modern criticism has entirely neglected her. I cannot find that any writer of authority has mentioned her name with interest since Keats, in 1817, when he was writing *Endymion*, came across her poems at Oxford, and in writing to Reynolds remarked that he found "a most delicate fancy of the Fletcher kind" in her poems, and quoted one piece of ten stanzas to prove it. In Mr. Ward's *English Poets*, where so many names owe their introduction to one or two happy compositions which have survived the body of their works, I find no page dedicated to Orinda; and I suppose she may fairly be considered as dead to the British public. If I venture to revive her here, it is not that I greatly admire her verses, or consider her in the true sense to have been a poet, for even the praise just quoted from Keats seems to me exaggerated; but it is because of the personal charm of her character, the interest of her career, and its importance as a chapter in the literary history of the Restoration. Nor was she, like so many of her contemporaries, an absurd, or preposterous, or unclean writer: her muse was uniformly pure and reasonable; her influence, which was very great, was exercised wholly in favour of what was beautiful and good; and if she failed, it is rather by the same accident by which so many poets of less intelligence have unexpectedly succeeded.

Katherine Fowler was born on New-Year's Day, 1631, in a respectable cockney family of Bucklersbury. Of her father, who was a Presbyterian, nothing else is known save that he was a prosperous merchant. She was baptized at the font of St. Mary Woolchurch on

January 11, 1631. John Aubrey, the antiquary, who was her exact contemporary and one of her numerous friends, has preserved various traditions of her childhood. Like Cowley, another cockney child of the period, she was very eager and precocious in the pursuit of letters. The imaginative bias of her mind first took a religious form. She had read the Bible right through before she was five years old; she would pray aloud—rather ostentatiously, one fears—by the hour together, and had a potent memory for the actual text of the florid sermons that she heard on Sundays. At school she was a prodigy of application; she would commonly say, by heart, many chapters and passages of Scripture, and began at a very early age to write verses. As she grew old enough to form convictions of her own, she threw off the Presbyterian and Parliamentary traditions of her home, and announced herself an admirer of the Church and the King just as those stars were setting on the political horizon. Through the darkest period of the Commonwealth she remained stanchly Royalist; and we may fancy that she was well content to leave a home no longer sympathetic to her, when, in her seventeenth year, she married a Royalist gentleman of Wales, Mr. James Philips, of Cardigan Priory.

The early part of her life as Mrs. Philips is dark to us. None of her letters, and but few of her poems, from this period have been preserved. The earliest of her verses form an address to her neighbour Henry Vaughan, the Silurist, on the publication of his *Olor Iscanus* in 1651. These lines are interesting to the

student of versification as showing that Katherine
Philips, from the very first, had made up her mind to
look forwards and not backwards. There is no particular merit in these verses, but they belong to the
school of Waller and Denham, and prove that the
authoress had learned very exactly the meaning of the
new prosody. To the end of her career she never
swerved from this path, to which her constant study
of French poetry further encouraged her.

She seems to have adopted the melodious pseudonym
by which she had become known to posterity in 1651.
It would appear that among her friends and associates
in and near Cardigan she instituted a Society of Friendship, to which male and female members were admitted,
and in which poetry, religion, and the human heart
were to form the subjects of discussion. This society,
chiefly, no doubt, owing to the activity of Mrs. Philips,
became widely known, and was an object of interest to
contemporaries. Jeremy Taylor recognised it from afar,
and Cowley paid it elaborate compliments. In the eyes
of Orinda it took an exaggerated importance:—

> " Nations will own us now to be
>   A temple of divinity ;
>   And pilgrims shall ten ages hence
>   Approach our tombs with reverence,"

a prophecy which still waits to be fulfilled. On
December 28, 1651, Miss Anne Owen, a young lady of
Landshipping, entered the Society under the name of
Lucasia, it being absolutely necessary that each member
should be known by a fancy name. The husband of

the poetess, for instance, is never mentioned in her
poems or her correspondence except as Antenor.
Lucasia was the chief ornament of the Society, and
the affection of Orinda was laid at her feet for nearly
thirteen years, in a style of the most unbounded and
vivacious eulogy.   It is very delightful to contemplate
the little fat, ruddy, cockney lady, full of business and
animation, now bustling the whole parish by the ears,
now rousing her rather sluggish husband to ambition,
now languishing in platonic sentiment at the feet of
the young Welsh beauty who accepted all her raptures
so calmly and smilingly.   In Miss Owen, Mrs. Philips
saw all that can be seen in the rarest altitudes of
human character.

> " Nor can morality itself reclaim
> The apostate world like my Lucasia's name :
> . . . Lucasia, whose harmonious state
> The Spheres and Muses only imitate.
> . . . So to acknowledge such vast eminence,
> Imperfect wonder is our eloquence,
> No pen Lucasia's glories can relate."

Nor is Lucasia the only member of her little provincial quorum of whom she predicates such brave
things.   There is Ardelia, whose real name neglectful
posterity has forgotten to preserve; there is Miss
Mary Aubrey, who becomes Mrs. Montague as time
goes on, and whose poetical name is Rosania; there
is Regina, "that Queen of Inconstancy," Mrs. John
Collier; later on, Lady Anne Boyle begins to figure
as " adored Valeria," and Lady Mary Cavendish
as "dazzling Polycrite."   The gentlemen have very

appropriate names also, though propriety prevents
Orinda, in their cases, from celebrating friendship in
terms of so florid an eloquence.   The "excellent
Palæmon" was Francis Finch originally, but the name
was transferred, as the "noble Palæmon," to Jeremy
Taylor; the "noble Silvander," Sir Edward Dering,
was more fortunate in preserving his name of honour;
and last, but not least, the elegant Sir Charles Cotterel
achieved a sort of immortality as Orinda's greatest
friend, under the name of Poliarchus.

There are few collections of seventeenth century
verse so personal as the poems of Orinda.   Her
aspirations and sentimentalities, her perplexities and
quarrels, her little journeys and her business troubles,
all are reflected in her verse as a mirror.   She goes
from Tenby to Bristol by sea in September 1652, and
she gives Lucasia an account of the uneventful voyage
in verse:—

> " But what most pleased my mind upon the way,
>   Was the ships' posture that in harbour lay;
>   Which to a rocky grove so close were fixed
>   That the trees' branches with the tackling mixed,—
>   One would have thought it was, as then it stood,
>   A growing navy or a floating wood."

These are verses for which we have lost all taste,
but they were quite as good as those by which Waller
was then making himself famous, and in the same
modern manner.   These and others were handed about
from one friend to another till they reached London,
and gained the enthusiastic poetess literary and
artistic friends.   Among these latter were Henry

Lawes, the great musician, and Samuel Cooper, the finest miniature painter of the day, to both of whom she has inscribed flowing copies of verses, informed by her familiar stately wit.

But the subject that chiefly inspired her was the excellence of her female friends, and in treating this theme she really invented a new species of literature. She is the first sentimental writer in the English language, and she possesses to the full those qualities which came into fashion a century and a half later in the person of such authors as Letitia Landon. Orinda communes with the stars and the mountains, and is deeply exercised about her own soul. She is all smiles, tears, and sensibility. She asks herself if her affection has been slighted, she swears eternal truth, she yearns for confidences, she fancies that she is "dying for a little love." With Antenor, her husband, she keeps up all the time a prosaic, humdrum happiness, looking after his affairs, anxious about his health, rather patronisingly affectionate and wifely; but her poetical heart is elsewhere, and her leisure moments are given up to romantic vows with Rosania and Lucasia, and correspondence about the human heart with the noble Silvander. The whole society, one cannot help feeling, was entirely created and kept alive by the sensibility of Orinda, and nothing but her unremitting efforts could have sustained its component parts at the proper heights of sympathy. Mrs. Philips, in fact, had come to the conclusion that, as she put it, "Men exclude women from friendship's vast capacity," and she was determined, in spite of the difficulties in her path, to produce some shining specimens of female friendship. The seventeenth century was quite astonished, and looked on with respectful admiration, while the good Orinda laboured away, undeterred by the irritating circumstances that her *sociétaires* would get married at the very moment when they seemed approaching perfection, and that after marriage they were much more difficult for her to manage than before.

Her first great disappointment was the "apostasy" of Rosania, on which occasion she lifted up her voice to the "great soul of Friendship," and was rewarded by unusual response from Lucasia, on whom it is possible that the absence of Rosania had acted in an exhilarating manner. But it is time to quote some of those addresses to her friends by which she distinguishes herself so clearly from all the writers of her generation, and by which she must be known in future, if she be known at all. After receiving one of those compliments from the great men of her age, which began to flow in upon her retirement at Cardigan, Orinda thus expressed her satisfaction to Lucasia, and stirred her up to fresh efforts of sentiment :—

> "Come, my Lucasia, since we see
>   That miracles man's faith do move,
>   By wonder and by prodigy
>   To the dull angry world let's prove
>   There's a religion in our love.
>
> "We court our own captivity,—
>   Than thrones more great and innocent ;
>   'Twere banishment to be set free,
>   Since we wear fetters whose intent
>   Not bondage is, but ornament.

> " Divided joys are tedious found,
>   And griefs united easier flow ;
> We are ourselves but by rebound,
>   And all our titles shuffled so,—
>   Both princes, and both subjects too.

> " Our hearts are mutual victims laid,
>   While they,—such power in friendship lies,—
> Are altars, priests and offerings made,
>   And each heart which thus kindly dies,
>   Grows deathless by the sacrifice."

It cannot be denied that these are vigorous lines, full of ingenious fancy, nor were there many men then living in England who could surpass them. We are dealing with a school whose talent has evaporated, and we must not forget to judge such verse by the standards of its time. Of Milton nobody was thinking ; Dryden was still silent ; Herrick and Wither had ceased to write ; and it may safely be said that there was nothing in the lines just quoted which Cowley, or Waller, or Denham would have disdained to sign. Lucasia was also the theme of some verses which close, at all events, in a very delicate harmony :—

> " I did not live until this time
>   Crowned my felicity,
> When I could say, without a crime,
>   I am not Thine, but Thee.

> " For as a watch by art is wound
>   To motion, such was mine ;
> But never had Orinda found
>   A soul till she found thine.

> " Then let our flame still light and shine,
>   And no false fear control,
> As innocent as our design,
>   Immortal as our soul."

The piece which Keats admired so much that he took the trouble of copying it in full, was inspired by Miss Mary Aubrey, and may be given here as a final example of the manner of Orinda :—

> " I have examined and do find
>   Of all that favour me,
> There's none I grieve to leave behind,
>   But only, only thee :
> To part with thee I needs must die,
> Could parting separate thee and I.

> " But neither chance nor compliment
>   Did element our love ;
> 'Twas sacred sympathy was lent
>   Us from the Quire above.
> That friendship Fortune did create
> Still fears a wound from Time or Fate.

> " Our changed and mingled souls are grown
>   To such acquaintance now,
> That, if each would resume her own,
>   Alas ! we know not how ;
> We have each other so engrost,
> That each is in the union lost.

> " And thus we can no absence know,
>   Nor shall we be confined ;
> Our active souls will daily go
>   To learn each other's mind.
> Nay, should we never meet to sense
> Our souls would hold intelligence.

" Inspirèd with a flame divine,
    I scorn to court a stay ;
For from that noble soul of thine
    I ne'er can be away.
But I shall weep when thou dost grieve,
Nor can I die whilst thou dost live.

" By my own temper I shall guess
    At thy felicity,
And only like thy happiness,
    Because it pleaseth thee.
Or hearts at any time will tell
If thou or I be sick or well.

" All honour sure I must pretend,
    All that is good or great ;
She that would be Rosania's friend
    Must be at least complete ;
If I have any bravery,
'Tis cause I have so much of thee.

" Thy leiger soul in me shall lie,
    And all thy thoughts reveal,
Then back again with mine shall fly,
    And thence to me shall steal ;
Thus still to one another tend :
Such is the sacred name of Friend.

" Thus our twin souls in one shall grow,
    And teach the world new love,
Redeem the age and sex, and show
    A flame Fate dares not move :
And, courting Death to be our friend,
Our lives too shall together end.

" A dew shall dwell upon our tomb
    Of such a quality,
That fighting armies thither come
    Shall reconcilèd be.
We'll ask no epitaph, but say,
ORINDA *and* ROSANIA."

For ten years Katherine Philips continued to live at Cardigan in the midst of this enthusiastic circle of friends, and in a social quiet that was broken only by her own agitations of spirit. In 1654, in the seventh year of her marriage, she bore her first child, a son who was named Hector, and who lived only forty days. She bewails his loss in many verses, which are not the less affecting because they are stiff in form. She was ultimately consoled for her boy's death by the birth of a girl, who survived her, and eventually married a Mr. Wogan, of Pembrokeshire. It is unfortunate that we cannot trace the course of Orinda's intimacy with Jeremy Taylor, although it is most probable that he visited her Society at Cardigan during the years that he lived near to her in Carmarthenshire. At all events, when, in 1659, he dedicated his *Discourse on the Nature, Offices, and Measures of Friendship* to "the most ingenious and excellent Mrs. Katherine Philips," he paid her the most delicate and affectionate compliments, and showed himself well acquainted with the tenor of her mind. His treatise was, indeed, a public testimony, from a man of the highest authority, to the success with which she had proved women to be capable of the serene and exalted virtue of friendship.

This tribute from the famous Bishop of Down and Connor inaugurated that brief period during which Orinda ceased to be a provincial notoriety, and became for the small remainder of her life a prominent figure in contemporary society. At the Restoration she sang out loud and clear, in strains that were proved to be sincere by her long and unflinching resistance to the Commonwealth. As Arion she goes forth to meet his Majesty upon a dolphin :—

> " Whom does this stately navy bring?
> O, 'tis Great Britain's glorious King!
> Convey him then, ye Winds and Seas,
> Swift as desire and calm as peace.
> Charles and his mighty hopes you bear;
> A greater now than Cæsar's here,
> Whose veins a richer purple boast
> Than ever hero's yet engrossed,
> Sprung from a father so august
> He triumphs in his very dust."

She hails the fine weather for the coronation as a " bright parenthesis " placed by Heaven itself between two storms of rain, and she indites separate copies of verses to all the ladies of the royal family. Soon the Duchess of York becomes aware of this ardent poetess in the West, and commands her to send some specimens of her poems ; and in a little time we find Orinda, unable to stay at Cardigan when the world of London had suddenly become so distractingly interesting, on a visit to town. We find her the guest of Cowley at Barn Elms, and invited to inscribe her name on one of his ancient trees. And at the close of this visit to London in 1661 she suddenly becomes vividly present to us for the rest of her life.

We have already mentioned her friendship for Sir Charles Cotterel, whom she named Poliarchus. He was a Royalist courtier of great elegance and erudition, who had long been steward to the Queen of Bohemia, and was now master of the ceremonies at the Court of Charles II. He dabbled gracefully in literature, was a

Q

very accomplished linguist, and long after the death of Orinda achieved an ephemeral reputation as the translator of the novels of La Calprenède. He survived Katherine Philips nearly a quarter of a century, dying in 1687, and what then became of his collection of her letters does not appear. In 1705, however, forty years after her death, Bernard Lintott published, without any bibliographical information, forty-eight *Letters from Orinda to Poliarchus*, which are not only extremely well written and vivacious, but full of autobiographical matter, and amply furnished with dates. By means of these letters we can follow Orinda closely through the last and most interesting months of her life.

The first letter is dated from Acton, Dec. 1, 1661. She has come up to London to prosecute some business for her husband, and is staying with his brother, to the members of whose family she had at various occasions indited poems. Sir Charles Cotterel has paid her a visit, in the course of which he has confided to her his hopeless passion for a lady named Calanthe, and she is full of concern for his peace of mind. Mr. Matthew Arnold has pointed out how suddenly the prose of the Restoration threw off its traditional involutions and false ornament, and became in a great measure the prose that we wish to use to-day. The *Letters* of Orinda form a singular instance of the truth of this criticism, and compare very favourably with such letters as those of Howel in point of simplicity of style. Thus, for instance, she refers to Sir Charles Cotterel's agitation of mind :—

"The great disturbance you were in when you went hence, and the high and just concern I have for you, have made me take the resolution to trouble you with my most humble and earnest request to resist the attempts your present passion is like to make on your quiet, before it grows too imperious to be checked by the powers of either reason or friendship. There is nothing more easy than to captivate one's self to love or grief, and no more evident mark of a great soul than to avoid those bondages. I hope, therefore, you will not think it altogether unbecoming the friendship you have given me leave to profess for you, to entreat you to overcome those passions, and not give way to melancholy, which will unhinge your excellent temper, and bring so great a cloud on the happiness of your friends. Consider for how many important interests you are responsible, and exert all the powers of reason with which your excellent judgment abounds, to shake off your sorrows, and live cheerfully and long the delight of all who have the honour of your acquaintance."

Calanthe had been in correspondence with Orinda, and that faithless confidante had shown her letters to Poliarchus, hence many entreaties that her weakness may not be divulged to the injured fair. It is plain that Orinda greatly enjoyed her position as go-between in this interesting love affair, which, however, very shortly languished, and left upon the ensuing correspondence only this trace, that Sir Charles Cotterel having written such passages in his letters to Orinda as were not to be read by Calanthe in Italian, Orinda was obliged to learn that language, to which, indeed, she forthwith gave herself very assiduously. Her visit to London came to an end in March 1662, and she wrote to Poliarchus a sprightly letter from Gloucester on her return journey. A very interesting letter, dated Cardigan Priory, March 18th, announced her return. She found Wales exceedingly dull at first, after the

pleasures of courtly and literary society in London.
She complained that she could not find any satisfaction
in "my beloved rocks and rivers, formerly my best
entertainment," and she longed to be able once more
to enjoy Sir Charles Cotterel's conversation, which was
to her "above all the flights of panegyrick." Her one
consolation was that the faithful Lucasia was still at
Cardigan, though threatening every day to be gone
to her own home. Descending to mundane things,
poor Orinda confessed that she had been much disappointed in the condition of her husband. He is dull,
apathetic, and depressed, was roused to no interest
by her account of the conduct of his affairs in
London, and terrifies her by his absolute indifference
to business. From the sluggishness of Antenor she
turns again to the pleasures of literature, and by an
amusing affectation characteristic of the school she
belonged to, she tells Poliarchus that she is reading
English books with patience and French ones with
pleasure.

She spent the month of April with her beloved friend
at Landshipping, but, alas! the hour of the apostasy of
Lucasia was approaching. While Orinda was amusing
herself with the idea that Poliarchus was showing her
poems at Court, and while she was signing herself to
him "more than all the world besides your faithful
Valentine," Miss Anne Owen was herself accepting a
valentine in a less platonic sense. It seems to have
all happened at Landshipping under the very nose of
Orinda, without attracting the attention of that active
creature. When at last she found it out, she was

beside herself with chagrin and indignation. The bridegroom was a son of Sir Thomas Hanmer, and the match was one thoroughly approved of by both families. Orinda, as she says herself, "alone of all the company was out of humour; nay, I was vexed to that degree that I could not disguise my concern, which many of them were surprised to see, and spoke to me of it; but my grief was too deeply rooted to be cured with words." Her position, indeed, was a very trying one; nor ought we to smile at the disappointment of this worthy little lady, who had worshipped a divinity so long only to find her suddenly composed of common clay.

The event was certainly hurried, for before the middle of May Lucasia was married, Orinda meanwhile indulging herself in transports of jealousy, and in long correspondence on the subject with Rosania and Poliarchus. When the young people were actually married, Orinda remained with them at Landshipping, and when they prepared to go over to Ireland, where the bride's new home was, she announced her intention of accompanying them. The vigilance of friendship, however, was not the only or the main cause of this determination. There were several suits to be tried in Dublin, involving heavy gains or losses to her husband, and as he could by no means be roused to an interest in these, Mrs. Philips resolved to undertake them herself. On July 19th, 1662, she writes from Rosstrevor, in County Down, where she had been enjoying the society of Jeremy Taylor, who had been settled something less than two years in his diocese. This august companionship did not prevent Orinda from exercising a sharp supervision over the newly married pair. She informs Poliarchus, in a strain of the finest unconscious humour, that she believes the bridegroom to be of a most stubborn and surly humour, although, "to speak sincerely, she has not been able hitherto to detect in him the marks of any ill nature," and what exasperates her most of all, in her character of the social banshee, is that Lucasia herself "pretends to be the most satisfied creature in the world."

In July 1662, Mrs. Philips began what was evidently the happiest year of her life by taking up her abode in Dublin. At the Restoration the great difficulty of settling the claims of those Irish gentlemen who demanded the King's favour, and the endless litigations respecting the forfeited lands in Ireland, brought over to Dublin a large company of distinguished lawyers with their families, and gave the city a temporary show and glitter. It was many years before affairs were in any degree arranged, and the English colony in Dublin settled down to enjoy themselves as best they might. Orinda found herself thrown at once into the distinguished company which gathered round the Lord-Lieutenant, the great first Duke of Ormonde, and she received an exceptionally warm welcome in the family of the Countess of Cork. Of all the Boyles, however, at that moment, the most influential was Roger, Earl of Orrery, whose enthusiastic admiration for Orinda displayed itself at once in every species of compliment and hospitality. He was eminent alike as a soldier, a statesman, and a poet, was one of the most influential men in the three kingdoms, and at that moment was engaged in Ireland upon a most arduous and painful office. He had just been appointed Lord Chief-Justice of Ireland under the Duke of Ormonde, and his friendship was not merely flattering and agreeable to Orinda, but extremely advantageous. He placed her among the ladies of his family, obtained for her the protection and personal friendship of Lady Cork, and in fact did all that was possible to make her stay in Dublin pleasant.

Another distinguished person with whom she swore eternal friendship in Dublin was the young Earl of Roscommon, not yet famous as the author of the *Essay on Translated Verse*, and indeed only twenty-eight years of age, but already looked upon as a patron of poetry, and as a very agreeable and eligible bachelor, "distempered," unfortunately, "with a fatal affection for play." Another Dublin acquaintance was James Tyrell, the politician and historian; yet another was John Ogilby, a man belonging to a generation earlier than all these, who had successfully outwitted Sir William Davenant, and had contrived to persuade Charles II. to send him out to Dublin as Master of the Revels. Ogilby is still sometimes remembered as the translator of the *Odyssey* and of the *Æneid*. That Orinda impressed all these persons with a great sense of her intellectual power and moral excellence, is evident from the nature of the eulogies they poured upon her while she lived and long after she died. When a man in the position of Lord Orrery says in

print of a little plain Welsh lady of the middle
class—

> " Madam, when I but knew you by report,
> I feared the praises of the admiring Court
> Were but their compliments, but now I must
> Confess, what I thought civil is scarce just "—

we may be sure that he is trying to express with
sincerity a very genuine admiration. Nor is the Earl
of Roscommon, who addresses her as " Dear Friend,"
less sincere, though more ridiculous, when he states it
to be his experience that when he meets hungry wolves
in the Scythian snows,

> The magic of Orinda's name
> Not only can their fierceness tame,
> But, if that mighty word I once rehearse,
> They seem *submissively to roar in verse.*"

On one of the earliest occasions upon which Mrs.
Philips met Lord Orrery, in August 1662, she ventured to show him her latest effusion, a scene she had
translated from the third act of Corneille's tragedy of
Pompée. Orrery admired it excessively, and laid his
entreaties, almost his commands, upon her to complete
it in the same style—that is, in rhymed heroic verse.
She set to work and completed the task, a very considerable one, by the middle of October. She found
that it relieved her, in combination with select passages
from Seneca and Epictetus, from absolutely breaking
her heart over Lucasia, whose husband at last insisted
on taking her back to their house at Rosstrevor.
Orinda, ensconced in her snug nest of quality at

Dublin, full of literary ambition, and scribbling day
and night at *Pompey*, seems to have missed her friend
as little as could be expected. She was treated as a
very great celebrity; and when she had occasion to
hand round some manuscript verses which Cowley
had just sent her for approval, she must have felt that
her cup of literary importance was full.

Thus caressed by Lady Cork and complimented by
all the lettered earls, she passed the months of August
and September 1662 in a sort of golden dream,
scarcely finding time, amid all her avocations, to write
a hasty letter to the devoted Poliarchus, to whom,
however, *Pompey* was sent in quick instalments. She
gives him an interesting account, in October, of the
theatre which the new master of the revels, Ogilby,
was building at Dublin—a theatre that cost £2000 to
put up. She holds it to be much finer than Davenant's
in London; and she is present when the season opens
with a performance of Beaumont and Fletcher's comedy
of *Wit without Money*. As soon as the rough draft
of *Pompey* was finished, she busied herself with her
husband's affairs—" putting in Antenor's claim as an
adventurer in my father's right here in Ireland "—and
this, with two other minor lawsuits, occupies her spare
time until the summer of the ensuing year. Her most
serious attention, however, settles upon *Pompey*. Sir
Charles Cotterel takes so much interest in it that she
says, "I look on you as more a friend to me than
David was to Jonathan;" but she shows a little temper
when he offers some verbal criticism. For instance,
and this is interesting historically, he objects to the

word *effort* as not English, and she replies that it has been naturalised here these twelve years. She might have added that Cotgrave had included it in his dictionary, in 1660.

Orinda spent the winter of 1662 at Dublin, touching up the text of *Pompey*, writing songs for it, and having them put to music—not without regret that her friend, the great Henry Lawes, who died just as the first manuscript of the play reached London, could not adorn them with immortal strains. Lord Orrery, who looked upon himself as the "onlie begetter" of this tragedy, moved heaven and earth to bring it out upon the stage; and, when Ogilby had made arrangements for its representation, Orrery spent £100 out of his own pocket to buy handsome Egyptian and Roman dresses and bring out the tragedy in style. It was dedicated to his mother, Lady Cork. Lord Roscommon wrote the prologue, and Sir Edward Dering the epilogue; each of them so ordered their verses that they should be delivered by the actor while turning to the Duke of Ormonde's box. New dances and a masque were introduced here and there by Ogilby, and on the second week of February 1663 it was finally presented to the public. It enjoyed an unbounded success; but, unfortunately, the letter in which Mrs. Philips gave Sir Charles Cotterel an account of the performance has not been preserved. Her friends, however, pressed her to print the play, and from the success which attended this experiment we may judge of the reception of the piece on the boards. An edition of five hundred was printed, a

single packet only being sent to London, and in a
fortnight the whole of the impression was sold. In
London the demand was so great, that hardly had the
few copies sent arrived at the capital, than Mr. Herring-
man, the poets' publisher in those early days of the
Restoration, wrote to ask Orinda's leave to bring out
a London edition.

Meanwhile, Orinda had certain literary experiences.
She made the acquaintance of Samuel Tuke, whose
very successful play, the *Adventures of Five Hours*,
was awakening delusive hopes of a great new dramatist; and she welcomed in *Hudibras* the advent of
one much greater than Tuke. Her first impulse of
criticism was that which the world has endorsed: "In
my life I never read anything so naturally and so
knowingly burlesque." In May, her troubles as an
authoress began. A miscellany of poems by living
writers appeared, in which some of her lyrics were
pirated and widely advertised; and her serenity was
shaken, a week or two later, by the fact that two
London publishers were quarrelling for *Pompey*, and
did, in fact, bring out, in the month of June, two
simultaneous editions of that lucky play. And now it
came to her knowledge that, while she had been thus
busily employed, she had cut the ground from under
the feet of some of the most celebrated wits of the
day; for Waller had set his heart on translating
Pompée, and had finished one act before Orinda's
version was heard of. The other four acts had been
supplied by Sir Edward Fillmore, Sir Charles Sedley,
and the young men who were afterwards known as

the Earls of Dorset and Middlesex.   As early as January 1663 it was announced that this translation was complete and immediately to appear. The success, however, of the Irish version checked the London one; and Orinda, hearing nothing of her illustrious rivals, became frightened, and wrote to Waller a letter deprecating his anger. His reply, which reached her early in June, reassured her; the courtly poet was characteristically smooth, courteous, and obliging, and, if he felt annoyance, contrived most wittily to avoid the show of it. At last, on July 16, 1663, having gained the two most important of her three suits, Mrs. Philips set sail from Dublin to Milford, and went home to her husband at Cardigan after an absence of exactly twelve months.

She found the excellent Antenor much improved in health, and she settled down to spend the autumn and winter at home. Her new importance as a woman of letters, and her large London correspondence, however, exposed her to a fresh annoyance. The postmaster at Carmarthen scandalously neglected his duty, and letters were constantly delayed and lost. The gentry of the neighbourhood, however, stirred up by the ever-energetic Orinda, sent in a memorial to O'Neil, the Postmaster-General, and the indolence at Carmarthen received a sharp reprimand. She found the winter tedious after her happy life at Dublin; she does not complain, but her letters to Sir Charles Cotterel are dejected in tone, and her appeals to her friends to find something in London for her husband to do are constant and pathetic. And now another

annoyance occurred.   A piratical London publisher
managed to obtain copies of all her miscellaneous
poems, which she had refused to print, and brought
them out surreptitiously in November 1663, the title-
page dated 1664.   Her friends wrote to her to condole,
but did not send her the book, and her anxiety and
vexation, combined with the rumour that the verses
were very incorrectly printed, threw her into a sharp
attack of illness.   The volume, however, is not particularly incorrect, and it was prefaced by an ode of
Cowley's which should have been balm to the breast of
the wounded poetess.   In it that eminent rhetorician,
speaking in the consciousness of his enormous prestige,
addressed her in terms of the highest and most affectionate eulogy, and contrived to throw into one stanza,
at least, of his encomiastic ode, some of the most
delicately felicitous compliments that a poet ever
addressed to a sister in Apollo :—

> " Thou dost my wonder, would'st my envy raise,
>   If to be praised I loved more than to praise ;
>   I must admire to see thy well-knit sense,
>   Thy numbers gentle, and thy fancies high,
> These as thy forehead smooth, these sparkling as thine eye.
>   'Tis solid and 'tis manly all,
>   Or rather, 'tis angelical !
>   For, as in angels, we
>   Do in thy verses see
>   Both improved sexes eminently meet,—
> They are than Man more strong, and more than Woman sweet."

In January 1664 she took in hand another play of
Corneille's, and that the one most popular in England
through his lifetime—*Horace*.   It had been translated

before, by Sir William Lower, in 1656, and was attempted later on by Charles Cotton, in 1671. Orinda worked slowly at this, and brought four acts of it, all she was destined to complete, with her when she came to London in March. She was absolutely unable to stay any longer in suspense, and she thought that her energy and influence might secure some post for her husband if she came right up to town. The last three months of her life were brilliantly spent; she was warmly welcomed at court and in the best society. Her last verses, signed June 10, 1664, were addressed in terms of affectionate respect to the Archbishop of Canterbury. They breathe the old ardour, the old moral elevation, the old eager note of the enthusiastic Orinda. Twelve days later she was dead, a victim to smallpox, that frightful disease to which the science of the day saw no hope of resistance. She had but half completed her thirty-fourth year. She was buried under a great slab in the church of St. Bennet Sherehog, among the remains of her ancestors.

Thus, in the middle of a brilliant social and literary success, the abhorred shears slipped in and cut the thread. The memory of the matchless Orinda was celebrated in numberless odes. All the Royalist poets combined to do her honour. Cowley mourned her in a massive lyric. Denham demanded the privilege of concluding her *Horace*. Her name was mentioned with those of Sappho and Corinna, and language was used without reproach which might have seemed a little fulsome if addressed to the Muse herself.

For half a century Orinda was an unquestioned light

in English song; then she sank into utter darkness. But her memory is worthy of some judicious revival. She presents us with a clearly defined and curious type of the literary woman, and there are few such in our early literature. She secured the affectionate esteem of the principal people of her time, and we know enough of her character to see that she could not but secure it; and if she sinned against poetry, as we understand it, much may be forgiven her, for she loved it much.

———————

Fifteen years after the death of Orinda there was published in London a volume of *Female Poems*, which now forms one of the rarest books of the Restoration. This little volume was anonymous, but was said to be "written by Ephelia," and we are told that Ephelia was a certain Miss Joan Philips. I do not know whether I start too wild a theory when I acknowledge that it has several times crossed my mind that Ephelia may have been Orinda's only daughter, who, as we have said, eventually married a Mr. Wogan, of Pembrokeshire. This daughter seems to have been born about 1656, and accordingly would be twenty-three in 1679. The portrait of Ephelia affixed to her poems, and the description she gives of her person would tally closely enough with this hypothesis; and she expressly speaks of herself as deprived of her parents in early life, and as having soon after lost the property which they bequeathed to her. However this may be, the poems of Joan Philips are

closely modelled upon those of Katherine Philips, even
to the form of her addresses to royalty and to the
enthusiastic pseudonyms which she gives to her
friends. That she does not refer to any such relationship would be amply accounted for by her desire to
conceal her name, which the extremely confidential
nature of her effusions made imperative. Her little
book deserves mention as an appendix to Orinda's,
not merely because it may be written by a relation
and is certainly quite unknown to students, but also
on account of its inherent merit. It is a sincere page
out of the heart of a human being—a series of con-
fessions so true and so poignant that we seem to hear
a living voice across two centuries. In its warmth
and vivacity, its womanly passion and subtlety, I know
no utterance like it except the sonnets of Louise Labé.
A real human voice is so rare in Restoration literature,
that we may listen for a few moments to this not very
tuneful one.

Ephelia tells us her story without any maidenly
reserve, but with a great deal of nature. Her earliest
poems show her, as Orinda had been before her,
enslaved to a circle of fair friends of her own sex.
One day she meets Strephon, or J. G., whose surname
appears from an acrostic to have been Gilbert, and
she falls in love with him at first sight. He is much
older than she, and does not for some time respond to
her passion; but by degrees he melts to her, and they
are engaged to be married. J. G., however, is offered
a valuable appointment in the factory at Tangiers, and
he rides away under her bower-eaves, like a false

knight in a ballad, and sets sail without even bidding her farewell. She hears first a rumour that he is paying court to a lady of wealth in Morocco, and then that he had married This, " the best-born among the Afric maids." Ephelia loudly bewails her fate and Strephon's unkindness, and presents the public with a volume of poems in which every shade of emotion, as it passed through her mind, has been conscientiously transferred to verse. The result is extraordinary.

Joan Philips is a very unequal writer, but at her best she attains some undeniable vigour in the use of the heroic couplet. The following example gives as good an impression of her style as the reader can require ; it is a passage inspired by the first suspicion of J. G.'s unfaithfulness :—

> " Why do I love ? go, ask the glorious sun
> Why every day it round the world doth run ;
> Ask Thames and Tiber, why they ebb and flow ;
> Ask damask roses, why in June they blow ;
> Ask ice and hail, the reason why they're cold ;
> Decaying beauties, why they will grow old ;
> They'll tell thee, fate, that everything doth move,
> Inforces them to this, and me to love.
> There is no reason for our love or hate,
> 'Tis irresistible as Death or Fate ;
> 'Tis not his face ; I've seen enough to see
> That is not good, though doted on by me ;
> Nor is't his tongue that has this conquest won,
> For that at least is equalled by my own ;
> His carriage can to none obliging be,
> 'Tis rude, affected, full of vanity,
> Strangely ill-natured, peevish and unkind,
> Unconstant, false, to jealousy inclined ;
> His temper could not have so great a power,
> 'Tis mutable and changes every hour ;

R

Those vigorous years, that women so adore,
Are past in him, he's twice my age and more ;
And yet I love this false, this worthless man
With all the passion that a woman can,
Dote on his imperfections, though I spy
Nothing to love, I love, and know not why.
Save 'tis decreed in the dark book of fate,
That I should love, and he should be ingrate.

The artificial accent of the age is entirely absent here, as elsewhere in Ephelia, and her couplets are not without vigour. Dryden's *Aureng-Zebe* had not been acted without profit to the ear of this young lady, who might, one fancies, under proper training, have become a genuine poet. She mentions Waller and Cowley with enthusiasm, and addresses a copy of rhymes to Aphra Behn, complimenting her on her "strenuous polite verses." In all this she is the child of her age. But her misfortunes, her amazing frankness in the analysis of her feelings, and the possibility that she was Orinda's daughter, lift her out of the region of commonplace.

1881.   _____

There was a second edition of Ephelia's *Poems*, for a knowledge of which I am indebted to the courtesy of Mr. Edward H. Bierstadt, of New York. It consists of the sheets of the first edition, with a new title dated 1682, and twenty-eight additional leaves at the end containing thirty-two new poems. At least nine of these additional poems are taken from the first (1680) edition of Rochester, and many of the others are of such a character as to make us hope that the chaste Ephelia not merely did not write, but never read them.

SIR GEORGE ETHEREDGE

THAT Sir George Etheredge wrote three plays which are now even less read than the rank and file of Restoration drama, and that he died at Ratisbon, at an uncertain date, by falling down the stairs of his own house and breaking his neck after a banquet, these are the only particulars which can be said to be known, even to students of literature, concerning the career of a very remarkable writer. I shall endeavour to show in the following pages that the entire neglect of the three plays is an unworthy return for the singular part they enjoyed in the creation of modern English comedy; and I shall be able to prove that the one current anecdote of Etheredge's life has no foundation in fact whatever. At the same time I shall have the satisfaction of printing, mainly for the first time, and from manuscript sources, a mass of biographical material which makes this dramatist, hitherto the shadowiest figure of his time, perhaps the poet of the Restoration of whose life and character we know the most.

The information I refer to has been culled from two or three fields. Firstly, from the incidental references to the author scattered in the less-known writings of his contemporaries ; secondly, from an article published in 1750, and from manuscript notes still unprinted, both from the pen of that " busy, curious, thirsty fly " of polite letters, the antiquarian Oldys ; but mostly, and with far the greatest confidence, from a volume in the Manuscript Room of the British Museum, entitled *The Letterbook* of Sir George Etheredge, while he was Envoy Extraordinary at Ratisbon. This volume, which is in the handwriting of an unnamed secretary, contains drafts of over one hundred letters from Etheredge, in English and French, a certain number of letters addressed to him by famous persons, some of his accounts, a hudibrastic poem on his character, and, finally, some extremely caustic letters, treacherously written by the secretary, to bring his master into bad odour in England. I cannot understand how so very curious and important a miscellany has hitherto been overlooked. It was bought by the British Museum in 1837, and, as far as I can find out, has been never referred to, or made use of in any way. It abounds with historical and literary allusions of great interest, and, as far as Etheredge is concerned, is simply a mine of wealth. Having premised so much, I will endeavour to put together, as concisely as possible, what I have been able to collect from all these sources.

On January 9, 1686, Etheredge addressed to the Earl of Middleton an epistle in octosyllabics, which eventually, in 1704, was printed in his *Works*. Readers of Dryden will recollect that a letter in verse to Sir George Etheredge by that poet has

always been included in Dryden's poems, and that
it begins :—

> " To you who live in chill degree,
> As map informs, of fifty-three,
> And do not much for cold atone
> By bringing thither fifty-one."

That Etheredge was fifty-one at the date of this
epistle has hitherto been of little service to us, since
we could not tell when that letter was composed.
The Letterbook, however, in giving us the date of
Etheredge's epistle, to which Dryden's poem was an
immediate answer, supplies us with an important item.
If Etheredge was fifty-one in the early spring of 1686,
he must have been born in 1634, or the first months
of 1635. He was, therefore, a contemporary of Dryden,
Roscommon, and Dorset, rather than, as has always
been taken for granted, of the younger generation of
Wycherley, Shadwell, and Rochester. Nothing is
certainly known of his family. Gildon, who knew him,
reported that he belonged to an old Oxfordshire family.
He was at school at Thame, and, therefore, may probably have been a descendant of Dr. George Etheredge,
the famous Greek and Hebrew scholar, who died about
1590, and whose family estate was at that town. A
Captain George Etheredge, who was prominent among
the early planters of the Bermudas Islands from 1615
to 1630, was presumably the poet's father. Oldys very
vaguely conjectures that he was educated at Cambridge.
Gildon states that for a little while he studied the law,
but adds, what external and internal evidence combine
to prove, that he spent much of his early manhood in

France. My own impression is that from about 1658
to 1663 he was principally in Paris. His French, in
prose and verse, is as fluent as his English; and his
plays are full of allusions that show him to be intimately at home in Parisian matters. What in the
other Restoration playwrights seems a Gallic affectation seems nature in him. My reason for supposing
that he did not arrive in London at the Restoration,
but a year or two later, is that he appears to have
been absolutely unknown in London until his *Comical
Revenge* was acted; and also that he shows in this
play an acquaintance with the new school of French
comedy. He seems to have possessed means of his
own, and to have lived a thoroughly idle life, without
aim or ambition, until, in 1664, it occurred to him, in
his thirtieth year, to write a play.

At any critical moment in the development of a
literature, events follow one another with such head-
long speed, that I must be forgiven if I am a little tiresome about the sequence of dates. According to all
the bibliographers, old and new, Etheredge's earliest
publication was *She Would if She Could*, 1668, immediately followed by *The Comical Revenge*, first
printed in 1669. If this were the case, the claim of
Etheredge to critical attention would be comparatively
small. Oldys, however, mentions that he had heard
of, but never seen, an edition of this latter play of
1664. Neither Langbaine, Gildon, nor any of their
successors believe in the existence of such a quarto,
nor is a copy to be found in the British Museum. However, I have been so fortunate as to pick up two copies

of this mythical quarto of 1664,* the main issue of
which I suppose to have been destroyed by some one
of the many accidents that befell London in that decade,
and Etheredge's precedence of all his more eminent
comic contemporaries is thus secured.

The importance of this date, 1664, is rendered still
more evident when we consider that it constitutes a
claim for its author for originality in two distinct kinds.
The Comical Revenge, or Love in a Tub, which was
acted at the Duke of York's Theatre in Lincoln's Inn
Fields, in the summer of 1664, is a tragi-comedy, of
which the serious portions are entirely written in
rhymed heroics, and the comic portions in prose.   The
whole question of the use of rhyme in English drama
has been persistently misunderstood, and its history
misstated.   In Mr. George Saintsbury's life of Dryden,
for the first time, the subject receives due critical attention, and is approached with the necessary equipment.
But while I thoroughly agree with Mr. Saintsbury's
view of the practice, I think something may be added
from the purely historical side.   The fashion of rhyme
in the drama, then, to be exact, flourished from 1664
until Lee and Dryden returned to blank verse in 1678.
Upon this it suddenly languished, and after being occasionally used until the end of the century, found its last
example in Sedley's *Beauty the Conqueror*, published
in 1702.   The customary opinion that both rhymed
dramatic verse and the lighter form of comedy were
introduced simultaneously with the Restoration is one

* I have also in my collection an issue of 1667, so that the edition
of 1669 must really be the third, and not the first.

of those generalisations which are easily made and slavishly repeated, but which fall before the slightest historical investigation. When the drama was re-organised in 1660, it reappeared in the old debased forms, without the least attempt at novelty. Brome and Shirley had continued to print their plays during the Commonwealth, and in Jasper Mayne had found a disciple who united, without developing, their merits or demerits. During the first years of the Restoration the principal playwrights were Porter, a sort of third-rate Brome, Killigrew, an imitator of Shirley, Stapylton, an apparently lunatic person, and Sir William Lower, to whom is due the praise of having studied French contemporary literature with great zeal, and of having translated Corneille and Quinault.

Wherever these poetasters ventured into verse, they displayed such an incompetence as has never before or since disgraced any coterie of considerable writers. Their blank verse was simply inorganic, their serious dialogue a sort of insanity, their comedy a string of pothouse buffooneries and preposterous "humours." Dryden, in his *Wild Gallant*, and a very clever drama-tist, Wilson, who never fulfilled his extraordinary promise, tried, in 1663, to revive the moribund body of comedy, but always in the style of Ben Jonson; and finally, in 1664, came the introduction of rhymed dramatic verse. For my own part, I frankly confess that I think it was the only course that it was possible to take. The blank iambics of the romantic dramatists had become so execrably weak and distended, the whole movement of dramatic verse had grown so flaccid, that a little restraint in the severe limits of rhyme was absolutely necessary. It has been too rashly taken for granted that we owe the introduction of the new form to Dryden. It is true that in the 1664 preface to *The Rival Ladies*, a play produced on the boards in the winter of 1663, Dryden recommends the use of rhyme in heroic plays, and this fact, combined with the little study given to Dryden's dramas, has led the critics to take for granted that that play is written in rhyme. A glance at the text will show that this is a mistake. *The Rival Ladies* is written in blank verse, and only two short passages of dialogue in the third act exhibit the timid way in which Dryden tested the ear of the public.

Of course lyrical passages in all plays, and the main part of masques, such as the pastorals of Day, had, even in the Elizabethan age, been written in decasyllabic rhymed verse; but these exceptions are as little to the point as is the example under which Dryden shelters himself, *The Siege of Rhodes*. This piece was an opera, and therefore naturally in rhyme. As a point of fact Dryden was the first to propose, and Etheredge the first to carry out, the experiment of writing ordinary plays in rhyme. Encouraged by the preface to *The Rival Ladies*, and urged on by the alexandrines he was accustomed to listen to on the French stage, Etheredge put the whole serious part of his *Comical Revenge* into dialogue, of which this piece from the duel scene is an example :—

> " *Bruce.* Brave men ! this action makes it well appear
> 'Tis honour and not envy brings you here.

> *Beaufort.* We come to conquer, Bruce, and not to see
> Such villains rob us of our victory ;
> Your lives our fatal swords claim as their due,
> We'd wronged ourselves had we not righted you.
> *Bruce.* Your generous courage has obliged us so,
> That to your succour we our safety owe.
> *Lovis.* You've done what men of honour ought to do,
> What in your cause we would have done for you.
> *Beaufort.* You speak the truth, we've but our duty done ;
> Prepare ; duty's no obligation.   [*He strips.*
> None come into the field to weigh what's right,
> This is no place for counsel, but for fight."

And so on. The new style was at once taken up by
the Howards, Killigrews, and Orrerys, and became, as
we have seen, the rage for at least fourteen years.

But the serious portion of *The Comical Revenge* is
not worth considering in comparison with the value of
the prose part. In the underplot, the gay, realistic
scenes which give the play its sub-title of the " Tale of
a Tub," Etheredge virtually founded English comedy,
as it was successively understood by Congreve, Goldsmith, and Sheridan. The Royalists had come back
from France deeply convinced of the superiority of
Paris in all matters belonging to the business of the
stage. Immediately upon the Restoration, in 1661, an
unknown hand had printed an English version of the
Menteur of Corneille. Lower had translated the tragedies of that poet ten years before, and had returned
from his exile in Holland with the dramas of Quinault
in his hand. But the great rush of Royalists back to
England had happened just too soon to give them an
opportunity of witnessing the advent of Molière. By
the end of 1659 the exiled Court, hovering on the Dutch

frontier, had transferred their attention from Paris to London. A few months before this, Molière and his troop had entered Paris, and an unobtrusive performance of *L'Étourdi* had gradually led to other triumphs and to the creation of the greatest modern school of comedy. What gave *The Comical Revenge* of Etheredge its peculiar value and novelty was that it had been written by a man who had seen and understood *L'Étourdi*, *Le Dépit Amoureux*, and *Les Précieuses Ridicules*. Etheredge loitered long enough in Paris for Molière to be revealed to him, and then he hastened back to England with a totally new idea of what comedy ought to be.

The real hero of the first three comedies of Molière is Mascarille, and in like manner the farcical interest of *The Comical Revenge* centres around a valet, Dufoy. When the curtain went up on the first scene, the audience felt that a new thing was being presented to them, new types and an unfamiliar method. Hitherto Ben Jonson had been the one example and theoretical master of all popular comedy. The great aim had been to hold some extravagance of character up to ridicule, to torture one monstrous ineptitude a thousand ways, to exhaust the capabilities of the language in fantastic quips and humours. The comedian had been bound to be in some sort a moralist, to lash himself into an ethical rage about something, and to work by a process of evolution rather than by passionless observation of external manners. Under such a system wit might flourish, but there was no room for humour, in the modern acceptation of the word ; for humour takes things quietly, watches unobtrusively, and is at heart sublimely indifferent. Now, the Royalists had come home from exile weary of all moral discussion, apt to let life slip, longing above all things for rest and pleasure and a quiet hour. It was a happy instinct that led Etheredge to improve a little on Molière himself, and simply hold up the mirror of his play to the genial, sensual life of the young gentlemen his contemporaries. The new-found motto of French comedy, *castigat ridendo mores*, would have lain too heavily on English shoulders; the time of castigation was over, and life flowed merrily down to the deluge of the Revolution.

The master of Dufoy, Sir Frederick Frollick, is not a type, but a portrait; and each lazy, periwigged fop in the pit clapped hands to welcome a friend that seemed to have just strolled in from the Mulberry Garden. He is a man of quality, who can fight at need with spirit and firmness of nerve, but whose customary occupation is the pursuit of pleasure without dignity and without reflection. Like all Etheredge's fine gentlemen, he is a finished fop, although he has the affectation of not caring for the society of fine friends. He spends hours at his toilet, and "there never was a girl more humoursome nor tedious in the dressing of her baby." It seems to me certain that Etheredge intended Sir Frederick as a portrait of himself. Dufoy gives an amusing account of his being taken into Sir Frederick's service. He was lounging on the new bridge in Paris, watching the marionettes and eating custard, when young M. de Grandville drove by in his chariot, in company with his friend Sir Fred. Frollick, and recommended Dufoy as a likely fellow to be entrusted with a certain delicate business, which he carried out so well, that Sir Frederick made him his valet. *The Comical Revenge* is a series of brisk and entertaining scenes strung on a very light thread of plot. Sir Frederick plays fast and loose, all through, with a rich widow who wants to marry him; a person called Wheedle, with an accomplice, Palmer, who dresses up to personate a Buckinghamshire drover, plays off the confidence-trick on a stupid knight, Sir Nicholas Cully, quite in the approved manner of to-day. This pastime, called "coney-catching" a century earlier, was by this time revived under the title of "bubbling." By a pleasant amenity of the printer's the rogues say to one another, "Expect your Kew," meaning "cue."

Meanwhile high love affairs, jealousies, and a tremendous duel, interrupted by the treachery of Puritan villains, have occupied the heroic scenes. The comedy grows fast and furious; Sir Nicholas rides to visit the widow on a tavern-boy's back, with three bottles of wine suspended on a cord behind him. Sir Frederick frightens the widow by pretending to be dead, and Dufoy, for being troublesome and spiteful, is confined by his fellow-servants in a tub, with his head and hands stuck out of holes, and stumbles up and down the stage in that disguise. A brief extract will give a notion of the sprightly and picturesque manner of the dialogue. A lady has sent her maid to Sir Frederick's lodgings to remonstrate with him on his boisterousness.

"*Beaufort.* Jenny in tears! what's the occasion, poor girl?
Maid. I'll tell you, my Lord.

Sir Fred. Buzz ! Set not her tongue a-going again ; she has made more noise than half a dozen paper-mills ; London Bridge at low water is silence to her ; in a word, rambling last night, we knocked at her mistress's lodging, they denied us entrance, whereat a harsh word or two flew out.

Maid. These were not all your heroic actions ? pray tell the consequences, how you marched bravely at the rear of an army of linkboys ; upon the sudden, how you gave defiance, and then, having waged a bloody war with the constable, and having vanquished that dreadful enemy, how you committed a general massacre on the glass windows. Are not these most honourable achievements, such as will be registered to your eternal fame by the most learned historian of Hicks's Hall ?

Sir Fred. Good, sweet Jenny, let's come to a treaty ; do but hear what articles I propose."

The success of *The Comical Revenge* was unprecedented, and it secured its author an instant popularity. While it was under rehearsal, it attracted the attention of the young Lord Buckhurst, then distinguished only as a parliamentary man of promise, but soon to become famous as the poet Earl of Dorset. To him Etheredge dedicated his play, and by him was introduced to that circle of wits, Buckingham, Sedley, and the precocious Rochester, with whom he was to be associated for the rest of his life.

Four years later he produced another and a better play. Meanwhile English comedy had made great advances. Dryden and Wilson had proceeded; Sedley, Shadwell, the Howards, had made their first appearance ; but none of these, not even the author of *The Mulberry Garden*, had quite understood the nature of Etheredge's innovation. In *She Would if She Could* he showed them more plainly what he meant, for he

had himself come under the influence of a masterpiece
of comedy. It is certain to me that the movement of
She Would if She Could is founded upon a reminiscence of *Tartuffe*, which, however, was not printed
until 1669, "une comedie dont on a fait beaucoup de
bruit, qui a esté longtemps persecutée." Etheredge
may have been present at the original performance of
the first three acts, at Versailles, in May 1664; but
it seems to me more probable that he saw the public
representation at Paris in the summer of 1667, and
that he hastened back to England with the plot of his
own piece taking form in his brain.

The only direct similarity between the French and
English plays is this, that Lady Cockwood is a female
Tartuffe, a woman of loud religious pretensions, who
demands respect and devotion for her piety, and who
is really engaged, all the time, in the vain prosecution
of a disgraceful intrigue. Sir Oliver Cockwood, a
boisterous, elderly knight, has come up to town for
the season, in company with his pious lady, who leads
him a sad life, with an old friend, Sir Jocelyn Jolly,
and with the wards of the latter, two spirited girls
called Ariana and Gatty. These people have taken
lodgings in St. James's Street, at the Black Posts, as
Mrs. Sentry, the maid, takes pains to inform young
Mr. Courtall, a gentleman of fashion in whom Lady
Cockwood takes an interest less ingenuous than she
pretends. The scene, therefore, instead of being laid
in Arcadia or Cockayne, sets us down in the heart of
the West End, the fashionable quarter of the London
of 1668. The reader who has not studied old maps,

or the agreeable books of Mr. Wheatley, is likely to
be extremely ill informed as to the limits and scope of
the town two hundred years ago.   St. James's Street,
which contained all the most genteel houses, ran, a
sort of rural road, from Portugal Street, or Piccadilly,
down to St. James's Park.   One of Charles II.'s first
acts was to beautify this district.   St. James's Park,
which then included Green Park, had been a kind of
open meadow.   The King cut a canal through it,
planted it with lime-trees, and turned the path that
led through St. James's Fields into a drive called Pall
Mall.   In St. James's Street rank and fashion clustered,
and young poets contended for the honour of an invi-
tation to Mr. Waller's house on the west side.   Here
also the country gentry lodged when they came up to
town, and a few smart shops had recently been opened
to supply the needs of people of quality.

Such was the bright scene of that comedy of fashionable life of which *She Would if She Could* gives us
a faithful picture.   In a town still untainted by smoke
and dirt, with fresh country airs blowing over it from
all quarters but the east, the gay world of Charles II.'s
court ran through its bright ephemeral existence.
There is no drama in which the physical surroundings
of this life are so picturesquely brought before us as
that of Etheredge.   The play at present under discussion distinguishes itself from the comic work of
Dryden, or Wycherley, or Shadwell, even from that
of Congreve, by the little graphic touches, the intimate
impression, the clear, bright colour of the scenes.   The
two girls, Sir Jocelyn's wards, finding life dreary with

Lady Cockwood and her pieties, put on vizards, and
range the Parks and the Mall without a *chaperon*.
This is an artful contrivance, often afterwards imitated
—as notably by Lord Lansdowne in his *She Gallants*
—but original to Etheredge, and very happy, from the
opportunity it gives of drawing out naïve remarks on
familiar things; for in the second act the girls find
their way to the Mulberry Garden, a public place of
entertainment, adjoining Lord Arlington's mansion of
Goring House, afterwards Buckingham Palace, and
much frequented by a public whom Cromwell's sense
of propriety had deprived of their favourite Spring
Garden. Here Ariana and Gatty meet Lady Cockwood's recalcitrant spark Courtall, walking with his
friend Freeman, and from behind their masks carry
on with them a hazardous flirtation. The end of this
scene, when the two sprightly girls break from their
gallants and appear and reappear, crossing the stage
from opposite corners, amid scenery that reminded
every one in the theatre of the haunt most loved by
Londoners, must have been particularly delightful and
diverting to witness; and all these are circumstances
which we must bear in mind if we wish the drama of
the Restoration to be a living thing to us in reading
it. It was a mundane entertainment, but in its earthly
sincerity it superseded something that had ceased to
be either human or divine.

The two old knights are "harp and violin—nature
has tuned them to play the fool in concert," and their
extravagances hurry the plot to its crisis. They
swagger to their own confusion, and Lady Cockwood

encourages their folly, that she herself may have an opportunity of meeting Courtall. She contrives to give him an appointment in the New Exchange, which seems to have been a sort of arcade leading out of the Strand, with shops on each side. When the curtain rises for the third act, Mrs. Trinkett is sitting in the door of her shop inviting the people of quality to step in : " What d'ye buy ? What d'ye lack, gentlemen ? Gloves, ribbands, and essences ? ribbands, gloves, and essences ? " She is a woman of tact, who, under the pretence of selling " a few fashionable toys to keep the ladies in countenance at a play or in the park," passes letters or makes up rendezvous between people of quality. At her shop the gallants " scent their eyebrows and periwigs with a little essence of oranges or jessamine ; " and so Courtall occupies himself till Lady Cockwood arrives. Fortunately for him, Ariana and Gatty, who are out shopping, arrive at the same moment ; so he proposes to take them all in his coach to the Bear in Drury Lane for a dance. The party at the Bear is like a scene from some artistically-mounted drama of our own day. Etheredge, with his singular eye for colour, crowds the stage with damsels in sky-blue, and pink, and flame-coloured taffetas. To them arrive Sir Oliver and Sir Jocelyn ; but as Sir Oliver was drunk overnight, Lady Cockwood has locked up all his clothes except his russet suit of humiliation, in which he is an object of ridicule and persecution to all the bright crowd, who

"Wave the gay wreathe, and titter as they prance."

In this scene Etheredge introduces a sword, a velvet coat, a flageolet, a pair of bands, with touches that remind one of Metzu or Gheraerdt Douw. Sir Oliver, who is the direct prototype of Vanbrugh's Sir John Brute, gets very drunk, dances with his own wife in her vizard, and finally brings confusion upon the whole company. The ladies rush home, whither Freeman comes to console Lady Cockwood ; a noise is heard, and he is promptly concealed in a cupboard. Courtall enters, and then a fresh hubbub is heard, for Sir Oliver has returned. Courtall is hurried under a table just in time for the old knight to come in and perceive nothing. But he has brought a beautiful China orange home to appease his wife, and as he shows this to her it drops from his fingers, and runs under the table where Courtall lies. The maid, a girl of resource, promptly runs away with the candle, and, in the stage darkness, Courtall is hurried into the cupboard, where he finds Freeman. The threads are gradually unravelled ; Courtall and Freeman are rewarded, for nothing in particular, by the hands of Ariana and Gatty, and Lady Cockwood promises to go back to the country and behave properly ever after. The plot of so slight a thing is a gossamer fabric, and scarcely bears analysis ; but the comedy was by far the most sprightly performance at that time presented to any audience in Europe save that which was listening to Molière.

Etheredge had not dedicated *She Would if She Could* to any patron ; but the grateful town accepted it with enthusiasm, and its author was the most popular of the hour. It was confidently hoped that he

would give his energies to the stage; but an indolence
that was habitual to him, and against which he never
struggled, kept him silent for eight years.   During
this time, however, he preserved his connection with
the theatres, encouraged Medbourne the actor to trans-
late *Tartuffe*, and wrote an epilogue for him when
that play was produced in England in 1670.   He
wrote, besides, a great number of little amatory pieces,
chiefly in octosyllabics, which have never been collected.   Oldys says, in one of his manuscript notes,
that he once saw a *Miscellany*, printed in 1672,
almost full of verses by Etheredge, but without his
name.   I have not been able to trace this; but most
of the numerous collections of contemporary verse
contained something of his, down to the *Miscellany*
of 1701.   If any one took the trouble to extract
these, at least fifty or sixty poems could be put
together; but they are none of them very good.
Etheredge had but little of the lyrical gift of such
contemporaries as Dryden, Rochester, and Sedley;
his rhymed verse is apt to be awkward and languid.
This may be as good an opportunity as any other of
quoting the best song of his that I have been able
to unearth :—

> " Ye happy swains, whose hearts are free
>   From love's imperial chain,
>   Take warning and be taught by me
>   To avoid th' enchanting pain ;
>   Fatal the wolves to trembling flocks,
>   Fierce winds to blossoms prove,
>   To careless seamen, hidden rocks,
>   To human quiet—love.

> " Fly the fair sex, if bliss you prize—
>   The snake's beneath the flower ;
> Who ever gazed on beauteous eyes
>   And tasted quiet more ?
> How faithless is the lovers' joy !
>   How constant is their care !
> The kind with falsehood do destroy,
>   The cruel with despair."

We learn from Shadwell, in the preface to *The Humorists* of 1671, that the success of *She Would if She Could* was endangered by the slovenly playing of the actors. This may have helped to disgust the fastidious Etheredge. At all events, the satirists began to be busy with the name of so inert a popular playwright ; and, in 1675, Rochester expressed a general opinion in the doggerel of his *Session of the Poets :*—

> " Now Apollo had got gentle George in his eye,
> And frankly confessed that, of all men that writ,
> There's none had more fancy, sense, judgment, and wit ;
> But i' the crying sin, idleness, he was so hardened
> That his long seven years' silence was not to be pardoned."

" Gentle George " gave way, and composed, with all the sparkle, wit, and finish of which he was capable, his last and best-known piece, *The Man of Mode, or Sir Fopling Flutter*, brought out at the Duke's Theatre in the summer of 1676. Recollecting his threatened fiasco in 1668, Etheredge determined to put himself under powerful patronage, and dedicated his new play to Mary of Modena, the young Duchess of York, who remained his faithful patroness until fortune bereft her of the power to give. Sir Car Scroope wrote the prologue, Dryden the epilogue, and the play was acted by the best company of the time—Betterton, Harris, Medbourne, and the wife of Shadwell, while the part of Belinda was in all probability taken by the matchless Mrs. Barry, the new glory of the stage.

The great merit of *The Man of Mode* rests in the brilliance of the writing and the force of the characterisation.   There is no plot.   People of the old school, like Captain Alexander Radcliffe, who liked plot above all other things in a comedy, decried the manner of Etheredge, and preferred to it "the manly art of brawny Wycherley," the new writer, whose *Country Wife* had just enjoyed so much success; but, on the whole, the public was dazzled and delighted with the new types and the brisk dialogue, and united to give Sir Fopling Flutter a warmer welcome than greeted any other stage-hero during Charles II.'s reign.   There was a delightful heroine, with abundance of light-brown hair, and lips like the petals of "a Provence rose, fresh on the bush, ere the morning sun has quite drawn up the dew;" there was a shoemaker whom every one knew, and an orange-woman whom everybody might have known — characters which Dickens would have laughed at and commended; there was Young Bellair, in which Etheredge drew his own portrait; there was the sparkling Dorimant, so dressed that all the pit should know that my Lord Rochester was intended; there was Medley, Young Bellair's bosom friend, in whom the gossips discovered the portrait of Sir Charles Sedley; above all, there was Sir Fopling Flutter, the monarch of all beaux and dandies, the froth of Parisian affectation—a delightful personage, almost as alive to us to-day as to the enchanted audience of 1676. During two acts the great creature was spoken of, but never seen. Just arrived from France, all the world had heard about him, and was longing to see him, "with a pair of gloves up to his elbows, and his periwig was more exactly curled than a lady's head newly dressed for a ball." At last, in the third act, when curiosity has been raised to a fever, the fop appears. He is introduced to a group of ladies and gentlemen of quality, and when the first civilities are over he begins at once to criticise their dress :—

"*Lady Townley*. Wit, I perceive, has more power over you than beauty, Sir Fopling, else you would not have let this lady stand so long neglected.

Sir Fopling (to Emilia). A thousand pardons, madam! Some civilities due of course upon the meeting a long-absent friend. The *éclat* of so much beauty, I confess, ought to have charmed me sooner.

Emilia. The *brilliant* of so much good language, sir, has much more power than the little beauty I can boast.

Sir Fop. I never saw anything prettier than this high work, on your *point d'Espagne*.

Emilia. 'Tis not so rich as *point de Venise*.

Sir Fop. Not altogether, but looks cooler, and is more proper for the season. Dorimant, is not that Medley?

Dori. The same, sir.

Sir Fop. Forgive me, sir, in this *embarras* of civilities, I could not come to have you in my arms sooner. You understand an equipage the best of any man in town, I hear!

Medley. By my own you would not guess it.

Sir Fop. There are critics who do not write, sir. Have you taken notice of the *calèche* I brought over?

Medley. O yes ! it has quite another air than the English make.

Sir Fop. 'Tis as easily known from an English tumbrel as an inns-of-court man is from one of us.

Dori. Truly there is a *bel-air* in *calèches* as well as men.

Medley. But there are few so delicate as to observe it.

Sir Fop. The world is generally very *grossier* here indeed.

Lady Townley. He's very fine (*looking at Sir Fop*.).

Emilia. Extreme proper.

Sir Fop. O, a slight suit I had made to appear in at my first arrival—not worthy your admiration, ladies.

Dori. The pantaloon is very well mounted.

Sir Fop. The tassels are new and pretty.

Medley. I never saw a coat better cut.

Sir Fop. It makes me look long-waisted, and, I think, slender.

Lady Townley. His gloves are well-fingered, large and graceful.

Sir Fop. I was always eminent for being *bien-ganté*.

Emilia. He must wear nothing but what are originals of the most famous hands in Paris !

Sir Fop. You are in the right, madam.

Lady Townley. The suit ?

Sir Fop. Barroy.

Emilia. The garniture ?

Sir Fop. Le Gras.

Medley. The shoes?

Sir Fop. Piccat.

Dori. The periwig?

Sir Fop. Chedreux.

Lady Townley and Emilia (*together*). The gloves?

Sir Fop. Orangerie (*holding up his hands to them*). You know the smell, ladies ? "

The hand that throws in these light touches, in a key of rose-colour on pale gray, no longer reminds us of Molière, but exceedingly of Congreve. A recent critic has very justly remarked that in mere wit, the continuity of brilliant dialogue in which the action does not seek to advance, Molière is scarcely the equal of Congreve at his best, and the brightest scenes of *The Man of Mode* show the original direction taken by Etheredge in that line which was more specially to mark the triumph of English comedy. But the author of *Love for Love* was still in the nursery when *The Man of Mode* appeared, as it were, to teach him how to write. Until Congreve reached manhood, Etheredge's example seemed to have been lost, and the lesson he attempted to instil to have fallen on admiring hearers that were incapable of repeating it.

The shallowness, vivacity, and vanity of Sir Fopling are admirably maintained. In the scene of which part has just been quoted, after showing his intimate knowledge of all the best tradesmen in Paris, some one drops the name of Bussy, to see if he is equally at home among literary notabilities. But he supposes that Bussy d'Ambois is meant, and is convicted of having never heard of Bussy Rabutin. This is a curiously early notice of a famous writer who survived it nearly twenty years, it does not seem that any French critic has observed this. Sir Fopling Flutter is so eminently the best of Etheredge's creations that we are tempted to give one more sample of his quality. He has come with two or three other sparks to visit Dorimant at his rooms, and he dances a *pas seul*.

" *Young Bellair.* See! Sir Fopling is dancing!

Sir Fop. Prithee, Dorimant, why hast thou not a glass hung up here? A room is the dullest thing without one.

Y. Bell. Here is company to entertain you.

Sir Fop. But I mean in case of being alone. In a glass a man may entertain himself,——

Dori. The shadow of himself indeed.

Sir Fop. Correct the errors of his motion and his dress.

Medley. I find, Sir Fopling, in your solitude you remember the saying of the wise man, and study yourself!

Sir Fop. 'Tis the best diversion in our retirements. Dorimant, thou art a pretty fellow, and wearest thy clothes well, but I never saw thee have a handsome cravat. Were they made up like mine, they'd give another air to thy face. Prithee let me send my man to dress thee one day. By heavens, an Englishman cannot tie a ribband.

Dori. They are something clumsy-fisted.

Sir Fop. I have brought over the prettiest fellow that ever spread a toilet ; he served some time under Merille, the greatest *génie* in the world for a *valet de chambre*.

Dori. What, he who formerly belonged to the Duke of Candolle ?

Sir Fop. The very same—and got him his immortal reputation.

Dori. You've a very fine brandenburgh on, Sir Fopling !

Sir Fop. It serves to wrap me up after the fatigue of a ball.

Medley. I see you often in it, with your periwig tied up.

Sir Fop. We should not always be in a set dress ; 'tis more *en cavalier* to appear now and then in a *deshabille.*"

In these wholly fastastical studies of manners we feel less than in the more serious portions of the comedy that total absence of moral purpose, high aim, or even honourable instinct which was the canker of the age. A negligence that pervaded every section of the upper classes, which robbed statesmen of their patriotism and the clergy of their earnestness, was only too exactly mirrored in the sprightly follies of the stage. Yet even there we are annoyed by a heroine who is discovered eating a nectarine, and who, rallied on buying a "filthy nosegay," indignantly rebuts the accusation, and declares that nothing would induce her to smell such vulgar flowers as stocks and carnations, or anything that blossoms, except orange-flowers and tuberose. It is a frivolous world, Strephon bending on one knee to Cloe, who fans the pink blush on her painted cheek, while Momus peeps, with a grimace, through the curtains behind her. They form an engaging trio, *mais ce n'est pas de la vie humaine.*

The Man of Mode was licensed on June 3, 1676; it enjoyed an unparalleled success, and before the month was out its author was fleeing for his life. We learn this from the *Hatton Correspondence*, first printed in 1879. It seems that in the middle of June, Etheredge, Rochester, and two friends, Captain Bridges and Mr. Downes, went to Epsom on a Sunday night. They were tossing some fiddlers in a blanket for refusing to play, when a barber, who came to see what the noise was, as a practical joke induced them to knock up the constable. They did so with a vengeance, for they smashed open his door, entered his house, and broke his head, giving him a severe beating. At last they were overpowered by the watch, and Etheredge having made a submissive oration, the row seemed to be at an end, when suddenly Lord Rochester, like a coward as he was, drew his sword on the constable, who had dismissed his men. The constable shrieked out "Murder!" and the watch returning, one of them broke the skull of Downes with his staff. The others ran away, and the watchmen were left to run poor Downes through with a pike. He lingered until the 29th, when Charles

Hatton records that he is dead, and that Etheredge and Rochester have absconded.

Four years afterwards the *Hatton Correspondence* gives us another glimpse of our poet, again in trouble. On January 14, 1680, the roof of the tennis-court in the Haymarket fell down. "Sir George Etheredge and several others were very dangerously hurt. Sir Charles Sidley had his skull broke, and it is thought it will be mortal." Sidley, or Sedley, flourished for twenty years more; but we may note that here, for the first time, our dramatist is "Sir George." It is evident that he had been knighted since 1676, when he was plain "George Etheredge, Esq." In a manuscript poem called *The Present State of Matrimony*, he is accused of having married a rich widow to facilitate his being knighted, and with success. The entries in *The Letterbook* give me reason to believe that he was not maligned in this. But he seems to have lived on very bad terms with his wife, and to have disgraced himself by the open protection of Mrs. Barry, after Rochester's death in 1680. By this famous actress, whose name can no more be omitted from the history of literature than that of Mrs. Gwynn from the history of statecraft, he had a daughter, on whom he settled five or six thousand pounds, but who died young.

The close of Etheredge's career was spent in the diplomatic service. When this commenced is more than I have been able to discover. From *The Letterbook* it appears that he was for some time envoy of Charles II. at the Hague. It would even seem that he was sent to Constantinople, for a contemporary satirist speaks of

> " Ovid to Pontus sent for too much wit,
> Etheredge to Turkey for the want of it."

Certain expressions in *The Letterbook* make me suspect that he had been in Sweden. But it is not until the accession of James II. that his figure comes out into real distinctness. In this connection I think it would be hard to exaggerate the value of *The Letterbook*, which I am about to introduce to my readers. After reading it from end to end I feel that I know Sir George Etheredge, hitherto the most phantasmal of the English poets, better than I can know any literary man of his time, better than Dryden, better, perhaps, than Milton.

In February 1685, James II. ascended the throne, and by March, Mary of Modena had worked so assiduously for her favourite that this warrant, for the discovery of which I owe my best thanks to Mr. Noel Sainsbury, was entered in the Privy Signet Book :—

"Warrant to pay Sir Geo. Etheredge (whom his Maj. has thought fit to employ in his service in Germany), 3*l*. per diem."

On March 5 *The Letterbook* was bought, and Etheredge and his secretary started for the Continent. Why they loitered at the Hague and in Amsterdam does not appear, but their journey was made in so leisurely a manner that they did not arrive in Ratisbon until August 30. It does appear, however, that the dissipated little knight behaved very ill in Holland,

and spent one summer's night dead drunk in the streets of the Hague.   On his arrival at Ratisbon, he had two letters of recommendation, one from Barillon to the French ambassador, the other from the Spanish ambassador to the Burgundian minister.*   The first of these he used at once, and cultivated the society at the French Embassy in a way that would have been extremely impolitic if it had not, without doubt, been entered upon in accordance with instructions from home.   It was doubtless known to Etheredge, although a secret at the German court, that James had commenced his reign by opening private negotiations with France.   The poet settled in a very nice house, with a garden running down to the Danube, set up a carriage and good horses, valets, and "a cook, though I cannot hope to be well served by the latter" in this barbarous Germany.   On December 24 he wrote two letters, parts of which may be quoted here.   To Lord Sunderland he writes :—

"Since my coming here I have had a little fever, which has been the reason I have not paid my duty so regular as I ought to do to your Lordship. I am now pretty well recovered, and hope I am quit at a reasonable price for what I was to pay on the change of climate, and a greater change in my manner of living. Is it not enough to breed an ill habit of body in a man who was used to sit up till morning to be forced, for want of knowing what to do with himself, to go to bed in the evening ; one who has been used to live with all freedom, never to approach any

---

* There was no Burgundy known to history at this date. Mr. Samuel R. Gardiner suggests to me that this was an agent of the Spanish governor at Brussels, the Spanish Netherlands being part of the old circle of Burgundy.

one without ceremony ; one who has been used to run up and
down to find variety of company, to sit at home and entertain
himself in solitude? One would think the Diet had made a
Reichsgutachten to banish all pastimes in the city. Here was
the Countess of Nostitz, but malice would not let her live in
quiet, and she is lately removed to Prague. Good company
met at her house, and she had a little *hombre* to entertain them.
A more commode lady, by what I hear, never kept a basset
[table] in London. If I do well after all this, you must allow
me to be a great philosopher ; and I dare affirm Cato left not
the world with more firmness of soul than I did England."

And to a friend in Paris, on the same date :—

" Le divertissement le plus galant du pays cet hiver c'est le
traîneau, où l'on se met en croupe de quelque belle Allemande,
de manière que vous ne pouvez ni la voir, ni lui parler, à cause
d'un diable de tintamarre des sonnettes dont les harnais sont
tous garnis."

In short, he very soon learned the limitations of the
place. His letters are filled with complaints of the
boorish manners of the people, the dreary etiquette
which encumbers the Court and the Diet, and the
solitude he feels in being separated from all his literary
friends. The malice of the secretary informs us that
Sir George soon gave up his precise manner of living,
and adopted a lazier style. He seldom rose until two
or three p.m., dined at five or six, and then went to
the French ambassador's for three or four hours.
Finding time hang heavy on his hands, he took to
gaming with any disreputable Frenchman that happened to pass through the town. Already, early in
1686, a scoundrel called Purpurat, from Vienna, has
got round him by flatteries and presents of tobacco,

and has robbed him of ten thousand crowns at cards. When, however, things have come to this pass, Etheredge wakes up, and on the suggestion of M. Purpurat that he will be going back to Vienna, detains him until he has won nearly all his money back again, and finally is quit with the loss of a pair of pistols, with his crest upon them, which Purpurat shows in proof of his ascendency over the English ambassador.

These matters occupy the spring and summer of 1686, but there is nothing said about them in the letters home. These letters, however, are cheerful enough. In January he encloses, with his despatches to the Earl of Middleton, a long squib in octosyllabic verse, which the English minister, who is ill at these numbers, gets Dryden to answer in kind. A cancelled couplet in the first draft of the former remarks :—

> " Let them who live in plenty flout ;
> I must make shift with sauer kraut."

In June 1686 he writes to Middleton that he has "not this week received any letter from England, which is a thing that touches me here as nearly as ever a disappointment did in London with the woman I loved most tenderly." Middleton comforts him by telling him that the king, after a performance of *The Man of Mode*, remarked to him that he expected Etheredge to put on the sock, and write a new comedy while he was at Ratisbon. Once or twice, in subsequent letters, the poet refers to this idea ; but the weight of affairs, combined with his native indolence, prevented his attempting the task. Meanwhile, he does not seem to have neglected his duty as it was understood in those days. He writes, so he says at least, twice every week about state matters to Middleton, and, notwithstanding all the spiteful messages sent home about him, he does not seem to have ever lost the confidence of James and his ministers. These latter were most of them his private friends, and in his most official communications he suddenly diverges into some waggish allusion to old times. His attitude at Ratisbon was not what we should now demand from an envoy. The English people, the English Parliament, do not exist for him; his one standard of duty is the personal wish of the king. By indulging the bias of James, which indeed was his own bias, an excessive partiality for all things French, he won himself, as we shall see, the extreme ill-will of the Germans. But the only really serious scrape into which he got, an affair which annoyed him throughout the autumn and winter of 1686, does not particularly redound to his discredit.

It is a curious story, and characteristic of the times; *The Letterbook*, by giving Etheredge's own account, and also the secretary's spiteful rendering, enables us to follow the circumstances pretty closely. A troop of actors from Nuremberg came over to Ratisbon in the summer of 1686, with a star who seems to have been the leading actress of her time in South Germany. This lady, about whom the only biographical fact that we discover is that her Christian name was Julia, seems to have been respectability itself. Even the enemies of Etheredge did not suggest that any immoral connection

T

existed between them, and on the last day of the year, after having suffered all sorts of annoyance on her behalf, he still complains that she is as *fière* as she is fair. But actors were then still looked upon in Germany, as to some extent even in France, as social pariahs, vagabonds whom it was disgraceful to know, except as servants of a high order; artistic menials, whose vocation it was to amuse the great. But England was already more civilised than this; Etheredge was used to meet Betterton and his stately wife at the court of his monarch, and even the sullied reputation of such lovely sinners as Mrs. Barry did not shut them out of Whitehall. Etheredge, therefore, charmed in his Abdera of letters by the art and wit and beauty of Julia, paid her a state visit in his coach, and prayed for the honour of a visit in return. Ratisbon was beside itself with indignation. Every sort of social insult was heaped upon the English envoy. At a *fête champêtre* the lubberly Germans crowded out their elbows so as to leave him no place at table; the grand ladies cut him in the street when their coaches met his, and it was made a subject of venomous report to England that, in spite of public opinion, he refused to quit the acquaintance of the *comédienne*, as they scornfully named her.

At last, on the evening of November 25, a group of students and young people of quality, who had heard that Julia was dining with the English ambassador to meet the French envoy and one or two guests, surrounded Etheredge's house in masks, threw stones at the windows, shouted "Great is Diana of the English envoy!" and, on Etheredge's appearing, roared to him to throw out to them the *comédienne*. The plucky little poet answered by arming his lacqueys and his maids with sword-sticks, pokers, and whatever came to hand, and by suddenly charging the crowd at the head of his little garrison. The Germans were routed for a moment, and Etheredge took advantage of his success to put Julia into his coach, jump in beside her, and conduct her to her lodging. The crowd, however, was too powerful for him ; and though she slept that night in safety, next day she was thrown into prison by the magistrates, for causing a disturbance in the streets.

Etheredge, not knowing what to do, wrote this epistle to the ringleader of the attack on his house, the Baron Von Sensheim :—

" J'estois surpris d'apprendre que ce joly gentil-homme travesty en Italien hier au soir estoit le Baron de Senheim. Je ne savois pas que les honnetes gens se méloient avec des lacquais ramassez pour faire les fanfarons, et les batteurs de pavéz. Si vous avez quelque chose à me dire, faites le moy savoir comme vous devez, et ne vous amusez plus à venir insulter mes Domestiques ni ma maison, soyez content que vous l'avez échappé belle et ne retournez plus chercher les récompences de telles follies pour vos beaux compagnons. J'ay des autres mesures à prendre avec eux."

To this he received a vague and impertinent reply in German. Opinion in the town was so strongly moved, that for some time Etheredge never went out without having a musketoon in his coach, and each of his footmen armed with a brace of pistols ready charged. Eventually the lady was released, on the understanding that she and her company should leave

the town, which they did, proceeding in the last days
of 1686 across the Danube to Bayrischenhoff,* where
Etheredge visited them. It was in the midst of this
turmoil that Etheredge composed some of his best
occasional verses. I do not think they have ever been
printed before :—

> " Upon the downs when shall I breathe at ease,
>   Have nothing else to do but what I please,
>   In a fresh cooling shade upon the brink
>   Of Arden's spring, have time to read and think,
>   And stretch, and sleep, when all my care shall be
>   For health, and pleasure my philosophy ?
>   When shall I rest from business, noise, and strife,
>   Lay down the soldier's and the courtier's life,
>   And in a little melancholy seat
>   Begin at last to live and to forget
>   The nonsense and the farce of what the fools call great."

There is something strangely Augustan about this
fragment; we should expect it to be dated 1716 rather
than 1686, and to be signed by some Pomfret or Tickell
of the school of Addison.

On New-Year's Day, 1687, Etheredge encloses in a
letter to the Earl of Middleton a French song, inspired
by Julia, which may deserve to be printed as a
curiosity. I give it in the author's spelling, which
shone more in French than English :—

> " Garde le secret de ton ame,
>   Et ne te laisse pas flatter,
>   Qu'Iris espargnera ta flamme,
>   Si tu luy permets d'éclater ;

---

* That is to say, I suppose, the modern Stadt-am-Hof.

Son Humeur, à l'amour rebelle,
  Exile tous ses doux desirs,
Et la tendresse est criminelle
  Qui veut luy parler en soupirs.

" Puis que tu vis sous son empire,
  Il faut luy cacher ton destin,
Si tu ne veux le rendre pire
  Percé du trait de son dédain ;
D'une rigeur si delicate
  Ton cœur ne peut rien esperer,
Derobe donc à cette ingrate
  La vanité d'en trionfer."

In February a change of ministry in London gives him something else to think about ; he hears a report that he is to be sent to Stockholm ; he writes eagerly to his patrons for news. On the eleventh of the month he receives a tremendous snub from the Treasury about his extravagance, and is told that in future his extra expenses must never exceed fifty pounds every three months. He is, indeed, assailed with many annoyances, for his wife writes on the subject of the *comédienne* from Nuremberg, and roundly calls him a rogue. Upon this Etheredge writes to the poet, Lord Mulgrave, and begs him to make up the quarrel, sending by the same post, on March 13, 1687, this judicious letter to Lady Etheredge :—

"My Lady,—I beg your pardon for undertaking to advise you. I am so well satisfied by your last letter of your prudence and judgment that I shall never more commit the same error. I wish there were copies of it in London that it might serve as a pattern to modest wives to write to their husbands ; you shall find me so careful hereafter how I offend you that I will no more subscribe myself your loving, since you take it ill, but,—Madam, Y^r. most dutyfull husband,   G. E."

His letters of 1687 are very full of personal items and scraps of literary gossip. It would be impossible on this, the first introduction of *The Letterbook*, to do justice to all its wealth of allusion. He carefully repeats the harangue of the Siamese ambassadors on leaving the German court; he complains again and again of the neglect of the Count of Windisgrätz, who represents the Prince of Nassau, and is all-powerful in the Palatinate; he complains still more bitterly of the open rudeness of the Countess Windisgrätz; he is anxious about the welfare of Nat Lee, at that time shut up in a lunatic asylum, but about to emerge for the production of *The Princess of Cleve*, in 1689, and then to die; he writes a delightful letter to Betterton, on May 26, 1687, asking for news of all kinds about the stage. He says that his chief diversion is music, that he has three musicians living in the house, that they play all the best operas, and that a friend in Paris sends him whatever good music is published. One wonders whether Etheredge knew that Jean Baptiste Lully had died a week or two before this letter was written. News of the success of Sedley's *Bellamira* reaches him in June 1687, and provokes from him this eloquent defence of his old friend's genius :—

"I am glad the town has so good a taste as to give the same just applause to S^r. Charles Sidley's writing which his friends have always done to his conversation. Few of our plays can boast of more wit than I have heard him speak at a supper. Some barren sparks have found fault with what he has formerly done, only because the fairness of the soil has produced so big a crop. I daily drink his health, my Lord Dorset's, your own, and all our friends'."

A few allusions to famous men of letters, all made in
1687, may be placed side by side :—

"Mr. Wynne has sent me *The Hind and the Panther*, by
which I find John Dryden has a noble ambition to restore
poetry to its ancient dignity in wrapping up the mysteries of
religion in verse. What a shame it is to me to see him a
saint, and remain still the same devil [myself].

"Dryden finds his *Macflecknoe* does no good : I wish him
better success with his *Hind and Panther*.

"General Dryden is an expert captain, but I always thought
him fitter for execution than council.

"Remind my Lord Dorset how he and I carried two
draggled-tailed nymphs one bitter frosty night over the Thames
to Lambeth.

"If he happens in a house with Mr. Crown, John's songs will
charm the whole family."

A letter from Dryden, full of pleasant chat, informs
Etheredge in February that Wycherley is sick of an
apoplexy. The envoy begs leave, later in the year, to
visit his friend, the Count de Thun, whose acquaintance
he made in Amsterdam, and who is now at Munich, but
permission is refused. In October the whole Electoral
College invites itself to spend the afternoon in Sir
George Etheredge's garden, and he entertains them so
lavishly, and with so little infusion of Danube water in
the wine, that next morning he is ill in bed. His in-
disposition turns to tertian ague, and towards the end
of the month he asks to be informed how quinine should
be prepared. He compares himself philosophically to
Falstaff, however, and by Christmas time grows pensive
at the thought of the "plum-pottage" at home, and is
solicitous about a black laced hood and pair of scarlet

stockings which he has ordered from London.   In
January 1688 he laments that Sedley has grown
temperate and Dorset uxorious, but vows that he will
be on his guard, and remain foppish.   The last extract
that has any literary interest is taken from a letter
dated March 8, 1688 :—

"Mrs. Barry bears up as well as I myself have done ; my
poor Lord Rochester [Wilmot, not Hyde] could not weather
the Cape, and live under the line fatal to puling constitutions.
Though I have given up writing plays, I should be glad to read
a good one, wherefore pray let Will Richards send me Mr.
Shadwell's [*The Squire of Alsatia*] as soon as it is printed,
that I may know what is being done. . . . Nature, you know,
intended me for an idle fellow, and gave me passions and
qualities fit for that blessed calling, but fortune has made a
changeling of me, and necessity now forces me to set up for
a fop of business."

Three days after this he writes the last letter preserved in *The Letterbook*, and, but for an appendix to
that volume, we might have believed the popular story
that Etheredge fell downstairs at Ratisbon and broke
his neck.   But the treacherous secretary continues to
write in 1689, and gives us fresh particulars.   He
states that his quarrel with Sir George was that he had
been promised £60 per annum, and could only get £40
out of his master.   He further declares that to the last
Etheredge did not know ten words of Dutch (German),
and had not merely to make use of a French interpreter,
but had to entrust his private business to one or other
of his lacqueys ; and that moreover he spent a great
part of his time "visiting all the alehouses of the town,
accompanied by his servants, his *valet de chambre*, his

hoffmaster, and his dancing and fighting master, all with their coats turned inside outwards."

In his anger he lets us know what became of Etheredge at the Revolution, for in a virulent Latin harangue at the close of *The Letterbook* he states that after a stay at Ratisbon of "tres annos et sex menses," accurately measured, for the secretary's cry is a cry for gold, Etheredge fled to Paris. This flight must therefore have taken place early in March 1689. "Quando hinc abijt ad asylum apud Gallos quærendum," the poet left his books behind him, a proof that his taking leave was sudden and urgent. The secretary gives a list of them, and it is interesting to find the only play-books mentioned are Shakespeare's *Works* and the *Œuvres de Molière*, in two vols., probably the edition of 1682. I note also the works of Sarrazin and of Voiture.

At this point, I am sorry to say, the figure of Etheredge at present eludes me. There seems no clue whatever to the date of his death, except that in an anonymous pamphlet, written by John Dennis, and printed in 1722, Etheredge is spoken of as having been dead "nearly thirty years." Dennis was over thirty at the Revolution, and is as trustworthy an authority as we could wish for. By this it would seem that Etheredge died about 1693, nearer the age of sixty than fifty. But Colonel Chester found the record of administration to the estate of a Dame Mary Etheredge, widow, dated Feb. 1, 1692. As we know of no other knight of the name, except Sir James Etheredge, who died in 1736, this was probably the poet's relict; and it may yet appear that he died in 1691.   He was a short, brisk man, with a quantity of fair hair, and a fine complexion, which he spoiled by drinking.   He left no children, but his brother, who long survived him, left a daughter, who is said to have married Aaron Hill.

[It is to the kindness of my friend Mr. Edward Scott that I owe the discovery of *The Letterbook*. I have also to acknowledge valuable help from Mr. W. Noel Sainsbury, who has examined the State Papers for me.   The late Colonel Joseph Chester courteously consented to search his invaluable catalogues of the registers.   I have acknowledged in the body of the chapter my debt to Oldys' manuscript notes and conjectures.   To protect myself from the charge of plagiarism, I may add that the anonymous article on Etheredge in the new edition of the *Encyclopædia Britannica*, in which the critical view I have here taken was first propounded in outline, is from my pen.   In all cases my dates are new style.]

THOMAS OTWAY

WE gaze at the range of wooded hills that rises
between us and the sky, and we think we
perceive clearly enough of what the blue-grey
wall consists. It appears to be a single mass, diversi-
fied no doubt by upland and hollow, but in its general
character solid and complete. Yet we approach nearer
and nearer, we scale a line of hills, we descend into a
valley, and still the old loftier range is before us. We
begin to understand that what seemed a solitary barrier
was in fact only a series of independent ranges, each
distinct in itself, but all melted together in the harmonious perspective. So it is in literature. But even
as the apparent extent of a mountain range, though
not strictly accurate, is yet a good general type of
the tendency of incline in the particular district, so
the wide groups that form themselves in the history
of letters, though curiously inexact to the minute
observer, are yet excellent landmarks in the large
field of study.

In reviewing the dramatic literature of England we
are accustomed to speak loosely of the drama of the
Restoration, as of a school of playwrights flourishing
from 1660 to 1700, and we attribute certain qualities
without much distinction to all the plays of this wide

period. We are not incorrect in this rough classification; there are certain obvious features which all the dramatists who survived the first date and were born within the second unite in displaying. A Gallican vein runs through tragedy and comedy, just as surely as an Italian vein ran through the Elizabethan drama.

From Davenant to Cibber the aims are the same, the ideal the same, the poetic sentiment the same. But when we look a little closer, we are ready to forget that this general coincidence exists. When the drama was publicly reinstituted under Charles II. it was a pompous and gorgeous thing, with a new panoply of theatrical display. Under the auspices of Davenant, a set of fashionables wrote stilted pieces of parade which hardly belonged to literature at all. The two families of the Killigrews and the Howards were the main supporters of this rustling, silken school, and the year 1665 was the approximate date of its decay. Dryden sprang, a somewhat tawdry Phœnix, from its ashes, and, in company with Etheredge, Wilson, and Shadwell, recalled the drama to something like good sense. This was the first epoch of the Restoration, and for five years these four names were the only tolerable ones in English drama.

Between 1670 and 1675 this group received a sudden accession of number so remarkable, that it has had no parallel since the days of Marlowe. Within four years Crowne, Aphra Behn, Wycherley, George, Duke of Buckingham, Lacy, Settle, Otway, and Lee published each his first play, and in company with these more or less distinguished men, a whole army of forgotten playwrights burst upon the world. After this efflorescence, this aloe-blossoming of bustling talent, twenty years passed quietly on without a single new writer, except Southerne, who belonged in age to the earlier, and by genius to the later, school. Then, again, between 1693 and 1700, there ripened simultaneously a new crop of dramatists,—Congreve, Cibber, Mary Pix, Vanbrugh, Farquhar, and Rowe. It is plain that some designation should distinguish the first group from the second.

I would propose retaining the name of Restoration dramatists for the men of the earlier period, to entitle the contemporaries of Congreve the Orange dramatists: thus getting rid of the deceptive impression that the excesses and the elegances of these last writers were in any way connected with the reign of Charles II., who died when most of them were children. It will be found that something of the bluff wit of Jonson still lingered about the humour of Wycherley and Shadwell; there was not a trace of it in the modern and delicate sparkle of Congreve; the tragedians, too, even such dull dogs as Crowne, retained a tradition of the sudden felicities and barbaric ornament of the Elizabethan, though in an extremely modified form: a roughness which has entirely disappeared from the liquid periods of *Tamerlane* and *The Mourning Bride*. It may be shortly said that the younger school were as easily supreme in comedy as the elder in tragedy, since Congreve represents the one and Otway the other.

Thomas Otway was the son of the Rev. Humphrey Otway, rector of Woolbeding, a parish near Midhurst,

in the western division of Sussex.   The poet was born
at Trotton, on March 3, 1651, in the midst of the Civil
War, a few months before the decisive battle of
Worcester.   An error in geography has crept into our
literary history, to the effect that Otway was born on
the banks of the poetic Arun—

> " But wherefore need I wander wide
> To old Ilissus' distant side,
>   Deserted stream, and mute?
> Wild Arun, too, has heard thy strains,
> And Echo, 'midst my native plains,
>   Been soothed by Pity's lute.
>
> " There first the wren thy myrtles shed
> On gentlest Otway's infant head,
>   To him thy cell was shown ;
> And while he sang the female heart,
> With youth's soft notes unspoiled by art,
>   Thy turtles mixed their own."

So Collins sang, addressing Pity ; but, unhappily for
this charming fancy, Trotton is a hamlet on the north
bank of the Rother, embowered in the billowy woods
of Woolmer Forest.   There remain no traditions of
the boy's early life.   A brief passage in one of his
poems is all we possess :—

> " My Father was (a thing now rare)
>   Loyal and brave : my Mother chaste and fair.
> The pledge of marriage-vows was only I ;
> Alone I lived their much-loved fondled boy ;
>   They gave me generous education ; high
> They strove to raise my mind, and with it grew their joy.

He was sent to school at Winchester, and in 1669 he
was entered as a commoner of Christ Church College,

Oxford. His early life at the University was so easy
and brilliant, that in the bitterness of after days it
seemed in retrospect to have been without a shadow.
He was loved, courted, and flattered; his quick parts
pleased his teachers and attracted to him the dangerous
society of young wits belonging to a richer station
than his own. Lord Falkland and the Earl of Plymouth were among his intimate friends at Oxford; we
know their names, while others are forgotten, because
they remained true to their companion in after life. It
was probably among these golden youths that Otway
gained and nourished a taste for pleasure and the
lighter arts of life. Already he versified, and no
doubt there were plenty of flatterers ready to promise
him a career in the newly reawakened literary life of
London.

It was probably in the Long Vacation, 1671, being
twenty years of age, that he managed, we cannot tell
how, to introduce himself at the Duke's Theatre, in
Lincoln's Inn Fields. His first literary friend seems
to have been Aphra Behn, and to her he confided his
intense desire to appear on the public stage. His face
and figure, for he was singularly comely, were greatly
to his advantage, and the heart of the good-natured
poetess was touched. She gave him a part in her new
tragi-comedy of *The Forc'd Marriage*. The circumstances were amusing. Betterton, already an actor in
the prime of life, had to enter as a young lover; Otway,
the tender undergraduate, posed as the venerable king.
Yet the choice of the part showed the kindly tact of the
shrewd Mrs. Behn. The king had to speak the few

first words, to which the audience never listens, to make some brief replies in the first scene, and then not to speak again until the end of the fourth act. In the fifth act he had to make rather a long speech to Betterton, explaining that he was "old and feeble, and could not long survive," and this is nearly all he had to say till the very end, where he was in great force as the kind old man who unites the couples and speaks the last words. It was quite a crucial test, and Otway proved his entire inability to face the public. He trembled, was inaudible, melted in an agony, and had to leave the stage. The part was given to Westwood, a professional actor, and Otway never essayed to tread the boards again.

After this blow to his vanity he went back to Oxford again, somewhat crestfallen, we cannot doubt. But this visit must have produced an immense impression on his character. To have been spoken to on terms of equality by Mr. and Mrs. Betterton, even though they may have laughed at him behind his back, was a great distinction for the ambitious lad, and to have been received by Mrs. Behn, the greatest female wit since Orinda, this must indeed have marked an epoch. And he had tasted the fierce, delicious wine of theatrical life, he had seen the green-room, associated with actors, trodden the sacred boards themselves. No doubt this early escapade in 1671 (Downe incorrectly dates it 1672) set the seal upon his glittering and melancholy career. He himself darkly alludes to the death of a friend, whom he calls Senander, as deeply moving him about this time; but all we know, even by hearsay, is that he finally deserted the University in 1674, having refused an opening in the Church which was offered him if he would take holy orders. He obtained instead a cornetcy in a troop of horse, in that year, and sold it again before twelve months were over.

It seems that somewhat about this date he visited Duke, the poet, at Cambridge, and this in all probability originated the rumour that he became a scholar of St. John's College in that University. At all events we find him, in 1675, settled in London, without collegiate honours, and with no visible care to gain a livelihood by any honest means. That the poor lad was gulled by flatterers and idle companions is plain enough; it is obvious, also, that at first he must have possessed some fortune or received a liberal allowance from his father, for he tried to retain his aristocratic friends and vie with them in extravagance as long as he could. It was natural that he should gravitate to his old friends at the Duke's Theatre, and though they remembered his ill-success as an actor, they were ready to receive him as a poet. In 1675 each of the theatres accepted a tragedy from an unfledged dramatist; one was the *Alcibiades* of Otway, the other the *Nero* of Nat Lee, a youth of only twenty, but of precocious talent.

We must pause a few moments to review the condition of the stage in England since the Restoration. During the last years of the Commonwealth, Sir William Davenant had managed, by a clever subterfuge, to introduce in London lyrico-dramatic entertainments, which he called "operas," a new word to the

U

English public. These were given somewhat under
the rose, but when Charles II. arrived, Davenant posed
as the guardian of the drama, and claimed exclusive
privileges. The King took counsel with Clarendon,
and it was decided that only two theatres should be
licensed, one under his own direct patronage and the
other under that of the Duke of York. The King's
Theatre was placed under the censorship of Sir
Thomas Killigrew, and the Duke's was put in Davenant's hands. In April 1663 the former company took
up their abode in Drury Lane, and Dryden thereupon
was regularly attached as dramatist to their house after
1667, until which time he sometimes wrote for Davenant also. In 1668 Davenant died, and the house in
Lincoln's Inn Fields came into the far abler hands of
Betterton, a young actor of remarkable energy, who
had studied carefully at the Théâtre Français with the
definite prospect of taking the command of the Duke's
company. It is true that for a short time Dr. Charles
Davenant, the amiable son of the late poet-laureate,
nominally undertook the direction, but Betterton was
the life and soul of the concern.

This great actor and excellent man was one of the
brightest characters of his time. In that jarring age
of quarrelling, debauchery, and disloyalty, the modest
and serene figure of Betterton appears in the centre of
the noisy, boisterous crowd, always erect, always un-
stained. The greatest actor the English stage saw
until Garrick, it was the singular art of Betterton to
give nobility and life to the pompous and shadowy
figures of mere lath and paper which the poor tragedians

of the day called heroes: a thankless task which he
fulfilled with such amazing success, that the pit shrieked
applause at the trembling conscious poet whom the
genius of the actor had saved from being damned.
Hence Betterton was alike the darling of the world
before and behind the foot-lights. In 1670 he
strengthened his position by marrying Mrs. Sanderson,
an actress of the company, whom in time he trained
to play most admirably. Mrs. Betterton was a woman
worthy of her husband, and under their conjoint
supervision the Duke's Theatre rivalled the King's in
success, despite the attractions of Mr. Hart, the
tragedian, and the lovely Mrs. Eleanor Gwynn. The
style of acting patronised at Lincoln's Inn Fields was
pure and severe. It was a saying of Betterton's that
he, when he was acting a good part, "preferred an
attentive silence to any applause," and it is by such
slight phrases as these, handed down by casual
auditors, that we learn how to value the sincerity and
artistic devotion of the man.

When Otway visited the Duke's Theatre in 1675,
the company was familiar to him. One girl, known
in theatrical history as Mrs. Barry, had indeed been
received in 1674, but her delivery was so harsh and
her gait so uncouth, that she had been dismissed at
the end of the season. Her beauty, however, was
rapidly ripening, and she contrived to fascinate the
worst roué of the day, the notorious John Wilmot,
Earl of Rochester. It is probable that Rochester may
have made himself specially useful to the Duke's company in the year 1675. In order to spite Dryden, the

object of his animosity for the moment, the fretful young Earl had adopted the rival cause of John Crowne, and his exertions with the Queen had induced the latter to commission that poet to produce an opera for performance at court. *Calisto, or the Chaste Nymph* was the result of this unholy alliance, and it was brought out with great pomp at the palace. The daughters of the Duke of York performed the principal parts, and in order to give *éclat* to the affair, Betterton was invited to undertake the rehearsals and Mrs. Betterton to train the young amateurs. The princesses entered with spirit into the thing, *Calisto* was a great success, and Crowne a happy man. This was in 1675, and it seems likely that the immediate re-engagement of Mrs. Barry followed as a personal compliment to Rochester. It was no common chance by which her first appearance was arranged to be in Otway's *Alcibiades*. These two persons, who were to play Manon Lescaut and the Chevalier des Greux with a difference, began life together and after a strangely similar initial failure.

We may learn much of the under-current of feeling from prologues and epilogues, but the prologue of *Alcibiades* is a mere nervous experiment. The poet tries to conceal his trepidation by affecting indifference; he shows a want of tact and experience in ridiculing the labours of his predecessors. But there was nothing in his own play that could excuse such arrogance. Young Nat Lee, with his blood-and-thunder tragedy of *Nero* at the King's, was giving far better promise than this. It was the fashion of the hour to write tragedies in rhyme, and *Alcibiades* accordingly is in tagged couplets. Nothing could be flatter than the versification, nothing tamer than the action, nothing more conventional than the sentiments of this tiresome play. So entirely without salient features is it, that one has to hurry down one's impression of it immediately one closes it, for in five minutes not a waif of it remains in the memory. Charles Lamb remarked that nobody could say of Mrs. Conrady's countenance that it would be better if she had but a nose. No one could say of *Alcibiades* that it would be better if it had but a plot. Its entire deficiency in every kind of quality gives it quite a unique air of complete insipidity, which no positive fault could increase. If it were even indecent, it would lose its typical dulness; on the contrary, its extreme propriety gave much offence to the pit. But Betterton, we cannot doubt, clothed the poet's lay figure of Alcibiades with majesty, and in the small part of Draxilla, the hero's sister, the exquisite Mrs. Barry, now carefully trained to her business, won the applause of the audience. More than this, she won the weak and feverish heart of the young poet, who from this time fluttered like a moth towards the flame or star of her beauty.

Mrs. Barry was an ignoble, calculating woman; no generous act, even of frailty, is recorded of her. Whether or not, in rivalry with Mrs. Gwynn, she set her cap at royalty, she had a well-balanced sense of her own value, and smiled at nothing lower than an earl. Of the letters addressed to her through the remainder of his brief life by Otway, we possess only the few last, written, it is probable by internal evidence, in 1682.   We learn from these strange letters, which throb through and through with passion under the rhetorical ornament of fashionable expression, that for seven years she kept him in the torture of suspense. It is easy to understand why such a woman should reject a humble and penniless lover, and at the same time why she should have done her best, by little courtesies and partial coquettings, to keep by her side the poet who wrote the parts best suited to advance her fame.   It was universally acknowledged that no characters became Mrs. Barry so well as those which Otway wrote for her, and thus the poor tortured lover had the agony of weaving out of his own brain the robes that made his mistress lovely to his rivals.   The alliance between Mrs. Barry and Lord Rochester was probably sufficient to keep the poet at a distance at first, but as his passion grew and absorbed all other thoughts, he dared to lay his heart at her feet.   Like Propertius, standing in tears in the street, while Cynthia takes deep draughts of Falernian with her lover, amid peals of laughter, so is the picture we form of the unfortunate Otway, incurably infatuated, haunting the gay precincts of the Duke's Theatre.   As long as life and fortune lasted, he never abandoned the company of the Bettertons, and they acted in every play he wrote.

Although *Alcibiades* had been a partial failure, Betterton accepted another tragedy from the young author in the following year.   *Don Carlos* is as great an advance on its predecessor as it could possibly be.

It is difficult to believe that they were written by the same hand. The rhyming tragedies were on their last legs, but *Don Carlos* was a crutch that might have supported the failing fashion for years. The supple, strong verse, un-English in character, but worthy of Corneille or at least of Rotrou, assists instead of hampering the dramatic action : the plot is well considered, tragical, and moving ; the characters, stagey though they be, are vigorously designed and sustained. I think we should be justified in calling *Don Carlos* the best English tragedy in rhyme ; by one leap the young Oxonian sprang ahead of the veteran Dryden, who thereupon began to "weary of his long-loved mistress, rhyme." The story is familiar to all readers of Schiller ; in Otway's play the intrigue is simpler and less realistic, the object being, as always in tragedies of this class, to amuse and excite rather than to startle and to melt the audience.

The opening scene of *Don Carlos* is a fine declamatory piece of stage-business. The King, in full court, lavishes affection on the Queen, in order to excite jealousy in Don Carlos, and we are plunged at once in the middle of things. We soon become familiar with the two types which Otway incessantly presents to us. The Queen, a soft and simple creature, bewildered in the etiquette of a Spanish court, full of tenderness and womanly pity, is the spiritual sister of Monimia, Belvidera, and Lavinia. The hero is still more exactly the type which Otway drew, I cannot but believe, from his own heart. "An untamed, haughty, hot and furious youth," Don Carlos is yet full of

feminine weakness, irresolute, fevered, infatuate, unable
to give up the woman he loves though she is in the
hands of another man, yet lacking the force and temerity
to cut the Gordian knot by violence.   Unstable as
water, it is impossible that he should avoid the tragical
end that awaits him.   Such is Don Carlos, such again
in the *Orphan*; is Castalio; but the very prototype
of the character is Jaffier in *Venice Preserved*.   This
poetic, passionate, childish nature, born to sorrow as
the sparks fly upward, is as clearly depicted in the
love letters to Mrs. Barry as in the tragedies.   The
poet dipped his pen in his own heart.

The modern reader bears with impatience the rhetoric
of the Restoration.   But, if only to justify the statement
that *Don Carlos* is the best of the rhymed tragedies,
I must quote a few lines as an example of the nervous
English of the piece.   Don John, the King's profligate
brother, for whom Rochester probably sat, is speaking:—

> " Why should dull Law rule Nature, who first made
>   That Law by which herself is now betray'd ?
>   Ere Man's corruptions made him wretched, he
>   Was born most noble that was born most free ;
>   Each of himself was lord, and unconfined
>   Obeyed the dictates of his godlike mind.
>   Law was an innovation brought in since
>   When fools began to love obedience,
>   And called their slavery, safety and defence.
>   My glorious father got me in his heat,
>   When all he did was eminently great,
>   When warlike Belgia felt his conquering power
>   And the proud Germans called him Emperor.
>   Why should it be a stain then on my blood
>   Because I came not by the common road,
>   But born obscure and so more like a god ?"

This is not the language of nature, to be sure, but
it is vigorous, muscular verse, and the form was that
in which the age most delighted. The contemporaries
of Otway and Dryden would have scorned us for
objecting to this artificial diction as much as we
should ridicule a barbarian for finding fault with a
prima donna for singing instead of speaking. These
things go by fashion. It is an accepted idea nowadays
that a tragedy hero must talk as much as possible like
an ordinary person in extraordinary circumstances.
The same idea, fortunately, prevailed in the time of
Shakespeare. But always in France, and during the
Restoration in England also, a certain poetic phraseology was demanded from a tragedian, just as musical
expression is demanded from an actor at the opera;
and we must, if we would judge the productions of
that age, submit them to the standard which their own
time recognised. It is very interesting, too, to see the
flesh and blood peeping out under the rouge and tinsel.
The parting between the Queen and Don Carlos, at
the end of the third act, despite its staginess, is full
of passion and fervour. It was played by Betterton
and Mrs. Mary Lee; Mrs. Barry, for an unexplained
reason, having no part given her in this drama. The
wife of Shadwell the poet took the part of the
Countess of Eboli, and it was perhaps on this occasion
that Otway became acquainted with the man-mountain
who so much hated Dryden.

The Duke of York, it is difficult to conceive why,
had admired *Alcibiades*, and *Don Carlos* was dedicated
to him. The play was an immense success, and

brought in more money than any tragedy of the
period.   The folks at the King's Theatre became
jealous, and one legend says that Dryden had the
characteristic rashness to say spitefully, that he
" knew not a line in it he would be author of."
Otway, with schoolboy sprightliness, replied that he
knew a comedy—probably the *Marriage-à-la-Mode*—
that had not so much as a quibble in it which he would
be the author of.   We may see the Mephistopheles
hand of Rochester encouraging the youth to this
impertinence ; but at all events Otway was the successful poet of the season, and wonderfully flush of
money.   It was the one fortunate hour of his life,
and even this, we may believe, was spoiled by the
female Mordecai in the gate.   A slight reference to
the Fallen Angels, in the fourth act of *Don Carlos*,
is worth noting.   It seems to show consciousness
of the great epic of the poet who had just passed
away.

It is quite impossible to unravel the threads of personal animosity which confuse the dramatic history
of this period.   Everybody's hand was against everybody else, and no friendship seemed to last beyond
a year.   Almost the only writer who stood aloof from
the imbroglio was Mrs. Aphra Behn.   She kept on
good terms with every one ; the busiest *littérateur*
of the period had no time to defame the characters
of her contemporaries.   Settle had been the first of
Rochester's puppets, put up to annoy Dryden, and a
few years later, when the arch troubler was safe under-
ground, Settle still was sullenly firing blank cartridges

at the Laureate. But dire discord broke out in this joyous camp of assailants in the year 1676. Otway was then the reigning favourite with Rochester, Crowne was snubbed for having been too successful with his *Conquest of Jerusalem*, and Elkanah Settle was quietly dropped. But although "Doeg" had endured the insults of Crowne, the upstart Otway was more than his spirit could bear. He challenged Otway to a duel, and, if we may believe Shadwell, this terrible contest actually came off. Unhappily no lampooner and no caricaturist of the period seized the heroic moment for the laughter of ensuing generations.

Otway was better engaged in 1677, on the translation of a tragedy of Racine and a farce of Molière, which were performed the same night, and published in a single quarto. *Titus and Berenice* was affectionately dedicated to Lord Rochester. It is useless to analyse a play which owed little to its English garb. The versification is flowing and smooth, a little less vigorous, perhaps, than that of *Don Carlos*. There are only three important persons in the play, and Mrs. Barry took the unimportant part of Phœnice, Berenice's maid. Mrs. Lee was still the leading lady of the company. As an example of inanity and careless workmanship, the four opening lines of *Titus and Berenice* are worthy of a crown :—

> " Thou, my Arsaces, art a stranger here ;
> *This is th' Apartment of the charming Fair,*
> That Berenice, whom Titus so adores,
> The universe is his, and he is hers."

But I hasten to confess that they are by far the worst

in the whole play.   *The Cheats of Scapin* has not lost all its wit in crossing the Channel, and in this Mrs. Barry was allowed the best part, Mrs. Lee not appearing at all.

Otway's preface, with its incense burned before Rochester, had scarcely issued from the press, when he incurred the violent hatred of that dangerous person. The physical condition of the Earl of Rochester had by this time become deplorable.   For some years he had scarcely known what it was to be sober, and at the age of twenty-nine he was already a worn-out, fretful old man.   His excellent constitution, which he had supported by temperance until the unfortunate affair with the Earl of Mulgrave had undermined his self-respect, had now almost given way under the attacks of a frantic sensuality.   Lord Rochester had become a plague-spot in English literature and English society. He had begun by being an amiable debauchee, but he had ended as a petulant and ferocious rake, whose wasting hold on life only increased his malevolent licence.   The nominal cause of the split with Otway was the pretty Mrs. Barry.   As the Earl became more violent and more abominable, the agony that Otway felt in seeing her associated with him became unbearable, and the young poet was forced to sever his connection with the theatre.   To stay in London and not to be near the idol of his infatuation, was impossible. He applied to his old college friend, the Earl of Plymouth, for a post in the army.   Although the Treaty of Westminster, in 1674, had brought the war with Holland to a nominal close, fighting still went on on the Continent, and the Duke of Monmouth had an army at the service of the King of France. Otway obtained a cornet's commission under the Duke, and went over in a new regiment to fight in Flanders. He left behind him a comedy, which his quarrel with Rochester did not prevent Betterton from producing.

With the exception of Etheredge, who lived apart and seldom wrote, no very excellent comic dramatist flourished in the Restoration period, properly so called. But there were several poets who produced no one consummate work, but a bulk of comedies which in the aggregate were a notable addition to literature. Of these, three names will occur to every reader as the most praiseworthy. Wycherley had wit, Shadwell had humour, Aphra Behn had vivacity. In all these qualities the two principal tragedians, Dryden and Otway, were inferior to each of these writers in his or her own vein, and in point of fact Otway made a very bad second to Dryden, even in this inferior rank. Otway's three original comedies are simply appalling. The old comedy of whimsicality had died with Shirley and Jasper Mayne, and though Etheredge had invented or introduced the new comedy of intrigue, it had taken no root, and was to be inaugurated afresh by Congreve. There is no drearier reading than a series of early Restoration comedies. The greatest reward the reader can expect is a grain of wit here and there, a lively situation, a humorous phase of successful rascality. The general character of the pieces is given by Otway,

with singular frankness, through the mouth of his
Lady Squeamish :—

"And then their Comedies nowadays are the filthiest things,
full of nauseous doings, which they mistake for raillery and
intrigue : besides, they have no wit in 'em neither, for all their
gentlemen and men of wit, as they style 'em, are either silly
conceited impudent coxcombs, or else rude unmannerly drunken
fellows, faugh !"

The artificial comedy of the next generation was
loose and frivolous, indeed without any sense of
morality or immorality at all, but it was innocuous in
its fantastic and airy unearthliness, so that no one could
really be much injured by it, and only a pedant much
scandalised.   In Otway's atrocious comedies there is
equally little fear of injury to the moral sense of the
auditor or reader, for the characters bear scarcely the
faintest resemblance to human creatures, and their sins
fill us with the mere loathing of an ugly thing drawn
by an unskilful hand.   The horrible puppets, in fact,
like the figures in the base prints of the period, gibber
and skip over the stage with imbecile gestures and a
grin on their impossible faces.

The only legitimate *raison-d'être* of the persons in an
artificial comedy is that they should amuse.   The light
creations of Congreve and Vanbrugh completely justify
their creation, for they do amuse us heartily all through
—those of us, that is, who in this day of the worship of
realism can venture to be amused by pure literature
at all.   But Otway's comedies—and they are typical of
a class—do not perform the one slender function for
which they came into existence.   No faint shadow of

a smile passes over our faces as we drag through the dreary and repulsive scenes of *Friendship in Fashion*. It is the saddest fooling, and we wish at every scene that this were the last, and that the poor little marionettes might be decently shut up again in their box and forgotten. And yet there is evidence on record that this was an extremely successful play. It was revived in 1749, but the audience of that date could not endure it for an hour, and it was hissed off the stage for good and all.

There are some interesting points, however, connected with *Friendship in Fashion*. When it was printed, in 1678, it was dedicated to the Earl of Dorset; in this dedication Otway speaks of himself as working hard for his daily bread, and as surrounded by slanderous enemies. His tone is at once timorous and defiant, and he speaks of himself as worse treated by the critics than a bear is by the Bankside Butchers. The play was probably acted and printed while Otway was away in Flanders, for so autobiographical a writer could not have omitted to mention the sufferings of that ill-starred adventure. It seems that he was widely accused of libelling some person or persons in *Friendship in Fashion*; he strenuously denies the charge, and in an air so heavy with invective it would be difficult to determine the exact ground of the rumour. Those who will take the pains to read this tedious drama will perceive that Congreve deigned to remember it in the composition of his exquisite masterpiece, *Love for Love*. The hero in each case is named Valentine, and Malagene, Otway's tiresome button-holer and secret-monger, is a clumsy prototype of the inimitable Tattle. But the resemblance is very slight, and I almost owe the genius of Congreve an apology for suggesting it.

Otway's military excursion proved a lamentable failure. As we had declared peace with Holland, it was only in an underhand and unofficial manner that English soldiers could fight in the Low Countries as auxiliaries of France. On the 10th of August hostilities finally closed with the Peace of Nijmegen, signed in the Raadhuis between Louis XIV., Charles of Spain, and the States General. The English troops under the Duke of Monmouth were treated with infamous neglect; they were disbanded, and allowed to go whither they would, no means of transport home being provided. They were paid not in money, but with debentures, which it was extremely difficult to get cashed, and which are frequently ridiculed in the political lampoons of the period. The unlucky Otway got back to London, ragged and starved, with his tattered garments full of vermin, an unsavoury particular which was not missed by his rhyming enemies. The Earl of Rochester in particular had the indecency to introduce this mishap and its consequences into a doggerel *Session of the Poets*, which did equal discredit to his heart and head. Otway, however, was not yet crushed by adverse fate, and he sat down to write another comedy for his faithful allies at the Duke's Theatre. *The Soldier's Fortune*, acted probably in 1679, but not printed until 1681, is perhaps the only play of the time which is not dedicated to a person of quality. It is merely inscribed to Mr. Bentley, the stationer, or as we should now say, the publisher.

" I am not a little proud," Otway says, "that it has happened into my thoughts to be the first who in these latter years has made an Epistle Dedicatory to his Stationer. It is a compliment as reasonable as it is just. For, Mr. Bentley, you pay honestly for the copy, and an epistle to you is a sort of acquittance, and may probably be welcome ; when to a person of higher rank and order, it looks like an obligation for praises, which he knows he does not deserve, and therefore is very unwilling to part with ready money for."

It was the habit for every person of high rank to whom a book was dedicated to present the author with a gift of money. This noisome custom did not die out until late in the following century. In this instance the courtesies were reversed, for the prologue, very tolerably written, was contributed by Otway's old college friend, Lord Falkland. In the epilogue Otway describes himself as

" Full of those thoughts that make the unhappy sad,
And by imagination half grown mad,

and pours out a querulous complaint about "starving poets" wrecked by cruel fate, which must have struck a jarring chord at the close of a frivolous comedy. The play is full of autobiographical allusions to disbanded soldiers, debentures, ill food, and the hardships of war ; but perhaps the most curious point of all is in the preface, where, in answer to some great lady who objected to the indecency of the plot, he quotes Mrs. Behn, of all possible females, in defence of its propriety. " I have heard a lady, that has more modesty than any of these she-critics, and I am sure more wit, say she wondered at the impudence of any of her sex who would pretend to an opinion on such a matter." Poor Mrs. Behn, good honest creature, has come, in the whirligig of time, to be looked upon as the last person in all known literature to mark the standard of dramatic delicacy. And yet there was a time when a copy of light verses was considered in good taste if the fastidious Astræa could approve of it.

Hitherto Otway had subsisted upon the proceeds of one play a year. In 1680 he seems to have made a supreme effort to free himself from his liabilities, for in it he produced two plays and his only important poem. Moreover, one of these plays is so immeasurably superior to anything he had hitherto produced, as to justify his admirers in hoping that he had taken a new lease of his genius. His rival and enemy, the hated Rochester, had for some months been sinking under delirium tremens ; and, haunted by the terrors of his complaint, had sought ghostly comfort from Bishop Burnet. On July 26 he died, having ceased to be troublesome since the beginning of the year. There is an unusual sprightly hopefulness about the prologue and preface of *The Orphan*, as if a weight had been removed and the poet was nearing the fulfilment of his wishes. The dedication was accepted by " Her R.H. the Dutchess ; " not, of course, the Duchess of Cleveland, as Voltaire oddly enough supposed, but Mary d'Este, the unlucky Duchess of York.

The poetical reputation of Otway rests, or should rest, on his three best tragedies ; and of these it may be said that *The Orphan* is as far superior to *Don Carlos* as *Venice Preserved* is superior to it. The epoch of rhymed tragedies had passed away since *Don Carlos* was written. Dryden had inaugurated the return to blank verse with his *All for Love*, in 1678, and Lee with *Mithridates* in the same year. Otway followed their good example, and with no less zeal; for he also carefully studied the fountain-head of dramatic blank verse in Shakespeare. In *The Orphan* we feel at once that we breathe a freer air and tread on firmer ground; there is less rhetoric and more nature, less passion and more tenderness. The plot of this once so famous play is nowadays sufficiently unfamiliar to justify me in briefly analysing it. A retired nobleman, Acasto, lives at his country seat with his two sons Castalio and Polydore, men of great ambition and fiery purpose, but still very young and curbéd by their father's authority. They have, moreover, a sister—Serina. A young girl, Monimia, the orphan daughter of an old friend of Acasto's, has been brought up with these children, and is now a woman of the gentlest beauty. Castalio and Polydore have each fallen unawares into love with their father's ward, and in the opening scenes of the play we are introduced to their trustful mutual affection and then to the disturbing influence of this awakened passion. Castalio and Monimia, however, have secretly come to an understanding; but Castalio, from a foolish desire to let his brother down gently, feigns comparative indifference to Monimia, and even gives Polydore leave to win her if he can. At this moment Chamont, the brother of Monimia, appears on the scene and claims the ready hospitality of Acasto. He is a bluff, honest, but brutal and petulant soldier, and his presence is disturbing in the quiet household. He has formed a suspicion that Monimia has been wronged by one of the young men, and he annoys her with his rude and tactless questions. Meanwhile Acasto is taken suddenly ill, and Castalio and Monimia take advantage of the confusion to be privately married by the chaplain. Polydore, believing his brother to have no serious claim upon Monimia, happening to overhear them proposing a tryst in the night, comes beforehand in the darkness to Monimia's chamber, and is not discovered. Castalio, coming later, is excluded, and curses his wife for her supposed heartlessness and insubordination. The sequel may well be imagined. Ruin and anguish fall upon the brothers, but most of all on the innocent and agonised Monimia, who finally takes poison, while Castalio stabs himself.

There are many faults in the construction of this plot, besides the indelicacy of the main situation, which has long banished it from the stage. The foolish pretence of Castalio, the want of perception shown by Monimia, the impossible and ruffianly crime of Polydore—for which no just preparation is made in the sketch of his character—all these are radical faults which go near to destroy the probability of the story. But if we once accept these weak points and forget them, the play is full of delicate and charming turns of action, of decisive characterisation, and of intense and tear-compelling pathos. The old patriot Acasto, a study drawn, it is said, from the first Duke of Ormonde, is a noble figure of a patriotic servant of his country, shrinking in old age from the frivolity of a court, and studying rather a simple and patriarchal life among his tenantry. In the noisy soldier Chamont, a fierce and turbulent but not ill-meaning person, Otway produced a highly-finished portrait of a type with which his foreign adventures had no doubt made him only too familiar. Castalio is the veering, passionate, hot-headed man whom Otway invariably draws as his hero. This time the character is even more fervid and perverse than ever, and we are on the point of scorning him for his want of resolution, when the insupportable tide of sorrows that overwhelms him enforces our pity and sympathy.

Over the character of Monimia probably more tears have been shed than over that of any stage heroine. As long as the laxity of public speech still permitted the presentation of *The Orphan*, no audience of any sensibility could endure the fourth and fifth acts of this play without melting into audible weeping. It was one of Mrs. Barry's most celebrated parts, and it would seem as though Otway had wilfully put his breast to the torture by heaping up, with lingering hands, all the turns and phrases which could enhance the trembling agony and helpless beauty of his mistress. He, like poor Castalio, was left outside to the night and the storm; and he tried to console him-self by vainly imagining that his exquisite Monimia was unconscious of the wrong she did him.

The force of Otway's language does not consist in

flowery beauties that can be detached in quotation; he is not a poet from whom much of a very effective nature can be selected. His stroke was broad and bold, and when he did succeed, it was in figures of an heroic size and on a grand scale. The peculiar tenderness, and still more the lingering passion of grief which steep the whole play, are felt more intensely at a second reading than a first. *The Orphan* is not a masculine work, but it might be the crowning memorial of some woman whom great ambition and still greater sorrow had forged into a poet.

The other tragedy of the same year, *The History and Fall of Caius Marius*, is merely a kind of cento, the language of Shakespeare being transferred wholesale into the mouths of Otway's characters. There was no bad faith in this; the author announced in the prologue, which was a reverent eulogy on his great predecessor, that the audience would find that he had rifled Shakespeare of half a play—in point of fact, of *Romeo and Juliet*, with reminiscences of *Julius Cæsar*. Of course such a performance is scarcely to be mentioned among the original works of Otway, and it has no further importance than belongs to the curious fact that for a couple of generations it superseded *Romeo and Juliet* on the English stage. It was dedicated to the Earl of Falkland in a preface which contains a graceful allusion to the venerable Waller, the last survivor of the poets who had lived in Shakespeare's lifetime. Lavinia, the principal character, who spoke the words written for Juliet, was acted to perfection by Mrs. Barry, who had now attained that

majestic beauty and serenity, which she still retained
even in Colley Cibber's early days. From the epilogue
we learn that the poet usually had his benefit on the
third night, and that sometimes he mortgaged his
gains before they came into his pocket. The lines
are melancholy enough in all conscience.

> " Our Poet says, one day to a play ye come
> Which serves you half a year for wit at home,
> But which among you is there to be found
> Will take his third day's pawn for fifty pound ?
> Or, now he is cashier'd, will fairly venture
> To give him ready money for's debenture ?
> Therefore, when he received that fatal doom,
> This play came forth, in hope his friends would come
> To help a poor disbanded soldier home."

In the same year, 1680, the " poor·disbanded soldier "
published a poem in quarto, entitled *The Poet's Complaint of his Muse*, which gives some vague memoir of
himself, and much violent satire of his enemies. The
opening of his poem is vigorous and picturesque, like
a roughly-etched bit of barren landscape.

> " To a high hill, where never yet stood tree,
> Where only heath, coarse fern, and furzes grow,
>   Where, nipt by piercing air,
> The flocks in tattered fleeces hardly graze,
>   Led by uncouth thoughts and care,
> Which did too much his pensive mind amaze,
> A wandering Bard, whose Muse was crazy grown,
> Cloy'd with the nauseous follies of the buzzing town,
> Came, look'd about him, sighed, and laid him down."

The Bard, who is plainly Mr. Thomas Otway,
presently proceeds to give an account of his own early

life, and the tyrannous empire of his Muse, at once his mistress and his fate. He then proceeds to denounce, under thin disguises, his principal enemies, and in the forefront, Rochester, Shadwell, and Settle. The poem thus develops into a series of tolerably transparent political allegories, and closes with a passionate eulogy of the Duke of York, and a mournful description of his leaving England. The whole poem, which is well written and interesting, literally teems with the excitement of the Popish plots, then at the height of their vogue, and Otway was now a Tory, like Dryden.

There is still the same troubled sense of Titus Oates and his meaner brood of terrorists in the title of Otway's next play, *Venice Preserved, or a Plot Discovered*, which was produced in February 1682. The author only half deprecates such a belief in the prologue, as he briefly reviews the events that had excited popular apprehension. His preface does not tell us how he had been employed since 1680, but, in addressing the Duchess of Portsmouth, he extols her bounty, extended to her poet in his extremity. We are therefore justified in concluding that Otway had begun to suffer the last miseries of poverty. There is no diminution of power, however, in this drama, written out of the depths. In fact, as we all know, it is simply the greatest tragic drama between Shakespeare and Shelley. Out of the dead waste of the Restoration, with all its bustling talent and vain show, this one solitary work of supreme genius rose unexpected and unimitated.

There is nothing in any previous writing of Otway's,

nothing even in the moving and feminine pathos of *The Orphan*, which would lead us to await so noble and so solid a masterpiece as *Venice Preserved*. The poetic glow and irregular beauty of Elizabethan tragedy, its lyric outbursts, its fantastic and brilliant flashes of insight, its rich variety and varied melody, give the early plays a place in our affections which surpasses what is purely owing to their theatrical excellence. In *Venice Preserved* the poetic element is always severely subordinated to the dramatic; there are no flowers of fancy, no charming episodes introduced to give literary gusto to a reader. All is designed for the true home of the drama, the stage, and without being in the least stagey, this theatrical aim is carried out with the most complete success. There are few plays in existence so original and so telling in construction as this; the plot is in almost every respect worthy to be Shakespeare's. The only point in which any weakness can be traced is the motive actuating Jaffier to join the conspirators. The revenge of a merely private wrong upon a whole commonwealth is scarcely sane enough for the dignity of tragedy.

The story may be briefly given. Jaffier, a noble young Venetian, had secretly married Belvidera, the daughter of a proud and wealthy senator, Priuli, who in consequence disowns her. The young couple fall into great poverty, and at the opening of the piece Jaffier is begging Priuli to assist them, but his entreaties are met with injurious insults. His pride is up in arms, and at that moment he meets his friend Pierre, a soldier to whom the Senate of Venice has refused his just rewards, and who is embittered against the state. He enflames Jaffier by describing the fate of Belvidera, the injuries done to Jaffier, and the sorrows that will fall upon their children. They part with a promise to meet at midnight and consult still further. At midnight Jaffier accordingly meets Pierre on the Rialto, and after testing the temper of his friend, Pierre confides to him that a plot is on the eve of being hatched, and offers to introduce him to the conspirators. This is accordingly done, but as they are jealous of the honesty of the new-comer, Jaffier gives Belvidera into the charge of the leader, an old man named Renault. As it is impossible to explain the reason of this to Belvidera, she goes off in great distress, and as in the course of the night Renault offers to insult her, she breaks away, and flying to her husband, entreats him to explain to her his cruel and unaccountable conduct. He has sworn not to divulge the plot, but as she begs him to do so, and assures him of her complete devotion to his will, he gradually loses his self-control, and at last confides to her the secret. Her first thought is that her father is one of the Senate, and is therefore to be among the victims. She implores Jaffier to relent, and at last persuades him, much against his will, to go to the Senate and reveal the plot, claiming as his reward the lives of the conspirators.

Jaffier is finally convinced that it is his duty to do this, and, much as he loathes his bad faith, he actually goes before the Senate, and declares the plot. The conspirators are in consequence arrested in time, and

their design completely paralysed. At first the friends,
seeing Jaffier bound, believe him to be the partner of
their misfortune, but, discovering their mistake, they
load him with the heaviest reproaches, and, scornfully
rejecting pardon, they claim an instant death. Pierre
especially pours out the vials of his wrath on Jaffier,
and the unfortunate man breaks down in an agony
of humiliation and remorse. The faithless senators
decree a cruel death to the conspirators, and Jaffier
threatens Belvidera that he with his own hands will
stab her unless she forces a pardon for them from her
father Priuli. Her charms prevail, but Priuli's inter-
vention comes too late. Belvidera goes mad; Jaffier
struggles to the foot of the scaffold where Pierre is
about to be executed, and stabs his friend first and
then himself to the heart with a dagger. Belvidera
dies of a broken heart at their feet, and the scene
closes.

To give an idea of the vigour and beauty of this
play, it would be necessary to quote a longer fragment
than could conveniently be given here. A single
speech of Belvidera and the reply of Jaffier must
suffice; they are considering the necessity of a life in
poverty and exile.

> " *Bel.* O I will love thee, even in madness love thee !
> Tho' my distracted senses should forsake me,
> I'd find some intervals, when my poor heart
> Should 'swage itself, and be let loose to thine.
> Tho' the bare earth be all our resting-place,
> Its roots our food, some clift our habitation,
> I'll make this arm a pillow for thy head ;
> And as thou sighing ly'st, and swelled with sorrow,

> Creep to thy bosom, pour the balm of love
> Into thy soul, and kiss thee to thy rest,
> Then praise our God, and watch thee till the morning.
>   *Jaff.* Hear this, you Heavens! and wonder how you
>   made her ;
> Reign, reign, ye monarchs that divide the world :
> Busy rebellion ne'er will let you know
> Tranquillity and happiness like mine ;
> Like gaudy ships, the obsequious billows fall
> And rise again, to lift you in your pride ;
> They wait but for a storm, and then devour you :
> I, in my private bark already wrecked,—
> Like a poor merchant, driven on unknown land,
> That had by chance packed up his choicest treasure
> In one dear casket, and saved only that,—
> Since I must wander farther on the shore,
> Thus hug my little, but my precious store,
> Resolv'd to scorn, and trust my fate no more."

The character of Belvidera is one of the most exquisite, most lovable in literature. A thorough woman in her impulse, her logic, and her intensity of passion, she rules her husband by her very sweetness, and melts the scruples that no violence could have divided. The scene in which she persuades him that duty calls him to betray the conspirators, because her own heart yearns to save her father, is one of consummate skill and truth, and the gradual yielding of Jaffier's irresolute will before her feminine reasoning and absolute conviction is worthy of Shakespeare himself. No praise can possibly be withheld from the most delicate and vivid passages in *Venice Preserved ;* it is only where the interest of necessity flags, and above all in the nauseous comic passages, that we miss the presence of a great lyrical and a great humorous

genius.   Yet even here opinion may be divided, since
no less a critic than M. Taine has found a Shake-
spearian excellence in the comic scenes of this play.
Throughout, the spirit of the drama is domestic and
mundane ; there are no flights into the spiritual
heavens, no soundings of the dark and subtle secrets
of the mind.   The imagination of the poet is lucid,
rapid, and direct; there is the utmost clarity of statement and reflection ; in short, a masterpiece of genius
is not obscured, but certainly toned down, by a universal tinge or haze of the commonplace.   The political
bias of *Venice Preserved* is most clearly marked in the
comic character of Antonio, a lecherous old senator, in
whom the hated Shaftesbury was held up to ridicule,
the portrait being exact enough even to include that
statesman's weak ambition to be elected King of
Poland.

For the acting rights of *The Orphan* and for *Venice
Preserved*, two of the most brilliantly successful plays
of the period, Otway only received £100 a piece ; what
is still more astonishing is, that for the copyright of
the latter Jacob Tonson gave him only £15.   He
probably made a few pounds by a prologue for Mrs.
Behn's *City Heiress*, which was separately printed on
a single sheet, in 1682.   In Monimia and Belvidera
Mrs. Barry simply took the town by storm.   Her
acting was by this time perfection, and her personal
attractions were at their zenith.   " She had," we are
told by Cibber, "a presence of elevated dignity, her
mien and motion were superb and gracefully majestick,
and her voice was clear, full, and strong."   It seems

to have been in this year, 1682, that Otway made a
last effort to secure the love of this cold and beautiful
woman, whose worldly success he had done so much
to enhance : the letters we possess are six in number,
a waif preserved perhaps by accident, and first printed
long after his death.   In the first two he reminds her
of his unbroken constancy, of his patience and passion,
his indulgence and hope, and entreats her to take
mercy on a lover who has suffered the agonies of
desire for seven weary years.   He tells her that her
cruelty has driven him to find solace in noisy pleasures
and in wine, but that with solitude and sobriety her
torturing image has never ceased to return and tor-
ment him.   The third letter, sprightly and fantastic,
contrasts with the yearning and melancholy appeal of
the former two.   He rallies her on an idle threat to
leave the world, and takes upon himself, as a member
of that world, to divert her from so ill-natured an
inclination.   The fourth is brief and passionate ; he
wrestles with her, as though he would force her
frivolous coquetry into a serious declaration of love,
and he tells her he can bear no longer the alternation
of kind looks and cruel denials.   The fifth letter is
rough and inelegant in language ; he storms at her
with violent indignation, and denounces her vanity
and selfishness with the sharpest irony.   The sixth,
the shortest of all and the saddest, quietly remarks
that, in accordance with her promise to meet him in
the Mall, he was there at the appointed hour, but she
never came, and that he now begs her for the favour
of one genuine assignation, that he may really know

whether he may "hereafter, for your sake, either bless all your bewitching sex, or, as often as I henceforth think of you, curse womankind for ever."

Here this tantalising but priceless fragment of correspondence ceases, but we know that the answer was for cursing and not for blessing. From this point Otway's ruin was but a question of months; his genius did not long survive his passion. He had now few friends left to help him. His one faithful ally, the Earl of Plymouth, had died in 1680. Otway's conversion to the Tory party had softened Dryden's animosity a little, but not to the extent of any very warm recognition. Plunged in drunken misery, Otway remains almost invisible to us until 1684, when he seemed to make a final effort to regain a place in society. He wrote in that year a prologue to Lee's *Constantine the Great*, and produced a play of his own, *The Atheist*. This, his last drama, is a comedy, a sequel to *The Soldier's Fortune*, with the same characters, the vile company of the Dunces and Sir Jolly being happily excluded. It is, however, a very poor performance. The gross adulation of the preface to the eldest son of the Marquis of Halifax is enough to show how low the poet had fallen; the epilogue was written by Duke.

Charles II. died early in February 1685, and Otway instantly seized the opportunity to publish a quarto poem entitled *Windsor Castle*, in which he praised the dead king and exulted over the accession of James. He had been always loyal to the Duke of York, and he hoped now to be remembered, but scarcely was his poem published than he sank under the weight of destitution.   He found it impossible to borrow any more money; he was already £400 in the debt of Captain Symonds, a vintner.   It appears that he spent his last days in a wretched spunging-house on Tower Hill, a place known by the sign of the Bull.   According to one account he ventured out at the point of starvation, and begged a passer-by for alms, saying at the same time, " I am Otway the poet!"   The gentleman, shocked to see so great a genius in such a condition, gave him a guinea, with which Otway rushed to the nearest baker's, ravenously swallowed a piece of bread, and died at once, choked by the first mouthful.   This occurred on April 14, 1685.

Many years afterwards, apparently to cover the scandalous fact that the greatest tragic poet of the age was allowed to starve to death in London in his thirty-fourth year, a new story was circulated to the effect that Otway died of a fever caught by chasing the murderer of a friend of his from London to Dover on foot.   There seems no foundation, however, for this. No newspaper of the period is known to have announced his death.   In 1686 there appeared a sorry piece of hackwork under his name, *The History of the Triumvirate*, translated from the French ; and in November of the same year Betterton advertised for a tragedy by Mr. Otway, of which four acts were known to be written when he died.   During the winter of the same year the great manager repeated his advertisements, and then there was no more heard of this lost play. But more than thirty years later, in 1719, two obscure booksellers issued a tragedy, *Heroick Friendship*, which they attributed on the title-page to "the late Mr. Otway." They gave no sort of explanation of the means by which they obtained it, and their publication was at once discredited, and has been ridiculed by every editor of Otway. I lay myself open, I fear, to the charge of credulity if I confess that I am not quite ready to accept this universal verdict.

The play called *Heroick Friendship* is in blank verse of very unequal merit; some of it is of the very basest flatness, some of it has buoyancy and rhetorical vigour to a remarkable degree. It is most vilely edited, evidently from a cursive manuscript or first draft; on every page there are passages which the transcriber has misread, and phrases that are feebly finished, as though an unskilful hand had patched them. There are not a few lines that are absolutely unintelligible, and it is a noticeable fact that these corruptions occur only in the most poetical passages; the flat and insipid scenes are clear enough. If this play had been put before us without an author's name, we should be inclined to pronounce that two persons had been at work on it, and that it had been printed from a transcript of a rough, unfinished manuscript, the transcript being by the same person who completed the play. I do not think that it has been noticed that Betterton had not been long dead when this tragedy was printed by Mears and King. My own impression is that those booksellers obtained it by some underhand means from persons who had access to the effects of Betterton, and this would account for their silence

Y

when called upon to show the credentials of the play.
If it be asked why had Betterton concealed it for a
quarter of a century, when he had eagerly advertised
for it, the answer I would suggest would be that he
received the rough manuscript in answer to his advertise-
ment, set to work as well as he could to copy it out
and to complete it, and when he had finished was so
little pleased with the result that he put it on one side.
In an uncritical age no one cared for imperfect works
by a great man, unless they could be completed and
used.   There were no bibliographers to secure the
manuscript of Dryden's *Ladies à la Mode*, and no
interest would have been felt in a rough draft by
Otway.

So much for external speculation; of internal evidence I have also something to bring forward.   Imperfect as the execution is, the plot and idea of *Heroick
Friendship* are exceedingly characteristic of Otway.
The story is briefly told: it concerns itself with the
Roman occupation of Britain.   A mythical King
Arbelline has a brother Guiderius, of whose claim to
the throne he is jealous; this brother loves a British
lady, Aurosia, to whom the king makes overtures.   In
her terror she urges her lover to rebellion, to which
he is further pressed by his dearest friend, Decimus,
a Roman.   Arbelline, discovering the love of Aurosia
for Guiderius, determines on his ruin.   He is arrested
and sentenced to death.   In order that he may take a
farewell of his mistress, Decimus offers to take his
place in prison for a night and a day, which his
friend spends with Aurosia.   At the end of that time

Guiderius hurries back to release Decimus, but is followed and over-persuaded by Aurosia, who cannot bear to part with him. This vacillating lover, ever convinced against his will by feminine blandishments, is the fellow-creation, surely, of Castalio and Jaffier. The first act, I am convinced, is all Otway's, though doubtless patched and tagged by an inferior hand. The following passage, for instance, in spite of some textual confusion in the end of the first speech, is most characteristic of the author, who triumphs in a lover's parting :—

> " *Aur.* Go then, be every influence propitious,
> And all the stars as fond of thee as I am !
> May the Gods join with thee, and justly move
> Against a tyrant in the cause of love,
> Drive him to death, and when he breathless lies,
> Lead the dear victor to the Elysian Gardens.
> There on the river's brink, within his view,
> Haste, haste his way for me to crown his conquest.
>   *Guid.* But should the King by force !—by force !—O Gods !
>   *Aur.* Though everything should aid his hated passion,
> Doubt not Aurosia's spirit nor her faith ;
> But I must go, or be suspected here,—
> A worser evil, if a worse can be,
> Than that of parting with thee ; oh farewell !
>   *Guid.* Stay ! Let me take a lover's farewell of thee !—
> One dear embrace, firm as my faith ! O blessing !
> Thou balmy softness, as the morning sweet,
> When the glad lark with mounting music charms
> The mild unclouded heavens."

The rest of the play is unworthy of the first act, but there are passages throughout the second and third acts which may be confidently attributed to Otway. If the works of the poet are edited again, *Heroick Friendship* should by no means be omitted.

In person Otway was handsome and portly, with a fine air. Dryden, in tardy acknowledgment, admitted that " charming his face was, charming was his verse ; " and the best accredited portrait that we possess of him, that by John Ryley in the Chesterfield Collection, shows that " charming " was exactly the right adjective to use. The face is of a full clear oval, suave and bright. We see before us the countenance of a gracious, amorous person, with more wit than wisdom, unfit to battle with the world, and fallen on troublous times. My own impression of Otway is that he closely resembled the character of Valentine in *Love for Love*, save that, alas ! no beneficent deity crowned him with fortune and Angelica in the last act.

Any account of the writings of Otway would be incomplete without some allusion to his relation with the great French dramatists, his contemporaries ; and yet to enter into this at all fully would lead us beyond our limits. In point of time he was the coeval of Quinault and Racine, both of whom outlived him, but his intellectual kinship is much rather with Rotrou and Corneille. The masterpieces of *le grand Corneille* had a profound influence on Betterton, and through him on the English poets who wrote for him. Of these Otway kept the closest to the severity of the French classicists. Dryden, in his vain search for novelty, tried every species of tragic subject, and, until near his end, failed in each. Lee, with a great deal of inherent genius, struck at once on the rock of bombast. Otway alone understood the tragic force of pity and tears, and at this point he came very near excelling all the French tragedians.

It is impossible not to compare with the brief sad life of the young English poet that of the young French poet whose life ceased in such a noble apotheosis six months before Otway's birth. Rotrou and Otway each wrote many dramas; each produced one of great and another of supreme excellence; the career of each was cut off in youth by calamity. But while the one was the victim of his own weakness and of public neglect, the other freely surrendered his life to an adorable sentiment of duty. In mental as in moral fibre, the author of *Saint-Genest* and *Venceslas* surpassed the poet of *The Orphan* and *Venice Preserved*, but there is something similar in the character of their writings, with this curious exception, that in his highest beauties Rotrou approaches the English poetic type, while Otway's finest passages are those in which he is most French.

These passages led to his being early admired and imitated in Paris; and several French tragedies, particularly the *Manlius Capitolinus* of Antoine de la Fosse, published in 1698, show the influence which Otway exercised abroad. This partiality was rudely attacked by Voltaire, whose criticism of Otway was at one time famous, and did much to bring the poet into discredit. It is to be found in the same volume of the *Mélanges Littéraires* which contains the notorious analysis of *Hamlet*. The plot of *The Orphan* is what he mainly dwells upon. He has no words sufficiently contemptuous for these clumsy inventions of *le tendre Otway*, in whom he is not prepared to admit a single merit. Voltaire, rare and delicate critic as he was, was yet too profoundly out of sympathy with English verse to be able to judge it at all. French criticism in the present century has been far more just to the claims of Otway, and Taine in particular has given him praise which to an English ear sounds excessive.

APPENDIX

Page 216.—To this challenge Mr. Lowell replied in words which it gives me a melancholy pleasure to reprint :—

" Whatever my other shortcomings (and they are plenty, as none knows better than I), want of reflection is not one of them. The poems were all intended for public recitation. That was the first thing to be considered. I suppose my ear (from long and painful practice on ϕ. B. K. poems) has more technical experience in this than almost any. The least tedious measure is the rhymed heroic, but this, too, palls, unless relieved by passages of wit or even mere fun. A long series of uniform stanzas (I am always speaking of public recitation) with regularly recurring rhymes produces somnolence among the men and a desperate resort to their fans on the part of the women. No method has yet been invented by which the train of thought or feeling can be shunted off from the epical to the lyrical track. My ears have been jolted often enough over the sleepers on such occasions to know that. I know *something* (of course an American can't know much) about Pindar; but *his* odes had the advantage of being chanted. Now, my problem was to contrive a measure which should not be tedious by uniformity, which should vary with varying moods, in which the transitions (including those of the voice) should be managed without jar. I at first thought of mixed rhymed and blank verses of unequal measures, like those in the choruses of *Samson Agonistes*, which are in the main masterly. Of course, Milton *deliberately* departed from that stricter form of the Greek chorus to which it was bound quite as much (I suspect) by the law of its musical accompaniment as by any sense of symmetry. I wrote some stanzas of the *Commemoration Ode* on this theory at first, leaving some verses without a rhyme to match. But my ear was better pleased when the rhyme, coming at a longer interval, as a far-off echo rather than instant reverberation, produced the same effect almost, and yet was grateful by unexpectedly recalling an association and faint reminiscence of consonance. I think I have succeeded pretty well, and if you try reading aloud, I believe you will agree with me. The sentiment of the *Concord Ode* demanded a larger proportion of lyrical movements, of course, than the others. Harmony, without sacrifice of melody, was what I had mainly in view."

INDEX